The Vote

Vote

Bush, Gore, and the Supreme Court
Edited by Cass R. Sunstein and Richard A. Epstein

THE UNIVERSITY OF CHICAGO PRESS   CHICAGO & LONDON

The University of Chicago Press, Chicago 60637

The University of Chicago Press, Ltd., London

© 2001 by The University of Chicago

All rights reserved. Published 2001

Printed in the United States of America

10 09 08 07 06 05 04 03 02 01   1 2 3 4 5

ISBN: 0-226-21306-4 (cloth)

ISBN: 0-226-21307-2 (paper)

Library of Congress Cataloging-in-Publication Data

The vote : Bush, Gore, and the Supreme Court / edited by Cass R. Sunstein and
Richard A. Epstein.

    p. cm.

   Includes index.

   ISBN 0-226-21306-4 (cloth : alk. paper)—ISBN 0-226-21307-2 (paper : alk. paper)

    1. Bush, George W. (George Walker), 1946—Trials, litigation, etc. 2. Gore, Albert,
1948—Trials, litigation, etc. 3. Contested elections—United States. 4. Contested
elections—Florida. 5. Elections—United States—President—2000. I. Sunstein, Cass R. II.
Epstein, Richard Allen, 1943–

KF5074.2 .V68 2001

324.973'0929—dc21

2001037805

⊗ The paper used in this publication meets the minimum
requirements of the American National Standard for
Information Sciences—Permanence of Paper for Printed
Library Materials, ANSI Z39.48-1992.

CONTENTS

ACKNOWLEDGMENTS

We are grateful to the University of Chicago Law Review, which originally published most of the essays appearing here, and whose editors contributed editorial and logistical help of multiple sorts. For particular thanks, we would likely to single out Jonathan Mitchell, Gordon Mead, and Michael Edney. For help of various sorts, Cass Sunstein would like to give special thanks to Kim Gardiner, Anne Preshlock, Ashley March, Pam March, Tony March, Doc Holiday, and his other friends at Perfecta Farm. Richard Epstein owns no horses but would like to thank for inspiration, and for pointed political commentary, the many warhorses who help preserve his sanity through basketball on Monday evenings and Saturday mornings.

Richard A. Epstein is the James Parker Hall Distinguished Service Professor of Law at the University of Chicago. He is author of *Principles for a Free Society: Reconciling Individual Liberty with the Common Good* (1998).

Elizabeth Garrett is professor of law and deputy dean for academic affairs at the University of Chicago. She is coauthor, with William N. Eskridge, Jr. and Philip P. Frickey, of *Legislation and Statutory Interpretation* (2000).

Samuel Issacharoff is professor of law at Columbia University. He is coauthor, with Pamela S. Karlan and Richard H. Pildes, of *When Elections Go Bad: The Law of Democracy and the Presidential Election of 2000* (2001).

Pamela S. Karlan is the Kenneth and Harle Montgomery Professor of Public Interest Law at Stanford University. She is coauthor, with Richard H. Pildes and Samuel Issacharoff, of *When Elections Go Bad: The Law of Democracy and the Presidential Election of 2000* (2001).

Michael W. McConnell is the Presidential Professor of Law at the University of Utah.

Frank I. Michelman is the Robert Walmsley Professor of Law at Harvard University. He is author of *Brennan and Democracy* (1999).

Richard H. Pildes is professor of law at the University of Michigan. He is coauthor, with Pamela S. Karlan and Samuel Issacharoff, of *When Elections Go Bad: The Law of Democracy and the Presidential Election of 2000* (2001).

Richard A. Posner is senior lecturer in law at the University of Chicago and judge of the U.S. Court of Appeals, Seventh Circuit. He is author of *An Affair of State: The Investigation, Impeachment, and Trial of President Clinton* (2000).

David A. Strauss is the Harry N. Wyatt Professor of Law, Russell Baker Scholar, and director of the Legal Theory Program at the University of Chicago.

Cass R. Sunstein is the Karl N. Llewellyn Distinguished Service Professor of Jurisprudence at the University of Chicago. He is author of *One Case at a Time: Judicial Minimalism on the Supreme Court* (1999).

John C. Yoo is professor of law at the University of California, Berkeley.

Introduction

Of Law and Politics

CASS R. SUNSTEIN

On January 20, 2001, Chief Justice William H. Rehnquist administered the traditional oath of office to George W. Bush, the forty-third president of the United States. Always an extraordinary national event, this ceremony had a unique twist: what ultimately assured the election of George W. Bush was a 5–4 decision by the Supreme Court of the United States.

The Supreme Court's decision in *Bush v Gore* surely counts as the most controversial judicial decision in several decades. In the fullness of time, the decision is likely to rank among the most controversial decisions in the entire history of the Supreme Court.

The Court's decision is controversial for two reasons. First, it effectively ended the long struggle over the Florida vote, on which the presidential election ultimately turned. And second, people continue to disagree sharply about whether the result can be justified. Most of those who agree with the Court tend to emphasize the perceived need to respond to illegitimate action by the Florida Supreme Court and also to put an end to a controversy that was threatening to spiral out of control. Many of those who are unconvinced by the Court's rationale have accused the Court of acting on a partisan basis, and not like a court of law at all. Apart from the controversy, the Court's decision raises a host of fascinating questions for the future, involving the nature of the ideal of political equality—and the question whether existing practices, in the United States and elsewhere, serve or violate that ideal.

The essays in this book are written by many of the nation's leading figures in the fields of constitutional and electoral law. The authors offer a remarkably wide range of perspectives on the Court's decision in *Bush v Gore* and the numerous puzzles it raises. Some of the authors condemn the Court's decision as an egregious abuse of power. Others sharply disagree, urging that the Court's decision can be supported on legal grounds. Still others are not sure of its legal basis, but insist that the decision made pragmatic sense because it prevented a volatile situation from spiralling out of control. Some authors emphasize what they see as the great promise, for the future of voting rights, of the Court's ruling under the equal protection clause. Other authors view the Court's ruling as ominous, portending excessive federal intervention into the domain of the states.

My purpose in this introduction is twofold. In order to provide general background for the discussion to follow, I offer a general chronology of the events in *Bush v Gore*, with a quick glance at the legal issues. Also for general background, I offer some few words on a large puzzle: the fact that reactions to the Court's division are sharply divided, among specialists and nonspecialists alike, on political grounds. To oversimplify: Gore supporters tend to think that the Court was wrong, even ludicrously wrong; Bush supporters tend to think that the Court's decision was defensible, right, perhaps even heroic. If there is a distinction between law and politics, how can this be? What, if anything, does the Court's remarkable decision tell us about legal reasoning and about the division between politics and law?

But let us begin by seeing exactly what happened.

CHRONOLOGY

The presidential election of 2000 was held on November 7, 2000. Shortly before 8 P.M., the networks made a dramatic announcement: on the basis of exit polls, it was clear that Gore had won Florida. At 9:30 P.M., Bush told the networks, in no uncertain terms, that they had been mistaken. The outcome in Florida was unquestionably crucial because early returns suggested that, with Florida in hand, Gore was overwhelmingly likely to become the next president. Shortly before 10 P.M., the networks moved Florida into the undecided column. At 2:15 A.M. on November 8, the networks started to call Bush the winner in Florida, and hence in the electoral college. Fifteen minutes later Gore telephoned Bush to concede. At 3:45 A.M., Gore called Bush again, retracting his concession. Fifteen minutes later the networks retracted their claim that Bush had won, again putting Florida in the undecided column.

So much for November 7 and 8. What happened in the next five weeks is much more complicated.

In the initial battle, the Gore team sought to prevent a certification of the vote for Bush, whereas the Bush team, thinking that Bush had won every reasonable count, sought a prompt certification on his behalf. November 9 saw an automatic machine recount, required by Florida law, of all Florida ballots, producing a lead for Bush of less than three hundred votes.[1] At that stage, Gore's lawyers called for hand recounts in four crucial Florida counties, urging that the secretary of state not certify the Florida vote until the hand recount was completed.

On November 11, Bush's lawyers sought an injunction in state court to stop the hand counts; the injunction was denied on November 13. On the same day, Katherine Harris, Florida's secretary of state, insisted that state law imposed a deadline of November 14 for county returns—meaning that no votes submitted by the counties after that date would be counted in the Florida vote. Harris simultaneously announced a three-hundred-vote lead for Bush and insisted that she would not include hand-counted ballots in the final tally. Harris's announcements were viewed with skepticism, and worse, in some quarters, especially because she was not only a Republican, but also an active participant in the 2000 presidential campaign for Bush. Gore representatives urged that Harris had interpreted the law in an unmistakably partisan manner.

This was the starting point for a continuing struggle between the secretary of state and the Florida Supreme Court. Initially, Gore lost his action against the secretary of state in the trial court, but on November 17, the Florida Supreme Court unanimously ordered Harris not to certify a winner until "further order from this court." On November 20, that same court unanimously ruled that manual returns must be accepted from the four disputed counties. The court's rulings were viewed with skepticism, and worse, in some quarters, especially because the justices had generally been appointed by Democratic governors (of the seven justices, six had been Democratic appointees, and the seventh was a compromise choice). Bush representatives urged that the court had not followed the law, but changed it—in an unmistakable suggestion that partisanship had played a crucial role in the court's decision.

On November 22, Bush authorized an appeal to the United States Supreme Court. Bush's lawyers made three arguments. First, they contended that the Florida court had changed the law of Florida, in violation

---

1. According to an unofficial count by the Associated Press.

of a federal statute, 3 USC § 15, which, they said, required a state's electoral votes to be chosen in accordance with law enacted "prior to" the election. Second, they contended that by changing the law of Florida, the Florida Supreme Court had violated the federal Constitution—in particular, Article 2, Section 5, which, they argued, required the state legislature, and not the state judiciary or even the state constitution, to establish the rules governing the selection of electors. Third, they contended that the standardless hand recount would violate the due process and equal protection clauses. Most observers believed that the United States Supreme Court would refuse to involve itself in the proceedings. But on November 24, the Supreme Court granted certiorari, limited to the first two questions raised by Bush.

On November 30, a whole new institution became involved, as a legislative committee in Florida urged the Florida legislature to meet in special session in order to appoint its own slate of electors. On December 4, a unanimous Supreme Court vacated the decision of the Florida Supreme Court, but did so in a narrow ruling that resolved very little. In a nutshell, the Supreme Court suggested that a change in legislatively enacted law would be unacceptable, but remanded to "clarify" whether the Florida Supreme Court really sought to interpret that law or instead relied on the state constitution to change it.

On the same day, a lower court judge in Florida refused to require a manual hand-count of votes in the four disputed counties. On December 8, the Florida Supreme Court, by a slim 4–3 majority, reversed the lower court and ordered immediate recounts of votes in the state. The court also concluded that 383 votes would have to be added to Gore's total, reducing Bush's lead to a mere 154 votes. At this point, matters seemed quite chaotic and unsettled. It was most unclear what would ultimately happen in the Florida recount.

At this stage, the United States Supreme Court asserted itself. On December 9, the Court issued a stay, by a 5–4 vote, effectively stopping the manual counting in Florida. The dramatic, election-ending 5–4 ruling in *Bush v Gore* came just three days later, on December 12. Gore conceded the election to Bush on December 13.

LAW OR POLITICS?

One of the most striking features of the decision in *Bush v Gore* is the much-remarked fact that the most conservative justices made up the five-person majority, with the least conservative justices constituting the four-person minority. Before and after the Court's final decision, it was easy to detect a similar division within the nation.

People who supported Gore, or who identified themselves as left of center, tended to be enraged by the Supreme Court's involvement; people who supported Bush, or who identified themselves as right of center, tended to approve of it. A similar division could be found over assessments of the Florida Supreme Court. Observers who supported Bush tended to think that the Florida court had not interpreted Florida law, but instead changed it. Observers who supported Gore tended to think that the Florida court had acted well within the legitimate bounds of interpretation. Of course, few of these people were experts in Florida law. But the same pattern seems to have held among those who knew nothing about Florida law and those who studied it in some detail.

Much the same division can be found in the essays in this book. Of course, there are exceptions and qualifications. But in general, there is, even among the academics represented here, a clear and sharp difference between Gore supporters, or left-of-center people, and Bush supporters, or right-of-center people: the former are generally skeptical of the Court's decision, whereas the latter think, broadly speaking, that it was correct. How can we account for this?

The most natural way would be to acknowledge the enduring truth in the view conventionally associated with the legal realist movement of the 1930s: the line between legal judgment and political judgment is far from crisp and simple. At least where the legal materials leave gaps, people will do what they like, on political grounds. In *Bush v Gore*, perhaps the legal materials left gaps, and thus people did what they liked, on political grounds. A more elaborate and appealing view of the situation is set out in Ronald Dworkin's conception of law as "integrity."[2] In Dworkin's view, legal reasoning consists of an effort to put the preexisting legal materials in the "best constructive light." Where the materials leave gaps, those engaged in legal reasoning try to make the materials seem sensible and rational by knitting them together into what is (to them) an appealing pattern. If this is what legal reasoning is, different people will disagree about what makes for an appealing pattern, and that disagreement will be reflected in different judgments about what the law is.

But there is a special problem for *Bush v Gore:* it seems obvious that if

2. Ronald Dworkin, *Law's Empire* (1985).

the parties were reversed, we could not possibly have seen the overall pattern of reactions found within the Supreme Court, among general observers, and among the contributors to this book.

Suppose, for example, that there is a parallel world, one culminating not in *Bush v Gore,* but in *Gore v Bush.* Here is what happened in that world: Gore won the initial count in Florida, but Bush challenged the count, with a plausible argument that a manual recount would show that Bush, not Gore, was the real winner. The secretary of state, a high-level official in the Gore campaign, refused to allow the manual recount. But the Florida Supreme Court, consisting of Republican nominees, re- jected the secretary of state's decision, agreeing with Bush. And so on.

Is it even possible to maintain that in the parallel world the same peo- ple would have the same reactions to *Gore v Bush* as to *Bush v Gore?* Is it not more likely that a majority of the observers would shift position? Is it unfair to suggest that more than half of United States Supreme Court justices, and more than half of academic commentators, would shift po- sition as well?

I am not sure of the answers to these questions. But I am sure that, at the very least, most people's reactions to *Gore v Bush* would be very differ- ent from their reactions to *Bush v Gore*—and hence that judgments about this case have a great deal to do with the identity of the parties. This may be less obvious for legal specialists than for nonlawyers, but it is certainly true for specialists, too. At the very least, this fact seems to be an embar- rassment for those who believe in the separation between law and politics.

To understand what is going on here, I would like to venture, very briefly and tentatively, what might be called a *neorealist account of legal judgment.* The core of the account is that in certain cases, people's ini- tial evaluations dominate their ultimate judgments, and their initial evaluations are highly emotional. Often the relevant emotion involves indignation or outrage. Take, for example, another high-profile legal dispute: whether President Clinton had committed an impeachable of- fense. The Congress was split down the middle on that issue, with party identification being a near-perfect determinant of people's votes. It de- fies belief to think that we would have seen the same pattern of evalua- tions if President Clinton had been a Republican.

In the impeachment case, legal evaluations were greatly affected by an intense emotional reaction, in the form of either "It's outrageous that a president of the United States has committed such acts" or, instead, "It's outrageous that Kenneth Starr's investigation has gone so far with essentially private misconduct." Now it is important to be careful with the idea of "emotions" here. With respect to law, as elsewhere, emotions are not cognition-free. They are based on and surrounded by thoughts—in the case of impeachment, thoughts about the character and performance of President Clinton. What is crucial is that an emotional reaction tends to dominate people's reaction to the topic at hand, dampening their responsiveness to other considerations, even making it hard for people on both sides to answer this question: What would I think if the person alleged to have committed these acts were someone of a different political party? What would I think if the parties were reversed? The difficulty of answering such questions is a characteristic feature of emotional reactions to certain political and legal events, and it ensures that the relevant judgments will be more or less impervious to further thinking.

There are three other factors here. First, when like-minded people talk with one another, they tend to move toward extremes.[3] If three members of a group tended to think that the Florida Supreme Court was stealing the election from George W. Bush, their discussions would push them toward a more extreme version of what they already thought. The effect would be heightened if such people thought of themselves as alike along some dimension: Republican, liberal, conservative, and so forth. At the same time, people engaged in deliberation are not likely to be much moved by people who disagree with them *if* those people can be said to fall in a different social category. Deliberating Republicans are not likely to be moved by deliberating Democrats, or vice versa, even if the same arguments might have some appeal if labels were not assigned to those who make those arguments. I speculate that in *Bush v Gore,* and in other cases involving politically charged legal questions, like-minded people, including like-minded judges and specialists, fortified one another's opinions, thus contributing to the neo-realist model that I have outlined.

Second, it is well established that while people care about fairness, their judgments about what is fair are systematically self-serving and hence biased. When an observer favors one or another side in a sport-

3. See Roger Brown, *Social Psychology* (2d ed 1986); Cass R. Sunstein, *Deliberative Trouble? Why Groups Go to Extremes,* 110 Yale LJ 71 (2000)

ing event, in politics, or in law, his prejudices greatly affect his judgments about what is right. Where legal materials are ambiguous, a similar effect is at work: judgments about what is fair, and about what is lawful, will partly be a function of what is in people's interests, broadly understood.

Now one of the purposes of legal reasoning, and even of the ideal of the rule of law, is to quiet the intense emotional reactions that often crowd out other factors. Perhaps we can see the ancient image of justice, equipped with blindfold, as a signal that certain considerations—above all, the identity of the parties—are not a legitimate basis for judgment. And it seems clear that well-trained lawyers and judges are, as a rule, less susceptible to emotions of this kind. But they are not entirely impervious to them, and in politically charged cases, justice is not blind in the least.

Third, people are subject to confirmation bias, in the sense that when they hear two contending sides in an argument, they will often be fortified in their preexisting belief, thinking that the debate has only served to confirm what they thought before.[4] For example, people who favor capital punishment are likely, after hearing arguments for and against capital punishment, to be fortified in their belief, because they will see the strength in the arguments on their side and stress the weaknesses in the opposing position. To the extent that Gore supporters were able to talk to Bush supporters, and vice versa, the discussion might well have failed to break down disagreements, partly because positions had become congealed when like-minded people spoke, at first, largely with one another. Judges and academics, like ordinary people, are not immune from confirmation bias.

I think that these factors were extremely important in the debate over *Bush v Gore* and that initial emotional reactions drove people's ultimate judgments about the law, including the judgments of Supreme Court justices and academic commentators. Perhaps outsiders to the national debate—in Europe? in Canada?—can escape some of the relevant pressures. Perhaps the perspective of time will help.

CONCURRENCES AND DISSENTS

I now offer a brief outline of the papers to come.

Richard Epstein offers an examination of the two major grounds on

---

4. Charles Lord, Lee Ross, and Mark R. Lepper, *Biased Assimilation and Attitude Polarization*, 37 J Personality & Soc Psychol 2098, 2102–4 (1979).

which the United States Supreme Court overturned the decision of the Florida Supreme Court in *Bush v Gore*. He first argues that the equal protection rationale, which commended itself to the five justices, was deeply flawed in relation to past cases. In Epstein's view, the most that the rationale could do was to demand equal standards across different precincts. But it could not compel the adoption of any single standard and thus required a remand to the Florida Supreme Court for a determination of how the votes would come out. But the second argument, involving the allegedly unconstitutional deviation from Florida law by the Florida Supreme Court, is far stronger. Epstein explores these points in some detail as they relate to both of the Florida court's decisions.

Elizabeth Garrett argues that there was a unique need for judicial restraint in *Bush v Gore* because of the inherent conflict of interest that the Supreme Court justices faced. In her view, this conflict makes *Bush v Gore* different from the election law cases and political process cases in which the Court has intervened often. Garrett focuses on the first opinion remanding the case and the decision to stay the recount, arguing that both were unnecessary and shaped the resulting decisions in ways that have opened the Court to charges of partisanship. She also argues that judicial restraint was appropriate in this context because this was a dispute that should have been resolved by Congress. Garrett disagrees sharply with those who argue that the Court saved us from a political or constitutional crisis. Such claims reveal a distaste for politics that is unfortunate and unwarranted. In her view, the nation would have been better served in this matter by the House and Senate, the politically accountable branches, than by the unelected Supreme Court.

Samuel Issacharoff urges that it is possible to measure the constitutional pedigree of *Bush v Gore* apart from the partisan issue of who won and who lost the 2000 election. In his view, *Bush v Gore* is the most dramatic departure from the Supreme Court's historic reluctance to enter the political fray or to proclaim the winner or loser of a specific election. Issacharoff measures the Supreme Court's recent handiwork against the arguments made for circumventing the political question barrier in the 1960s. Looking at the arguments that paved the way for courts to compel reapportionment and redistricting, he identifies two key features of those cases. First, the Court's successes in the political arena were always premised on clear constitutional commands, most notably the one-person, one-vote rule of reapportionment. Second, the Court intervened when it became apparent that there was no other institutional actor capable of providing redress. Measured against this two-part template, *Bush v Gore* is wanting on both counts. The core argument is not that courts may not intervene in highly charged political disputes, but that there are times when they should not. The final conclusion is that *Bush v Gore* is symptomatic of an insufficient commitment to modesty in the exercise of judicial power, much as argued by Justice Breyer in dissent in *Bush v Gore.*

Pamela Karlan suggests that *Bush v Gore* should be seen as part of the "newest" equal protection doctrine, which, in her view, reflects the Supreme Court's mistrust of almost all other actors in the political process. In Karlan's view, *Bush v Gore* fits with a number of other recent cases that attempt to protect the structure of voting without protecting either individual rights or the rights of members of disadvantaged groups. Karlan objects that the equality problems emphasized by the Court were far less serious than the equality problems that a manual recount promised to cure. She concludes that the Court is using equal protection to produce less, not more, in the way of equality and democracy.

Michael McConnell contends that the highly dubious decisions of the Florida Supreme Court put the United States Supreme Court in an awkward position. He argues that the seven justices of the Court were right to find that the standardless recount would violate the Fourteenth Amendment, but he objects to what he sees as the legal incorrectness and questionable judicial statesmanship of the 5–4 split on the issue of remedy. He contends that if the five justices in the majority had joined Justices Souter and Breyer to require a remand under strict constitutional standards, the outcome would have been more legitimate. McConnell emphasizes that the unequal treatment of identical voters was indeed a constitutional problem, and in his view, it would not be particularly unattractive to extend the Court's holding so as to ban vote-counting systems that are not uniform.

Frank Michelman asks whether, in retrospect, one could have predicted how the majority of justices would rule since, at any point in the proceedings and with the full support of their dissenting colleagues, they might have restrained or withdrawn the Court from any substantial involvement in the election. Those who find the majority opinion predictable, he argues, must be imputing to the majority either a plainly illicit or a conventionally inadmissible kind of motivation for this, or any, exercise of publicly entrusted judicial power. Those who are surprised by the majority's action should reconsider their own view of the Court's role in our national governance.

Richard Pildes urges that *Bush v Gore* be seen as the most dramatic moment in a constitutionalization of the democratic process that began forty years ago. By exploring *Bush v Gore* not as an isolated decision but in the context of this richer tapestry, Pildes identifies deeper patterns in the Court's approach to this increasingly important but understudied field of "the law of democracy." Rather than analyzing *Bush v Gore* in terms of formal legal doctrine, or in terms of what role, if any, partisan politics might be argued to have played in the decision, Pildes suggests that the case be seen as another manifestation of "cultural" attitudes toward democracy that currently divide the Supreme Court. As much as formal legal doctrine or narrow partisan calculations, it is competing cultural images, ideals, and fears of democracy that divide the current Supreme Court and that helped determine the Court's approach to the decision in *Bush v Gore*. Pildes sees *Bush v Gore* as a window into a more general and more enduring set of questions concerning how judges, including the current Supreme Court, imagine and picture the role of conflict, order, stability, and competition in democracy.

Judge Richard Posner explores one of the most frequently discussed questions arising out of the 2000 presidential election in Florida and the litigation that ensued: whether, if the hand recounts had been completed, Gore would have emerged as the "real" winner of the popular-vote plurality. Judge Posner argues no because the recounts violated Florida law and because responsible recounts of undervotes would not have been likely to produce enough new votes for Gore to overcome Bush's lead.

David Strauss asks a single question: what explains the decision of the United States Supreme Court in *Bush v Gore*? His hypothesis is that the United States Supreme Court had concluded that the Florida Supreme Court was going to try, by illegitimate means, to give the election to Vice President Gore and that the United States Supreme Court was determined not to allow that to happen. The United States Supreme Court did not, in any ordinary sense, follow the law; it cast about for a rationale that would permit it to stop the Florida Supreme Court. Strauss describes five actions taken by the United States Supreme Court that support this hypothesis because they can be justified not in conventional legal terms, but only as the product of a perceived need to stop the Florida Supreme Court. He also argues that the United States Supreme Court's perception of the Florida Supreme Court was not justified. But the principal point is that any effort to justify the United States Supreme Court's decision should recognize that it was not an action taken in accordance with the law.

Cass Sunstein examines *Bush v Gore* as a case study in "judicial minimalism." He contends that the decision had two virtues. It offered a prompt and authoritative end to a controversy that was rapidly threatening to become a crisis, and it provided an equal protection rationale that, while unprecedented, had a certain appeal. But in his view, the decision also had two vices. First, the Court's 5–4 split, with the five most conservative justices in the majority, suggested that the decision was not quite a product of law—a serious problem in a case of this kind. Second, the Court's decisions on the equal protection issue and (especially) on remedy are hard to defend in principle. The Court might well have created an equal protection problem more serious than the one it purported to prevent, and there was no sufficient reason not to remand the case to the Florida Supreme Court. In Sunstein's view, there are lessons here about both judicial minimalism and the nature of the right to vote, where *Bush v Gore* might spur some desirable initiatives, legislative and judicial, in the future. The Court probably did not intend to create the largest new voting right since one-person, one-vote, but it is possible that it did exactly that.

John Yoo explores whether *Bush v Gore* threatens the legitimacy of the Supreme Court in the American political system, as several have claimed. He urges that the historical circumstances of the case do not compare with those in previous periods in which the political branches and elements of the polity questioned the legitimacy of the judiciary and its decisions. *Bush v Gore* did not resolve some large issue of substance; it settled the rules whereby the players in the political system could be selected so that substantive choices about policy could be made. Because it was a narrow decision in a one-of-a-kind case, *Bush v Gore* is not likely to generate the sustained attention toward, and criticism of, the Court that occurred in periods where the Court's legitimacy was truly under assault.

One final note by way of introduction. In the face of such diverse perspectives, it is clear that there is no escaping the largest question raised by the contributions to this book: what do the underlying divisions say about the nature of legal reasoning and the possibility of distinguishing law from politics? On that question, the individual authors offer a remarkable range of answers, and readers are invited to draw their own conclusions.

1

"In such Manner as the Legislature Thereof May Direct"

The Outcome in *Bush v Gore* Defended

RICHARD A. EPSTEIN

For most American citizens, interest in the presidential election campaign of 2000 ended when the Supreme Court in *Bush v Gore*[1] refused to allow any further recount of the Florida votes. After a short flurry of heated debate over the soundness of the decision, the nation buckled down to business as usual. The attention of the media was, to say the least, short-lived. No longer did reporters seek out law professors to dissect past legal maneuvers and to predict future ones. Political attention quickly turned to John Ashcroft, Linda Chavez, and Gale Norton—all controversial Bush nominees for key cabinet positions. The public seems not to be composed of legal purists. It expected something ugly, and in a succession of divided opinions from the Florida and United States Supreme Courts, it got it. But resilience is the mark of a nation that quickly shrugged off one bruising legal and political struggle only to begin a second, and a third, and . . .

Constitutional law professors form a different breed, with longer memories and deeper resentments. Although the short-term issue of who counts as president has been resolved, letters and articles have voiced with varying degrees of indignation a common theme that the legitimacy of the Court has been effectively called into question by its political coup d'état.[2] The Court's decision in *Bush v Gore* has been regarded in many quarters as a travesty of constitutional law incapable of rational defense. Recently, for example, 585 law professors have signed a

1. 121 S Ct 525 (2000) (per curiam).

2. See, for example, Jeffrey Rosen, *Disgrace,* New Republic 18 (Dec 25, 2000) (arguing that the majority in *Bush v Gore* "have . . . made it impossible for citizens of the United States to sustain any kind of faith in the rule of law").

public letter attacking a conservative and mean-spirited Court for its devious and hypocritical judicial activism.[3] It is difficult to assess the potential influence of these harsh condemnations and dire predictions on public opinion and the political process. But, as the battles over the Bork and Thomas nominations show, old wounds are easily reopened in confirmation hearings of presidential Supreme Court nominees.

In this case, I think that overheated rhetoric has led to overstated charges. It is for this reason that I shall mount a qualified rear-guard defense of the outcome in *Bush v Gore*. I shall not do so on the equal protection grounds that carried the day with the five conservative justices who voted to end the recount. Quite simply, I regard that argument as a confused nonstarter at best, which deserves much of the scorn that has been heaped upon it. The same harsh judgment, however, cannot be made of the alternative ground for decision that was championed by Chief Justice Rehnquist in a concurring opinion joined only by Justices Scalia and Thomas, which would have overturned the decision of the Florida Supreme Court on the ground that its rulings ran afoul of Article II, Section 1, Clause 2 of the U.S. Constitution, which provides that "Each State shall appoint, in such Manner as the Legislature Thereof May Direct," the electors for the offices of President and Vice President. Unlike the equal protection phase of the case, any evaluation of this claim requires us to analyze the decision of the United States Supreme Court in relation to the two decisions of the Florida Supreme Court in the post-election period.[4] Part I discusses the equal protection arguments. Part II is devoted to the less conspicuous but more potent Article II argument.

I. THE EQUAL PROTECTION CLAIM

Any equal protection challenge to the Florida recount procedure quickly runs into insurmountable difficulties. The initial foray of the U.S. Supreme Court's per curiam opinion was to note the start-and-stop quality of the recount procedures throughout the state.[5] There was wide variation in standards across counties that used the paper ballots with their now-

3. See Dave Zweifel, *Court Decision Still Rankles Law Profs*, Cap Times 6A (Jan 24, 2001) (reprinting text of ad).

4. *Gore v Harris*, 772 S2d 1243 (Fla Dec 8, 2000) (overturning trial judge; ordering immediate statewide recount of undervotes), revd and remd as *Bush v Gore*, 121 S Ct 525; *Palm Beach County Canvassing Board v Harris*, 772 S2d 1220 (Fla Nov 21, 2000) (ruling that the Secretary of State had to take late-submitted totals from canvassing boards), vacd and remd as *Bush v Palm Beach County Canvassing Board*, 121 S Ct 471 (2000) (per curiam).

5. See *Bush v Gore*, 121 S Ct 525.

infamous chads. There were also wide variations in standards over time within a single county: Palm Beach, for example, had several different standards on the counting of chads, which veered from narrow to broad and back again.[6] There were also allegations that the Democrats (and doubtless the Republicans) placed pressure on the canvassing boards in Broward, Palm Beach, and Miami-Dade Counties to expand the definition of what votes could be counted.[7] None of the variations and switches that took place in time could be easily justified by differences in local equipment or local practices. There is also little doubt that uniformity in election procedures is highly desirable as a minimum, noncontroversial condition for procedural fairness. Indeed, Florida law charges the Secretary of State, as its chief election officer, with the responsibility to "[o]btain and maintain uniformity in the application, operation and interpretation of the election laws."[8]

Even against this troublesome backdrop, the equal protection claim runs into two serious challenges, one substantive and the other remedial. First, why does the inconsistent administration of the Florida election laws amount to a violation of the Equal Protection Clause? Second, why, if such is the case, was it appropriate or necessary to end the recount?

As to the first, there is an obvious gulf between the cases cited by the Supreme Court majority and the unfortunate electoral situation as it developed in Florida. *Harper v Virginia Board of Elections*[9] struck down a poll tax of up to $1.50 on the ground that it amounted to an implicit discrimination on account of wealth that bore no relation to voting qualifications proper.[10] To be sure, no one can doubt that any individual who cannot pay the tax is excluded from the polls. This free-form decision, which self-consciously sought to distance itself from *Lochner v New York*,[11] was itself something of a stretch under classical equal protection law given that a poll tax is facially neutral and, unlike literacy tests, can be applied in a mechanical way that eliminates the dangers of political discretion. At root it looks as though

6. See id at 531.

7. See Don Van Natta, Jr. and David Barstow, *Counting the Vote: The Canvassing Boards: Elections Officials Focus of Lobbying from Both Camps,* NY Times A1 (Nov 17, 2000) (reporting on pressure exerted on canvassing boards during the recount fight).

8. Fla Stat Ann § 97.012 (West 2000).

9. 383 US 663 (1966).

10. Id at 666.

11. 198 US 45 (1905) (ruling that a maximum hour law for bakers violated the Due Process Clause), noted in *Harper,* 383 US at 669.

Harper rests on the proposition that voting rights are so fundamental that they cannot be abridged on account of wealth. Be that as it may, *Harper* has scant relevance to the probity of Florida's recount procedures. It is one thing to find a serious affront to equal protection from a wealth test that is uniform in its application but disparate in its impact. It is quite another to find an equal protection violation in a process that does *not* take into account wealth (or for that matter, race) in deciding what counts as a valid vote. In a word, the Florida scheme is devoid of any suspect classification needed to trigger the equal protection analysis.

Likewise, the per curiam citation to *Reynolds v Sims*[12] also runs far afield. That case dealt with the refusal of state legislatures to reapportion themselves, in ways that perpetuated massive differences in the size of legislative districts.[13] The obvious imbalance is that all individuals who reside in populous counties systematically have much less political influence than their peers who reside in less populous counties. It is possible therefore to identify unambiguously the winners and losers from the state practice, and to demand in principle at least some justification for imbalances consciously perpetuated by the refusal of the dominant legislative coalition to initiate electoral reforms that would necessarily cut into its own power.

That situation bears scant resemblance to the Bush versus Gore dispute, in which all Florida voters, no matter where they lived, had equal say in the outcome of the election. No one in Florida practiced a conscious manipulation of the voting standard that necessarily skews the outcome in favor of one region, or even one group. To see why, start with the simple but realistic assumption that the election features only two candidates and that the winner is selected by a simple majority vote, with one vote per person. Under these circumstances it is sensible to treat the vote as though it were a share in some corporate enterprise, which is run by the party that commands just over 50 percent of the vote. On this view, *Harper* makes it impossible to exclude shareholders who cannot pay some minimum voting fee. *Reynolds* in turn holds that one share of stock cannot have ten votes while another share of stock only has one.

Bush v Gore, however, does not fall into either of these simple patterns of electoral skewing for there is no conscious form of ex ante discrimination. From the ex ante perspective no one can identify the determinate class of individuals who benefit from or are burdened by the choice of this or that

12. 377 US 533 (1964) (upholding district court orders to reapportion both houses of the Alabama legislature, noting that the failure to do so violated the Equal Protection Clause).

13. Id at 561–66.

standard for counting ballots. It is not as though one standard was used for Gore voters and another for Bush voters. It is thus no surprise that the per curiam opinion was unable to explain why this asserted equal protection violation worked to Bush's disadvantage. Here the key feature of any equal protection challenge is that it takes *no* position on the proper standard for counting votes. Rather, like any argument from distributive justice, it merely argues that *like* cases (or votes) should be treated *alike,* but remains agnostic on how any—indeed all—of these cases (or votes) ought to be treated.[14] Hence, even if it were conceded that the disparities in the recount processes between counties and within counties were indefensible, the equal protection analysis only demands that these anomalies be eliminated. But the equal protection critique offers no guidance as to *how* that should be done.

Accordingly, the appropriate remedy (at least if time is no constraint) is to remand the case to the Florida courts to decide which uniform standard should apply. At this point, Gore's prospects have to improve. The Florida Supreme Court made painfully clear that it held that the clear intention of the voter was the touchstone of Florida's election law.[15] It takes little imagination to predict that, if it had been forced to adopt a uniform standard for all punchcard ballots, the Florida Supreme Court could leap to that standard that maximized the number of undervotes that were included in the final tally. It was not just chance that Broward County had produced 567 net Gore votes and Palm Beach County only around 200.[16] No one could be certain that this change in the rules of the game would have erased the slender Bush advantage, but the recent reexamination of the

14. For an early expression of this limited ideal, see *Powell v Pennsylvania,* 127 US 678, 687 (1888) (ruling that state regulation of oleomargarine did not violate equal protection as it subjected all in the business to the same regulations).

15. See *Palm Beach County Canvassing Board v Harris,* 772 S2d 1220, 1238 (Fla Nov 21, 2000), vacd and remd as *Bush v Palm Beach County Canvassing Board,* 121 S Ct 471 (2000) (per curiam).

16. The extent of the differences is captured in this measure of Gore Yield prepared by Professor Jeffrey Milyo of the Harris School of Public Policy:
Gore Yield*

County	Gore Yield (1 % sample hand count)	Gore Yield (hand count)
Miami-Dade	4%	16% (partial)
Broward	1%*	8.5% (full)
Palm Beach	10%*	2% (full)

*estimated

"Gore Yield" = net Gore votes added divided by undervotes manually counted.

The obvious liberalization in Miami-Dade and Broward magnified the swing.

ballots by the Miami Herald suggests that Bush would have maintained his razor-thin advantage to the bitter end, even if the ballots had been recounted under the standards enunciated by the Florida Supreme Court.

The equal protection analysis thus does nothing to halt the recount process. What is needed is some anchor that locks the Florida Supreme Court into choosing a more restrictive rule. That anchor was available in Palm Beach County, where the local rule stated: "A chad that is fully attached, bearing only an indentation, should not be counted as a vote."[17] Indeed, there was no evidence that any other county in Florida had ever departed from that understanding. This anchor has two advantages. The first is that it offers a litmus test to determine what counts as a valid vote: if the light shines through, then the vote can count; otherwise it does not. The second is that the uniform past practice (especially in Palm Beach) resonates with the powerful notion of fairness that holds that you cannot change the rules after the race has been run.

This last concern probably accounts for the belated and undeveloped reference to possible due process violations in the per curiam opinion.[18] That maneuver runs into the potential doctrinal obstacle that a "vote" as such, notwithstanding its enormous institutional importance, may not rank as either "liberty" or "property" that is covered by the Clause. (There is no similar restriction in the Equal Protection Clause, which governs most voting cases.) Even the broad definitions of liberty and property do not explicitly cover voting rights.[19] Yet on the other hand, so long as corporate shares,

17. Guidelines on Ballots with Chads Not Completely Removed, Adopted by the November 6, 1990 Canvassing Board.

18. *Bush v Gore,* 121 S Ct at 532.

19. See, for example, *Meyer v Nebraska,* 262 US 390 (1923). The Court described its conception of liberty:

While this Court has not attempted to define with exactness the liberty thus guaranteed, the term has received much consideration and some of the included things have been definitely stated. Without doubt, it denotes not merely freedom from bodily restraint but also the right of the individual to contract, to engage in any of the common occupations of life, to acquire useful knowledge, to marry, establish a home and bring up children, to worship God according to the dictates of his own conscience, and generally to enjoy those privileges long recognized at common law as essential to the orderly pursuit of happiness by free men.

Id at 399. Those privileges generally did not include the right to vote. Likewise the right to vote has not been included in the expanded list of property interests that have been protected under the Due Process Clause. See, for example, *Goldberg v Kelly,* 397 US 254, 260–64 (1970) (using a definition of property rights expansive enough to include the statutory right to welfare benefits).

complete with voting rights, count as property, then it may well make sense to accept this broader reading here. Yet even this revised constitutional theory calls for a remand to the Florida courts, albeit with somewhat different instructions. Dimpled chads are out, and the Florida Supreme Court must run its recount under more restrictive rules. The U.S. Supreme Court's per curiam opinion did not pursue this issue further, but it segues neatly into the Article II issue to which I shall now turn.

II. WHAT DID THE FLORIDA LEGISLATURE DIRECT?

To the best of my knowledge no case, prior to *Bush v Gore*, had passed on the proper interpretation of the Article II, Section 1, Clause 2 requirement that Florida shall "appoint" its presidential electors "In such Manner as the [Florida] Legislature [ ] May Direct."[20] That question presumptively gives rise to many interpretive difficulties that were not raised in this case. To mention just two, it is not clear whether this provision requires that the "manner" for choosing electors be settled before the election or whether it allows Florida to change its mind after a popular election has been held but before the Electoral College meets. It would, to say the least, be very disconcerting to know that the Republican legislature could have voted to ignore the results of the popular vote if Gore had carried the state by one million votes. And if it could not intervene in that case, then could it intervene when the popular vote is much closer?

For our purposes, however, these difficulties can be mercifully skirted, because the root of the sensible challenge to the decisions of the Florida Supreme Court rests on the argument that the litigation phase of this election was not carried out in accordance with the substantive or procedural provisions of Florida's election law. To make this argument successfully, it is necessary to surmount some major pitfalls. Anyone who looks at this statute knows that it, like all complex legislation, calls out for interpretation. Even though the responsibility for interpretation is squarely given to the Secre-

---

20. This provision should be read in conjunction with Article I, § 4, cl 1: "The Times, Places and Manner of holding Elections for Senators and Representatives, shall be prescribed in each State by the Legislature thereof; but the Congress may at any time by Law make or alter such Regulations, except as to the Places of chusing Senators." The most obvious contrast is that between "holding" elections and "appointing" electors. Does this preclude the use of popular elections to "appoint" electoral slates for the presidency? Even if it does not, it seems that parallel concerns with federal judicial oversight in particular elections would apply here if the manner in which an election is held deviates substantially from the legislative plan.

tary of State under the Act,[21] at some level, this task falls into the province of the courts. It must therefore be shown, for there to be a violation of Article II, Section 1, Clause 2, that the state court's interpretation does not fall within the boundaries of acceptable interpretation, but rather represents what must be called, for want of a better term, a gross deviation from the scheme outlined in the statute. It should not be assumed, however, that this standard means that gross deviations from the legislative scheme can never be found so long as there are latent inconsistencies within the statutory framework. The courts may rightly query whether or not magenta counts as red, but they cannot do the same for green. Stated otherwise, the Florida Supreme Court can choose either *A* or *B* when both are plausible readings, but cannot choose *C*, which differs from both *A* and *B*, simply because it cannot decide between *A* and *B*. The size of the ambiguity limits the scope of judicial discretion.

Second, it does not appear that any gross deviation from the Florida statutory scheme must be intentional. Article II, Section 1, Clause 2 reads like a strict liability provision. The Florida legislature directs the manner in which the presidential electors are appointed, and all other actors within the Florida system have to stay within the confines of that directive. The word "direct" is a strong term whose sense is captured in the phrase "directed verdict," which refuses to let a jury stray beyond the area of permissible inferences.[22] It is not necessary that one allege or establish systematic bad faith on the part of the Florida Supreme Court to make the charge stick. It is only necessary to show that the gross deviation has in fact taken place.

Third, this dispute is not governed by the usual rule that gives state courts the last word on the interpretation of state law. That rule makes perfectly good sense when the matter in question is one that states regulate by virtue of their status as independent sovereigns within a federal system. But in this case, the strong federal interest in the selection of the President of the United States makes it appropriate for federal courts to see that all state actors stay within the original constitutional scheme. Given judicial review, the United States Supreme Court has the last word on whether any state has strayed from its constitutional path in choosing its presidential electors.

---

21. See Fla Stat Ann § 97.012, reproduced partially in text accompanying note 8.

22. See, for example, *Quinton v Farmland Industries, Inc,* 928 F2d 335, 338–39 (10th Cir 1991) (noting that a directed verdict is appropriate when "the evidence and *permissible inferences therefrom* indicate that reasonable minds could not differ") (emphasis added).

Surely, it would raise a federal question if the Secretary of State decided, contrary to state statutes, to ignore the state election returns in authorizing the slate of state electors even if the state courts remained silent. If therefore the state courts or state executive officials have failed properly to apply the state scheme, resulting in a gross deviation from the legislature's directives, then a federal court can review the matter under Article II.

Fourth, resort to Article II eliminates all doubts over the remedial fit that plagues the Court's equal protection argument. Once it is determined that the Florida Supreme Court has strayed from the legislative scheme, then the United States Supreme Court has no obligation to remand the case for another round. Rather, it becomes perfectly sensible to let the Secretary of State's determination stand since the Gore forces had not made any viable challenge to it.

With these preliminaries out of the way, it now becomes possible to identify some of the key mistakes of the Florida Supreme Court that support the charge that it created its own electoral scheme that substituted judicial authority for that of the Secretary of State. As an overarching objective, the main mission of the election law is to expand the franchise so that all eligible voters who choose to exercise their rights have a reliable means to do so. But an election code has to contend with grubby realities as well as lofty aspirations. Hence it must reconcile the desire for inclusion with the twin interests of finality and probity. Elections must be decided quickly enough so that the winners can prepare to assume public office. And the rules governing elections must be tight enough to prevent the use of fraudulent practices—before, during, and after an election—that might alter an outcome of an election for the worse. The key element in reading the Florida Election Code therefore is to see how these three concerns work themselves out in connection with particular statutory provisions. In this case it is instructive to look at three particular points. The first of these concerns the definition of what counts as an "error in the vote tabulation."[23] The second concerns the dispute over the date at which the local canvassing boards had to submit their tallies to the Secretary of State. The third element concerns the relationship between the (initial) protest phase of the proceedings and the (subsequent) contest phase. On each of these points, the Florida Supreme Court turned the original electoral system, as directed by the legislature, on its head.

23. Fla Stat Ann § 102.166(5) (West 2000).

A. ERRORS IN TABULATION

The first question of note involves the conditions that must be satisfied in order to have the hand recount that Gore requested. Here the basic statutory provision states that if the manual recount indicates an "error in the vote tabulation which could affect the outcome of the election, the county canvassing board shall:

> (a) Correct the error and recount the remaining precincts with the vote tabulation system;
> (b) Request the Department of State to verify the tabulation software; or
> (c) Manually recount all ballots."[24]

The entire recount procedure is thus predicated on a determination of an error in vote tabulation. Unless that is shown, no hand recount is authorized at all. In dealing with this issue, the administrative interpretation given to that phrase was that an "'error in the vote' tabulation only means a counting error resulting from incorrect election parameters or an error in the vote tabulating software."[25] The Florida Supreme Court also recognized, in line with federal principles on this same subject,[26] that it was bound to follow the interpretation that the Division of Elections gave to this phrase (and which the Secretary of State followed) unless it constituted clear error, which it promptly found:

> The plain language of section 102.166(5) refers to an error in the vote tabulation rather than the vote tabulation system. On its face, the statute does not include any words of limitation; rather, it provides a remedy for any type of mistake made in tabulating ballots. The Legislature has utilized the phrase "vote tabulation system" and "automatic tabulating equipment" in section 102.166 when it intended to refer to the voting system rather than the vote count. Equating "vote tabulation" with "vote tabulation system" obliterates the distinction created in section 102.166 by the Legislature.[27]

24. Id.

25. *Palm Beach County Canvassing Board v Harris,* 772 S2d 1220, 1229 (Fla Nov 21, 2000) (citing with disapproval the conclusion of the Division of Elections), vacd and remd as *Bush v Palm Beach County Canvassing Board,* 121 S Ct 471 (2000) (per curiam).

26. See, for example, *Chevron, USA, Inc v Natural Resources Defense Council, Inc,* 467 US 837, 866 (1984) (ruling that federal courts must defer to an administrative agency's reasonable interpretation of an ambiguous statute).

27. *Palm Beach County Canvassing Board v Harris,* 772 S2d at 1229.

This logic counts as pure sophistry, not plain meaning. The Florida Supreme Court drew a vacuous distinction between a vote tabulation and a vote tabulation system, without explaining why it matters in this case. At no point did it bother to offer any account as to the meaning of the term "tabulation" as it appears in both phrases. The clear sense of this term is captured in its dictionary definitions, which refer to the organization of data in tables or other accessible form.[28] That is exactly what the Secretary of State claimed. Her view allowed corrections to the extent that there were errors in addition and compilation; it also allowed correction to the extent that the tabulation system operated defectively so as to generate the wrong results. There is therefore perfectly good reason to use the phrase "automatic tabulating equipment" in some portions of the statute but not in others. But there is absolutely nothing in this provision that expands the word "tabulating" so that the statute "provides a remedy for any type of mistake made in tabulating ballots"—where the word tabulating no longer has its original restrictive meaning, but now covers the separate issue of standards: What counts as a valid vote?

The same point can be fortified when one looks at the three alternative remedies that are allowed once the canvassing board finds an error in tabulation. The first is that the errors that have been detected can be corrected. The remainder of the precincts can then be counted with the vote tabulation system in place.[29] It seems quite clear that the remedy in no way opens up the definitional question of what counts as a valid vote because the recount relies on the same machine reading used in the original counting process. The second remedy is again focused on how the mechanical task of counting could have gone awry, for it allows the canvassing board to ask the Department of State to verify the tabulation software.[30] This remedy does nothing whatsoever to change the initial definition of what counts as a valid vote. Its sole purpose is to debug the equipment used to tally votes.

All the action therefore swirls around the third option, which allows the canvassing board, if it chooses, to recount all the ballots manually.[31] The conjunction that separates alternative (b) from alternative (c) is "or," and

---

28. See, for example, the definition offered in *Merriam-Webster's Collegiate Dictionary* 1199 (10th ed 1993) ("tabulate 1 : to put into tabular form 2 : to count, record, or list systematically." "tabular . . . 2 a : of, relating to, or arranged in a table; *specif:* to set up in rows and columns b : computed by means of a table.").

29. See Fla Stat Ann § 102.166(5)(a).

30. See id § 102.166(5)(b).

31. See id § 102.166(5)(c).

this suggests that the choice of remedies lies within the sound discretion of the canvassing board, as the Florida Supreme Court itself recognized.[32] It defies comprehension, however, that the local canvassing board should have the power to make or break any candidate based simply on its choice among these three remedial options. The obvious structure of the entire provision is that the three remedies are *in pari materia*. They are all directed toward the same end—the correction of errors in tabulation that arise from either human or machine error. That program can be implemented only if the definition of a properly cast ballot does not vary with the method the canvassing board chooses to rectify the error in tabulation. On this view, the sole function of the hand recount is to examine ballots to see whether they meet the standards for a ballot that is machine readable.

At this point, the functions of the hand recount should be limited to two kinds of situations. The first is whether the chad has been so altered that it allows the passage of light through the opening. This test does not count dimpled chads, but counts partially hanging chads that have been displaced sufficiently to allow the light to shine through—the implicit requirement in the 1990 Palm Beach rule.[33] This test might have also been stretched (as had never been the case in Florida) to count some dimples on evidence of equipment malfunction that prevented the stylus from working—of which it appears that there was none.[34] A minimum condition for that approach is for the dimples to appear in a consistent fashion across the face of the ballot in which few, if any, of the chads are punched clear through. Under these circumstances, the argument can be made that the equipment failed to register votes whose intention can be discerned from the pattern of dimples that replicate the outcomes that are found in ballots that have been cleanly punched. But, to repeat, this conclusion is far from self-evident in the absence of some evidence of any systemwide failure of the ballot equipment. It is therefore a close question as to whether these "definite dimples in a coherent pattern" should count as errors in tabulation.

It is at this point that the distribution of powers between the Secretary of State, with her statutory responsibility for "interpretation" of the election

---

32. *Palm Beach County Canvassing Board v Harris*, 772 S2d at 1229.

33. Guidelines on Ballots with Chads Not Completely Removed (cited in note 17).

34. See *Gore v Harris*, 2000 WL 1790621, *3 (Fla Cir Ct Dec 3) (Sauls) (notice the lack of evidence of irregularity), revd and remd as *Gore v Harris*, 772 S2d 1243 (Fla Dec 8, 2000), revd as *Bush v Gore*, 121 S Ct 525.

law,[35] and the Florida Supreme Court comes into tension. Both the meaning of "tabulating" as well as the structure of the statute's remedial provisions wholly undermine the claim of the Florida Supreme Court that "the plain meaning" of the statute is such to allow a hand recount to take place under conditions in which dimples shall count, or at least be "considered," no matter what the condition of the voting machinery. The opposite conclusion more accurately captures the sense of the law. It thus counts as clear error to authorize the local canvassing boards to use a manual recount to remedy an "error in vote tabulation" as a pretext for adopting a broader definition of what counts as a valid vote. That decision belongs to the Secretary of State in her oversight function, not to the local canvassing boards, and not to the Florida courts.

The Florida Supreme Court sought to overcome the weight of the statutory language by noting the importance of guarding against error:

> Although error cannot be completely eliminated in any tabulation of the ballots, our society has not yet gone so far as to place blind faith in machines. In almost all endeavors, including elections, humans routinely correct the errors of machines. For this very reason Florida law provides a human check on both the malfunction of tabulation equipment and error in failing to accurately count the ballots.[36]

But once again this represents a complete misapprehension of how voting laws, and machines, work in Florida and elsewhere. The reason we have machine counts is to guard against the risk of human error and bias. The Florida Court thus wholly misstates the basic position by blithely assuming that it is possible to correct one type of error without introducing a second kind of error. The restricted types of review noted above constitute a sensible effort to take both human and machine error into account, and to guard against the possibility that zealous supporters of a given candidate or cause will invent votes where none exist.[37] A litmus test is not an impediment to justice but a bulwark against fraud. Watching election judges with political connections search for scratch marks on ballots is a somber reminder that both kinds of error exist.

35. See Fla Stat Ann § 97.012.

36. *Palm Beach County Canvassing Board v Harris*, 772 S2d at 1229–30.

37. On the risks, see Philip R. O'Connor, *Democrats, Hand-Count Gamble Un-American*, Chi Trib 23 (Nov 22, 2000) (noting the risk of human bias: "Machines don't have agendas. Humans do. Machines are honest.").

This reticence to rely on dimples is, moreover, ironically supported by the Illinois Supreme Court decision in *Pullen v Mulligan*,[38] which the Florida Supreme Court cited to support its own expansive views. In *Pullen* the Illinois Supreme Court wrote:

> To invalidate a ballot which clearly reflects the voter's intent, simply because a machine cannot read it, would subordinate substance to form and promote the means at the expense of the end.
>
> The voters here did everything which the Election Code requires when they punched the appropriate chad with the stylus. These voters should not be disfranchised where their intent may be ascertained with reasonable certainty, simply because the chad they punched *did not completely dislodge* from the ballot. Such a failure may be attributable to the fault of the election authorities, for failing to provide properly perforated paper, or it may be the result of the voter's disability or inadvertence. Whatever the reason, where the intention of the voter can be fairly and satisfactorily ascertained, that intention should be given effect.[39]

As a subsequent story in the Chicago Tribune reports,[40] this rhetoric did not cash out as a license for local boards to use whatever standards they chose in running the hand count. Rather, the hand count was done by shining lights through the ballot to see whether a human eye could pick up a beam of light that the machine might have missed.[41] Dimples, even definite dimples, were not counted, doubtless because of the risk of fraud and abuse of discretion that such a nebulous standard introduces. To my knowledge, there has never been an election in Florida in which dimples were counted as votes, given the need for some objective verification of the intention of a voter who can testify as to what he or she meant. On the merits therefore the

38. 138 Ill 2d 21, 561 NE2d 585 (1990).

39. Id at 611 (emphasis added) (citations omitted). "Did not completely" means "partially."

40. Jan Crawford Greenburg and Dan Mihalopoulos, *Bush Turns to Top U.S. Court: Republican Wants Florida's Manual Recount Stopped: Illinois Case Offers Shaky Precedent*, Chi Trib 1 (Nov 23, 2000) (noting that "the Illinois court actually affirmed a trial judge's order to exclude dented ballots, since he had decided he could not reasonably determine the voters' will by examining the ballots").

41. "[Circuit Court Judge Francis] Barth counted most of the ballots that had been perforated enough for light to shine through them, even if the paper tag known as a chad had not fallen out." Id.

Secretary of State relied on a far sounder interpretation of Florida law than did the Florida Supreme Court. If so, then the Florida Supreme Court abused its discretion in overriding the interpretation on which she relied with its own.

B. THE CUTOFF DATE

The second bone of contention in the first Florida Supreme Court case was whether the Secretary of State had discretion not to accept tallies from the various counties more than a week after the election. As a matter of administrative prudence, I think that it is clear that she made the wrong choice in cutting off the recount so precipitously. What she should have done in my view was to extend the period for the count while insisting on a standard of interpretation that precluded the use of the dimples, which was well within her discretion. But be that as it may, the question here is not whether she made the best possible choice, but whether she acted within the limits of her delegated powers. On this point the two key statutory provisions leave much to be desired. Section 102.111, which deals with the position of the Elections Canvassing Commission, provides:

If the county returns are not received by the Department of State by 5 P.M. of the seventh day following an election, all missing counties *shall* be ignored, and the results shown by the returns on file *shall* be certified.[42]

Thereafter Section 102.112 picks up the thread under the heading "Deadline for submission of county returns to the Department of State; penalties." It provides:

If the returns are not received by the department by the time specified, such returns *may* be ignored and the results on file at that time *may* be certified by the department.[43]

As the italicized words make clear, no one can doubt the conflict between these two sections. Section 102.111 is badly drafted because it seems to direct that all returns shall, in other words, must, be ignored if they are submitted after the seven-day period: nothing can be done to resurrect them. But if the returns are a dead letter, then it makes no sense to say in the next section that the Secretary of State may ignore them: for if she may

42. Fla Stat Ann § 102.111(1) (West 2000) (emphasis added).
43. Id § 102.112(1) (emphasis added).

ignore them, then she may also take them into account. In addition, to read the "shall" in Section 102.111 to control the "may" in Section 102.112 renders otiose and superfluous the penalties that the Secretary of State is empowered to impose on tardy local canvassing officials.

It is therefore incumbent to make some adjustment in the statutory language for the provisions to harmonize with each other. Truth be known that is not difficult to do. All that is required is to read the "shall" language so that it does not refer to the status of the late returns, but to the duty of the canvassing boards. The provision works, as it were, in personam and not in rem. The local canvassing officials are under a duty to submit the returns within the week under Section 102.111, but the Secretary of State has the power to extend that deadline if she so chooses, under, of course, the usual abuse of discretion standard that governs administrative officers generally. The upshot is that the local boards have a week to conduct a recount—no questions asked. But once they wish to go beyond that, then they must persuade the Secretary of State, who oversees the statewide process, to agree.

Unfortunately, at no point does the Florida Supreme Court acknowledge this obvious way to break the impasse. Instead it trots out every conceivable canon of statutory interpretation to

> conclude that, consistent with the Florida election scheme, the Secretary may reject a Board's amended returns only if the returns are submitted so late that their inclusion will preclude a candidate from contesting the certification or preclude Florida's voters from participating fully in the federal electoral process. The Secretary in the present case has made no claim that either of these conditions apply at this point in time.[44]

This order has no textual base whatsoever and it bears no relationship to either of the two sections that spawned the conflict in the first place. Surely, the Florida Supreme Court could not have defended its reading if Section 102.111 had been drafted to say, "The Canvassing Boards are under a Duty to Submit Returns within one week after the election unless this obligation is waived by the Secretary of State." By going far afield, the Florida Supreme Court invents its own standard that takes all the discretion away from the Secretary of State and puts her in a position where she *must* ac-

---

44. *Palm Beach County Canvassing Board v Harris*, 772 S2d 1220, 1239 (Fla Nov 21, 2000), vacd and remd as *Bush v Palm Beach County Canvassing Board*, 121 S Ct 471 (2000) (per curiam).

cept hand recounts completed after the statutory cutoff date so long as it remains possible to raise a contest, which is itself an odd rule given the inherent uncertainty over how long that contest might last. Yet even after this raw assumption of power, the court went further, taking it upon itself to determine when the protest phase of the electoral challenge is over. Here the Florida Supreme Court holds that it "must invoke the equitable powers of this Court to fashion a remedy that will allow a fair and expeditious resolution of the questions presented here."[45] The bottom line was 5:00 P.M. on Sunday, November 26, 2000. But this assertion of "equitable jurisdiction" has no textual referent: it looks like a fig leaf for judicial legislation, pure and simple.

In stressing this point, it is critical to note that "equitable jurisdiction" is not some formless field that gives all courts an implicit license to do as they please.[46] Traditionally, cases of equitable jurisdiction have been defined by the remedy afforded: damages were the province of the common law; specific performance, injunctions, foreclosure, and the like were equitable remedies that historically set out the scope of the Chancellor's jurisdiction. There is no question that equitable remedies could often be flexible; multiple parties were often involved, and remedies that operated on a defendant had to take into account their interests.[47] But by the same token equitable jurisdiction has never left courts with unchartered discretion to do what they choose: rather, it was constrained by its own set of rules, and I am aware of no general principle of equity that would allow a court to ride roughshod over a particular time limitation contained in a statute in favor of its own alternative date.[48] This is not a case where a court

45. *Palm Beach County Canvassing Board v Harris,* 772 S2d at 1240.

46. For the general principle, see *Albemarle Paper Co v Moody,* 422 US 405, 416–17 (1975) ("That the court's discretion is equitable in nature hardly means that it is unfettered by meaningful standards or shielded from thorough appellate review.") (citations omitted).

47. For a general discussion, see F.W. Maitland, *Equity: A Course of Lectures* (Cambridge 2d ed 1949) (revised by John Brunyate), in particular Lectures 1 and 2 (discussing the history and nature of courts of equity, particularly in England).

48. See, for example, *Cope v Anderson,* 331 US 461, 463–64 (1947) (noting that the same statute of limitations applies to legal and equitable remedies for the same underlying wrong). For a more general discussion, see Douglas Laycock, *Modern American Remedies: Cases and Materials* 931–34 (Little, Brown 2d ed 1994) (discussing interrelation between statutes of limitation and laches).

of equity invokes a principle of laches for an equitable cause of action in the absence of any specific time limitation. Nor is it even a case in which statutes of limitations are tolled to take into account specific disabilities of particular plaintiffs.

The reliance on equitable jurisdiction is a fig leaf, pure and simple, which allowed the Florida Supreme Court to impose its will on a Secretary of State who thought otherwise. The transfer of this power of discretion counts as arrogation by the judicial branch of powers reserved to the executive branch by statute. Had her decision been respected, the protest phase of this case would have ended as of November 14, 2000, and, as will become clear, her orders would have been immune from challenge. It makes good sense for the United States Supreme Court to enforce the result as of that date as the outcome that the legislature, by its articulation of general rules and its vesting of discretion in the Secretary of State, had directed.

C. PROTEST VERSUS CONTEST

The last feature of the Florida decisions that requires some comment concerns the relationship between the protest and contest phases of an election dispute. The protest phase, which has already been discussed, is directed toward the selection of administrative remedies prior to the certification of the election result by the Secretary of State. These remedies operate in much the same fashion as the initial administrative conduct of the election.[49] The contest phase begins only after the protest phase is over. Under Florida law the grounds for a contest after certification cover, in addition to issues of fraud, bribery, and eligibility, these two heads:

(c) Receipt of a number of illegal votes or rejection of a number of legal votes sufficient to change or place in doubt the result of the election.

. . .

(e) Any other cause or allegation which, if sustained, would show that a person other than the successful candidate was the person duly nominated or elected to the office in question or that the outcome of the elec-

---

49. The rules are contained in Fla Stat Ann § 102.168 (West 2000), enacted in 2000. The detailed rules governing these election contests are set out in *Gore v Harris,* 772 S2d 1243, 1253 n 4 (Fla Dec 8, 2000), revd and remd as *Bush v Gore,* 121 S Ct 525.

tion on a question submitted by referendum was contrary to the result declared by the canvassing board or election board.[50]

Once some violation of the statute has been found, the statute provides:

(8) The circuit judge to whom the contest is presented may fashion such orders as he or she deems necessary to ensure that each allegation in the complaint is investigated, examined, or checked, to prevent or correct any alleged wrong, and to provide any relief appropriate under such circumstances.[51]

Two features about the contest phase deserve immediate attention. The first is that one has contests about protests, so that the issues raised at the second phase are efforts to overturn incorrect decisions at the protest phase. It makes no sense to read the statute as though the contest phase is wholly unconnected with anything that went on at the protest stage. If so, then there is no need to bother to wait until the protest is over for the contest to begin. The second key feature is that the statute contemplates a judicial trial, not administrative action, at the contest phase. The minimum due process requirements of a trial in turn make it imperative that each party have the chance to raise the issues that it thinks appropriate, to present evidence to advance that contention, and to rebut contentions and evidence presented by the other side. Any sensible reading of the Florida statute seems to require that these elements be observed. The broad power of the circuit judge to issue orders that "each allegation in the complaint [be] investigated, examined, or checked, to prevent or correct any alleged wrong,"[52] surely means to give a broad scope to discovery in cases of this sort. But these provisions do not do away with the other elements of a trial, including the orderly presentation of evidence, under the usual rules of admissibility and cross-examination, before the court for its decision.

The order issued by the Florida Supreme Court did nothing to respect either of these key structural features about the relationship between these two phases of an integrated process. The threshold issue in its deliberation was to determine the standard of review that should be used during the contest phase. The statute itself is silent on the standard of review that the circuit court in an election contest should apply to the administrative re-

50. Fla Stat Ann § 102.168(3)(c)–(e).
51. Id § 102.168(8).
52. Id.

sults of the protest phase. Yet the Florida case law has read Florida law as calling for the abuse of discretion standard that Judge Sauls had applied, most recently in its first foray into this dispute.[53]

The internal logic of the Florida statute strongly confirms that this review should be done, as is the case with other administrative actions, under an abuse of discretion standard. After all, the initial statute gives the canvassing board the initial choice over the method that it wishes to use to correct errors in tabulation brought to light in the protest phase. Indeed in its first decision, the Florida Supreme Court stressed the word "or" in the choice of remedies. It seems odd in the extreme to reverse fields and now hold that the original protest was little more than a preliminary canter, so that the disappointed party can relitigate on demand in the contest phase all matters in the case solely on the assertion that the undervote had not been properly counted.

Once it chose the de novo review standard, the Florida Supreme Court simply took over the entire administration of the election challenge, trespassing on the functions allocated to either the canvassing boards or the Secretary of State. Thus the Florida Supreme Court took it upon itself to order a statewide recount of the undervote (but not the overvote).[54] Yet it nowhere explained where it received the power to make (as an appellate court no less) an order that neither side had requested. In support of its decision, it emphasized the words "investigated, examined, or checked," and it acted as though the prior referent to the phrase "each allegation contained in the complaint" did not limit their scope.[55] Trials do not allow an appellate court to set for itself the parameters of the initial complaint, and neither Gore nor Bush asked for a statewide recount. The Florida Supreme Court made a unilateral decision to order a statewide recount, which flies in the face of the structure of the statute, which conducts protests on a county-by-county level only, and which leaves it to the parties to determine

53. See *Broward County Canvassing Board v Hogan*, 607 S2d 508, 510 (Fla Dist Ct App 1992) (ruling that county canvassing boards had discretion to order or not to order a hand recount), quoted in *Gore v Harris*, 772 S2d at 1265 (Wells dissenting):

> Although section 102.168 grants the right of contest, it does not change the discretionary aspect of the review procedures outlined in section 102.166. The statute clearly leaves the decision whether or not to hold a manual recount of the votes as a matter to be decided within the discretion of the canvassing board.

54. *Gore v Harris*, 772 S2d at 1262.

55. Id at 1261.

the scope of any contest that they might wish to raise if they are disappointed with the outcome of the protest phase. It is hard to see how any remedy that goes beyond the boundaries of the complaint could count as "appropriate" for a judicial proceeding, even if the other requisites for a full-fledged contest had been satisfied, which, as noted above, they were not.

In order to secure this result, the Florida Court did not give due weight to the statutory words "rejection" and "legal." It wrote

> that a legal vote is one in which there is a "clear indication of the intent of the voter." We next address whether the term "rejection" used in section 102.168(3)(c) includes instances where the County Canvassing Board has not counted legal votes. Looking at the statutory scheme as a whole, it appears that the term "rejected" does encompass votes that may exist but have not been counted.[56]

This reading makes it appear as though voter failure is tantamount to official misconduct. As Chief Justice Rehnquist wrote, "Florida statutory law cannot reasonably be thought to *require* the counting of improperly marked ballots."[57] If the Florida legislature wanted to make the failure to ascertain the intention of the voter the standard for triggering a contest, it could have done so in just those words. But what it did do was to treat the exclusion of legally-cast ballots on a par with the inclusion of illegal ballots (for example, prisoner votes). A more sensible reading indicates that this provision is directed at local election officials who rejected, that is refused to accept or to count, votes that were properly cast. The image connoted is a blockade of legal voters from the polls. The paired use of the terms "legal" and "illegal" is designed to catch cases of misconduct of electoral officials, which is just not involved here. The section reads on a par with the provisions that allow contests over the question of candidate eligibility, fraud, and bribery.[58] It does not invite any decision not to count those ballots that do not meet the standards for validity that were set out in the election procedures themselves and then communicated clearly to voters.

In sum, then, Chief Justice Rehnquist draws blood when he writes: "It is inconceivable that what constitutes a vote that must be counted under the 'error in the vote tabulation' language of the protest phase is different from

---

56. Id at 1257.
57. *Bush v Gore,* 121 S Ct at 537 (Rehnquist concurring).
58. See Fla Stat Ann § 102.168(3)(a)–(b).

what constitutes a vote that must be counted under the 'legal votes' language of the contest phase."[59] The two sections cannot be read to use standards that are in flat contradiction with each other. Nor is the situation salvaged by appealing to Section 102.168(e), for the cause to be shown can only be the failure to adopt a broader definition of a countable ballot than that applicable in the protest phase, which makes no more sense here than it does with Section 102.168(e). Unfortunately, the Florida Supreme Court, once again, was happy to proceed simply on a showing that dimples were not counted on ballots somewhere inside the state, wholly without any showing of machine failure or electoral irregularity.[60]

This illicit expansion of the statutory grounds for a contest seems pretty clear. What is worse is that the maneuver wholly precludes the articulation of any coherent grounds to relate the protest to the contest provisions, even though the statutory scheme contemplates that the contest should be to review the protest stage, and commence within five days after it is finished.[61] But the difference matters. Given that an election contest is a trial, the Florida Supreme Court cannot simply conclude without a trial that the Broward County manual recount was correctly done. If it is appropriate in a de novo proceeding (assuming that was allowed under the statute) to count votes that have not been punched as required, then that de novo review cannot be selectively invoked, but must apply to all phases of the case. It is therefore wholly improper at the contest phase *not* to allow Bush to move—or indeed to raise the issue on its own motion—to exclude dimpled ballots on the grounds that they manifested no clear intention at all. The dual standard is not acceptable. The pro-Bush findings by the local canvassing boards were subject to de novo review. The pro-Gore findings were treated as res judicata.

The utter lack of any sense of continuity between protest and contest was only magnified by the Florida Supreme Court's treatment of the Miami-Dade decision not to continue the recount of the undervote when it decided that it could not do so accurately before the November 26, 2000,

---

59. *Bush v Gore,* 121 S Ct at 537 n 4 (Rehnquist concurring).

60. This point is repeatedly stressed in the dissent of Wells, C.J., see *Gore v Harris,* 772 S2d at 1263–64.

61. A party that wants to raise a contest must file a complaint "within 5 days after midnight of the date the last county canvassing board empowered to canvass the returns certifies the results of that particular election following a protest pursuant to s. 102.166(1)." Fla Stat Ann § 102.168(2), relied on in *Gore v Harris,* 772 S2d at 1270 (Wells dissenting).

deadline set by the Florida Supreme Court. The entire thrust of the first Florida Supreme Court decision was to hold that the discretion in the protest phase rested with the canvassing boards even after the seven-day deadline of November 14, 2000, had passed. But once this Canvassing Board decided that it could not recount all the ballots (as Section 102.166(5)(c) required), then its discretion vanished in favor of an *obligation* to recount all ballots even after the court-imposed November 26, 2000, deadline.[62] That overlap in processes makes it quite clear that what happens here is not an orderly progression between protest and contest, where the grounds of the contest are necessarily more limited than choices available in the protest stage. Rather, the entire statutory scheme is transmuted into one long recount that in the end was entrusted to the trial judge of Leon County, who was asked to assemble personnel to continue the recount on a statewide level, thereby assuming all the functions vested by statute in the Secretary of State. At this point, it seems clear that Chief Justice Rehnquist has it exactly right when he writes of the various maneuvers of the Florida Supreme Court:

> Underlying the extension of the certification deadline and the short-changing of the contest period was, presumably, the clear implication that certification was a matter of significance: The certified winner would enjoy presumptive validity, making a contest proceeding by the losing candidate an uphill battle. In its latest opinion, however, the court empties certification of virtually all legal consequence during the contest, and in doing so departs from the provisions enacted by the Florida Legislature.[63]

CONCLUSION

In sum, there is ample reason to believe, as the Rehnquist concurrence in *Bush v Gore* urges, that the Florida Supreme Court adopted, under the guise of interpretation, a scheme for conducting election challenges that deviates markedly from that which the Florida legislature had set out in its statutes. I have tried to indicate the multiple ways in which the Florida Court did violence to the state statutory scheme. To many modern mainstream constitutional scholars that conclusion might seem harsh because

62. *Gore v Harris,* 772 S2d at 1257–59.
63. *Bush v Gore,* 121 S Ct at 536–37 (Rehnquist concurring).

they find it hard to accept that weighty matters of constitutional interpretation do have right, and hence wrong, answers that can be gathered from a close examination of text, structure, and function. But accepting that view of pervasive skepticism disables them from intelligent criticism of the United States Supreme Court. If, conceptually, the Florida Supreme Court could not cross an imaginary line, then neither could the United States Supreme Court. If constitutional law is politics by another name, then it makes no more sense to condemn the United States Supreme Court for its political predilections than it does to condemn the Florida Supreme Court for its. All is politics and in that world rank alone becomes the sole arbiter of truth.

Effective criticism of the United States Supreme Court necessarily depends, then, on a view of language that allows for us to recognize that legal interpretation at any level could be wrong, indeed so wrong as to count as an abuse of discretion for partisan political ends. I think that charges of serious conceptual error do have a lot of force in dealing with the equal protection argument that five members of the United States Supreme Court found decisive. But by the same token, I hope that I have said enough to show that the alternative Article II argument has far more traction in light of what I regard to be the manifest errors in the Florida Supreme Court's decisions. Quite simply, if the canvassing boards and the Secretary of State did not abuse their discretion, then it seems as though the Florida Supreme Court abused its. And if it abused its discretion, then the United States Supreme Court did not abuse its.

Any Article II attack on the decision of the Florida Court would itself be quite unintelligible if statutory text did not limit, and limit sharply, the range of interpretive options open to a court. But so long as we can maintain the conceptual line between interpretation and legislation, then we must recognize that it is always possible for any court, at any level, to stray over that line so that its decrees can be regarded as judicial legislation. It is, to say the least, a regrettable truth that the outcome of a presidential election necessarily turns on a question of degree, by asking just how wrong is wrong enough to topple the decision of the Florida Supreme Court. But the peculiar determination to override at various times the decisions of Florida's canvassing boards, Secretary of State, and circuit court judges crosses that line.

Thus this tortured case draws to a close. It is tragic that on matters of this moment, no one can offer a mathematical demonstration of whether the mistakes of the Florida Supreme Court were large enough to constitute a gross deviation from the Florida statutory scheme, as I believe that they were. But even that uncertainty should prompt the outspoken critics of the United States Supreme Court to reign in their indignation a little bit. After all, in order to reach that conclusion, one has to think that the United States Supreme Court committed clear error in its decision. But owing to the sorry performance of the Florida Supreme Court, that conclusion cannot be maintained, which I think is why the United States Supreme Court's decision was greeted generally with widespread relief and not widespread protest. In the end it is regrettable, but true, that the all-or-nothing choice of the President of the United States could rest on what is in the end a question of degree, as so many vital questions are. Such is the way of the world, and it will not do to rail against it.

2

Leaving the Decision to Congress

ELIZABETH GARRETT

In *Bush v Gore*,[1] the majority defended the Court's aggressive role in the selection of the forty-third president:

> None are more conscious of the vital limits on judicial authority than are the members of this Court, and none stand more in admiration of the Constitution's design to leave the selection of the President to the people, through their legislatures, and to the political sphere. When contending parties invoke the process of the courts, however, it becomes our unsought responsibility to resolve the federal and constitutional issues the judicial system has been forced to confront.[2]

These words sound strange in the context of the Court's certiorari jurisdiction; the justices had the discretion to avoid hearing any or all of the cases they voted to take. Moreover, even if they felt compelled to exercise their discretion to hear the cases, they could have rendered decisions that offered the possibility of final resolution by state entities or political actors. The Court was not a necessary part of the election proceedings in 2000, so its decision to grant certiorari in two cases and to issue a stay of the Florida recount must be justified.

I will argue first that the Court should have done more than

I am grateful to Michael Bresson, Jack Goldsmith, Dennis Hutchinson, Daryl Levinson, Andrei Marmor, Efton Park, Rick Pildes, Eric Posner, and Adrian Vermeule for helpful comments; to Leslie Danks for exceptional research assistance; and to the James H. Douglas Fund for the Study of Law and Government and the Law and Government Program Endowment at the University of Chicago Law School for generous financial support.

1. 121 S Ct 525 (2000).
2. Id at 533.

admire the constitutional design; it should have adhered to that design and left the matter to the political sphere. More specifically, it was the responsibility of Congress to resolve any disputes that might have arisen from the election in Florida. Although the Court has a long history of involvement in the electoral process and in political matters, it often makes the situation it finds worse rather than better. Its rather undistinguished record in recent cases dealing with electoral issues results both from the limitations of case-by-case adjudication and from the Court's unsophisticated view of the political process. The Court should consider adopting a less intrusive stance in cases affecting the political process, intervening only to ensure free and equal access to that process. Certainly, it had ample opportunity to adopt a more modest role in this litigation.[3]

Some who have criticized the Court's reasoning in *Bush v Gore* or in its decision to stay the recount have nonetheless concluded that its intrusion into the political process was justified because it settled the presidential election dispute before the country was plunged into a constitutional or political crisis.[4] This distrust of the political branches to resolve controversies is part of a larger distrust of politics. For many legal academics and others in the intellectual elite, the messiness of the political process causes great concern. They are more comfortable with the reasoned decisionmaking and calm proceedings of the judiciary and thus look to the courts to save us from distasteful partisan wrangling. I will argue that there was no sign of a political crisis that would have done great damage to our institutions of governance. Instead, it was possible that the dispute would have worked itself out over time as state actors played their parts. If the controversy had lingered until January 6, 2001, the United States Congress would have been the appropriate forum to determine the outcome. In that way, citizens

3. I am focusing in this chapter on the role of the federal courts—in particular, of the United States Supreme Court. The appropriate role of the state courts in the 2000 election litigation is primarily a matter of state law, turning on whether the legislature has decided, through its election code, to leave the resolution of disputes to the judiciary. What the Florida legislature had decided in this case and whether the Florida courts followed legislative directives are issues beyond the scope of this analysis.

4. See, for example, Cass R. Sunstein, *Order Without Law,* in this volume; Dennis J. Hutchinson, *Law and Politics in the Supreme Court,* Chicago Trib 21 (Dec 17, 2000). Others who are more supportive of the Court's reasoning in the case also cite fears of a political crisis as a justification for judicial action. See, for example, Richard A. Posner, *Florida 2000: A Legal and Statistical Analysis of the Election Deadlock and the Ensuing Litigation,* 2000 Sup Ct Rev 1; John Yoo, *Bush Has a Federal Case,* Wall St J A26 (Nov 16, 2000).

could have held their representatives politically accountable for their actions, a result we are denied with respect to unelected justices. The long-term effect of the Court's premature imposition of order may be a further decline in the respect we have for the political branches. Continuing low expectations of our elected officials may well be a self-fulfilling prophecy.

I

The Supreme Court's role in shaping the electoral process is substantial. In some cases, notably the voting rights cases,[5] the judicial role can be defended as necessary to safeguard the equal access of every American to elected officials and institutions of governance.[6] Even if the institutional limitations of the adjudicatory process decrease the possibility that courts can provide comprehensive solutions, on balance the good done by the judiciary in these cases of political process failure outweighs the harm. Of course, even in the voting rights area, legislative involvement through the passage of the Voting Rights Act of 1965[7] was required for widespread and effective vindication of voting rights. In many other cases involving politics, it seems likely that judicial involvement is more detrimental than beneficial, a possibility that should counsel judges to take a more modest approach.

Two examples of judicial intrusion into the electoral sphere provide sobering evidence of the often deleterious results. First, the Court's decision in *Buckley v Valeo*,[8] which allowed limitations on campaign contributions, but not on expenditures, has resulted in a campaign finance system that virtually no one views as acceptable or sensible. The current regime is attacked from the right because of its limitations on campaign contributions,[9] and from the left because the jurisprudence makes a comprehensive regulatory scheme impossible.[10] Money in the political system has a hy-

5. See, for example, *Baker v Carr*, 369 US 186 (1962) (imposing one-vote, one-person principle); *Reynolds v Sims*, 377 US 533 (1964) (requiring redistricting in context of state legislative election to meet equipopulation principle).

6. See John Hart Ely, *Democracy and Distrust* 117 (1980); Michael J. Klarman, *The Puzzling Resistance to Political Process Theory*, 77 Va L Rev 747, 757–58 (1991).

7. 42 USC §§ 1971 et seq.

8. 424 US 1 (1976) (per curiam).

9. See, for example, Lillian R. BeVier, *Campaign Finance Reform: Specious Arguments, Intractable Dilemmas*, 94 Colum L Rev 1258 (1994); Bradley A. Smith, *Faulty Assumptions and Undemocratic Consequences of Campaign Finance Reform*, 105 Yale LJ 1049 (1996).

10. See, for example, Burt Neuborne, *Is Money Different?*, 77 Tex L Rev 1609 (1999).

draulic quality:[11] if laws leave possible avenues of spending unregulated, money tends to flow there, and sometimes these new streams are relatively hard to discover and publicize. Obstacles to complete disclosure are worrisome because information about the identity of contributors and the amount of their financial support improves voters' ability to cast their ballots for the people who most closely represent their views.

Recent campaign finance decisions are not appreciably better than *Buckley*. In *Nixon v Shrink Missouri Government PAC*,[12] for example, the Court affirmed the contribution/expenditure dichotomy, applying a less stringent standard of scrutiny to laws regulating campaign contributions. Furthermore, it required no evidence that contributions in excess of the extremely low statutory caps present a danger of quid pro quo corruption. Future challenges to the Court's capacity to render astute campaign finance decisions will be increasingly complex and difficult. As Justice Kennedy observed in his dissent in *Shrink Missouri Government PAC*, new methods of communication offer new possibilities for meaningful regulation, yet the Court does not consider these technological advances as relevant to its decisions.

> Among the facts the Court declines to take into account is the emergence of cyberspace communication by which political contributions can be reported almost simultaneously with payment. The public can then judge for itself whether the candidate or the officeholder has so overstepped that we no longer trust him or her to make a detached and neutral judgment. This is a far more immediate way to assess the integrity and importance of our leaders than through the hidden world of soft money and covert speech.[13]

The Court's ineffectual and often counterproductive jurisprudence in the campaign finance cases results in part from its institutional limitations, as the passage from Kennedy's dissent suggests. Effective campaign finance regulation demands comprehensive structures and extensive fact-finding. Policymakers must anticipate the reactions of sophisticated political players to the design and scope of regulation and either make adjustments in the original structure or make subsequent modifications. Courts are not insti-

---

11. See Samuel Issacharoff and Pamela S. Karlan, *The Hydraulics of Campaign Finance Reform*, 77 Tex L Rev 1705, 1708 (1999).

12. 528 US 377 (2000).

13. Id at 408 (Kennedy dissenting).

tutionally suited for this kind of decisionmaking. Instead, they work piece-meal, without sufficient awareness of the effects of their holdings, leading several scholars to point to the campaign finance cases as among the best examples of the law of unintended consequences.[14] Interestingly, similar institutional concerns led courts for decades to refuse to become involved in the mechanics of how states conduct their elections. As federal appellate courts have observed, intervention in state electoral processes, other than in extraordinary circumstances, would "thrust [federal judges] into the de-tails of virtually every election, tinkering with the state's election machinery, reviewing petitions, registration cards, vote tallies, and certificates of elec-tion for all manner of error and insufficiency under state and federal law."[15] In an early federal court challenge to the Florida recount, Judge Middlebrooks concluded that "[t]he central thrust of these decisions is that federal courts should tread cautiously in the traditional state province of electoral procedures and tabulations."[16] The new equal protection right es-tablished by the majority in *Bush v Gore* may result in a jurisprudence that looks very much like *Buckley* and its progeny, as courts rule occasionally on particular aspects of a comprehensive state election scheme and do so with-out much empirical basis.

One of the complexities inherent in the regulation of campaign finance concerns the role that political parties should play.[17] Here the Court's in-stitutional limitations are acute, and its general difficulty in dealing with po-litical parties further confounds the problem. Indeed, cases involving po-litical parties provide a second example of unfortunate judicial intrusion into the electoral system. The Court's unsophisticated view of political par-ties was placed in sharp relief recently when it struck down California's blanket primary law in *California Democratic Party v Jones*.[18] Whether adop-

14. See, for example, Steven M. Gillon, *"That's Not What We Meant to Do": Reform and Its Unintended Consequences in Twentieth-Century America* 234 (2000); Cass R. Sunstein, *Political Equality and Unintended Consequences,* 94 Colum L Rev 1390, 1395–96 (1994).

15. *Duncan v Poythress,* 657 F2d 691, 701 (5th Cir 1981) (quoting *Powell v Power,* 436 F2d 84, 86 (2d Cir 1970)), cert granted, 455 US 937, cert dismissed, 455 US 1012 (1982).

16. *Siegel v LePore,* 120 F Supp 2d 1041, 1051 (SD Fla), affd, 234 F3d 1163 (11th Cir 2000).

17. In the 2000 term, the Court is again faced with a dispute involving expenditures on behalf of candidates by political parties. *Federal Election Commission v Colorado Republican Federal Campaign Committee,* 213 F3d 1221 (10th Cir), cert granted, 120 S Ct 296 (2000).

18. 530 US 567 (2000).

tion of the blanket primary is a wise political reform is a difficult question. In a blanket primary, voters can vote in the primaries of more than one party; for example, a voter can choose among Democrats for governor and among Republicans for secretary of state. The people of California adopted the blanket primary through a popular vote, apparently to empower moderate candidates over more extreme partisans and to increase voter participation and confidence. The complexity of the case is evident in the unusual coalition of the challengers. Both major and minor parties attacked the blanket primary as an unconstitutional burden on the rights of association and free speech. Typically, the interests of minor and major parties diverge: minor parties seek ballot position, the right to participate in debates, the ability to campaign near polls on election day, or some other sort of access to the political system, while the major parties work to preserve their duopoly control of the political process.[19]

One would be hard-pressed to find in the majority opinion evidence of an awareness of the extensive political science and legal literature discussing the role of political parties in structuring voter choice in the voting booth.[20] Nor is there any mention of the substantial scholarly literature distinguishing between the interests of minor parties, which operate more as ideological groups, and the interests of major parties, which play a significant governance role in addition to their expressive activities.[21] Instead, the Court talks about political parties as though they all share the same characteristics and as though even major parties are akin to private organizations whose paramount concern is communicating a message rather than forming a government. The opinion would have been strengthened by a nuanced view of political parties and their fundamental importance in shaping the options presented to voters on the ballot and in organizing in-

19. See Richard L. Hasen, *Entrenching the Duopoly: Why the Supreme Court Should Not Allow the States to Protect the Democrats and Republicans from Political Competition,* 1997 Sup Ct Rev 331 (1997) (describing this divergence and critiquing the Court's ballot access jurisprudence); Samuel Issacharoff and Richard H. Pildes, *Politics as Markets: Partisan Lockups of the Democratic Process,* 50 Stan L Rev 643 (1998) (terming this a "partisan lockup" and urging a structural analysis of political process cases).

20. See, for example, Leon D. Epstein, *Political Parties in the American Mold* (1986); Nathaniel Persily and Bruce E. Cain, *The Legal Status of Political Parties: A Reassessment of Competing Paradigms,* 100 Colum L Rev 775 (2000).

21. See, for example, Steven J. Rosenstone, Roy L. Behr, and Edward H. Lazarus, *Third Parties in America: Citizen Response to Major Party Failure* (2d ed 1996).

stitutions of governance. Such a sophisticated view could have led to several different outcomes. Those who believe strong parties are necessary for effective governments might also have struck down the blanket primary;[22] those who are more concerned that the people determine how their choices at the polls are structured might have found the blanket primary to be an acceptable regulation of political parties.[23] One particularly interesting perspective was provided by an amicus brief that argued the blanket primary is unconstitutional as applied to minor parties and constitutional as applied to major parties.[24]

The point therefore is not that the Court got the result wrong in the blanket primary case, although the majority may well have erred. The problem is that we cannot be sure, nor can the justices, because their view of the political process is inaccurate and rather naïve. Moreover, the Court's institutional limitations and its inability to resolve problems comprehensively again undermined its effectiveness. The blanket primary case, like *Bush v Gore,* may have ramifications past those intended by the majority. Just as the new equal protection right in *Bush v Gore* may extend well past the facts of the case (despite the majority's unconvincing attempt to limit its reach[25]), *California Democratic Primary v Jones* casts into question the ability of states to impose open primaries on unwilling political parties. The majority provides a rather flimsy distinction between the two kinds of primaries[26] in an attempt to protect from attack the open primary used by many states, sometimes without the support of the regulated political parties.

In short, although the Court has entered the political thicket frequently, its performance in these cases is disappointing. *Bush v Gore* was even more problematic for the Court than most other cases dealing with election law. Usually, the Court's ruling benefits large groups of candidates

22. For such an argument, see Nathaniel Persily, *Toward a Functional Defense of Political Party Autonomy,* 76 NYU L Rev (forthcoming 2001).

23. See Richard L. Hasen, *Do the Parties or the People Own the Electoral Process?,* 149 U Pa L Rev 815 (2001).

24. Brief for the Brennan Center for Justice at the New York University School of Law as Amicus Curiae in Support of Neither Party, *California Democratic Party v Jones,* 530 US 567 (2000) (No 99-401).

25. 121 S Ct at 532 ("Our consideration is limited to the present circumstances, for the problem of equal protection in election processes generally presents many complexities.").

26. See 530 US at 2409 n 6.

or political actors. For example, in the campaign finance area, the Court's jurisprudence arguably benefits incumbents relative to challengers, or the independently wealthy relative to middle- and lower-income Americans. The blanket primary decision favors more extreme candidates over more moderate ones. Rarely does the Court actually know that its decision will result in the immediate election of one or the other individual who is a party in the case. In *Bush v Gore,* however, the Court must have been aware that each decision it rendered helped George Bush and harmed Al Gore. Stopping the Florida recount,[27] for example, destroyed any hope of the Gore campaign that the process would be completed by the time the electoral college voted. Moreover, the Court has a substantially greater and more direct interest in the winner of the presidential election than in the winner of a disputed congressional or local office. The next president is likely to select one or more justices, a decision in which all the current justices have a significant interest. In an institution that makes decisions collectively, the future membership determines whether a retiring justice's jurisprudential legacy will live on and whether remaining justices will be able to assemble majorities for their opinions. Supreme Court justices value their ability to shape policy while on the bench and afterward; they are therefore vitally and personally interested in who serves as the forty-third president. I am not arguing that this conflict of interest—felt by all nine justices, not just the five who joined in the per curiam opinion—should have disqualified them. But this factor was bound to open any decision to charges of partisanship.

The likelihood that any opinion in the 2000 election dispute would be credibly attacked as partisan, combined with the disappointing performance of the Court generally in this area, should have counseled in favor of judicial restraint. Certainly, the Court had the opportunity to adopt a much less aggressive role in the presidential election contest. The first decision it handed down[28] was unnecessary, and the petition for certiorari should have been dismissed as improvidently granted. By the time the case was argued, it was clear that the additional votes counted because certification

---

27. *Bush v Gore,* 121 S Ct 512 (2000) (order granting certiorari and stay pending further order of the Court).

28. *Bush v Palm Beach County Canvassing Board,* 121 S Ct 471 (2000) (per curiam) (remanding the decision on the date of certification to the Florida Supreme Court for clarification of its grounds for decision).

had been delayed by the Florida Supreme Court's decision had not changed the outcome. Bush remained the winner, albeit by 393 fewer votes. While the disparity in votes might matter in a subsequent election contest (if certified votes were given a presumption of correctness that votes found in subsequent recounts were not), this part of the controversy could have been determined later in the contest proceeding.

Moreover, it is not the case that the Court's failure to avoid a decision in this first case had minimal consequences for the rest of the litigation.[29] On the contrary, the Court drastically altered the substance and tone of future state court decisions by suggesting that the language in Article II of the Constitution, combined with provisions of the Electoral Count Act,[30] affected the way that state courts could interpret state election laws in presidential contests. It seems quite likely that the Florida Supreme Court would have provided more specific standards for determining a voter's intent in a recount, perhaps rejecting the controversial dimpled chads, had it not been convinced that such routine statutory interpretation would be struck down by the United States Supreme Court under an Article II analysis. Thus, in the guise of minimalism, the Court's remand decision had substantial ramifications, setting the Florida Supreme Court up for a reversal on the equal protection argument not deemed worthy of certiorari at the time the Court considered *Bush v Palm Beach County Canvassing Board*. In fact, so many courts had dismissed the equal protection argument, in part because precedent seemed to strongly disfavor this analysis, that the possibility of a reversal on this ground must have seemed a remote possibility to the state justices. These developments are particularly unfortunate because the Article II argument could not ultimately command a majority of the Court, and it had not been extensively briefed or argued before the remand was justified on this ground.

Similarly, the surprising decision of the Court to halt the recount, pending its decision on the merits of *Bush v Gore*, was unnecessary and gave rise to subsequent claims that the Court had acted in a partisan manner. In his separate opinion, Justice Scalia justified issuing the stay, an action that caused irreparable harm to Gore, particularly given the majority's ultimate disposition of the issue of remedy. He argued:

29. For an argument that this opinion was minimalistic, see Cass R. Sunstein, *The Broad Virtue in a Modest Ruling*, NY Times A29 (Dec 5, 2000).

30. 3 USC §§ 1–18.

The counting of votes that are of questionable legality does in my view threaten irreparable harm to petitioner, and to the country, by casting a cloud upon what he claims to be the legitimacy of his election. Count first, and rule upon legality afterwards, is not a recipe for producing election results that have the public acceptance democratic stability requires.[31]

This statement, apparently a product of Scalia's political intuition, is unconvincing. In some election disputes, recounts occur as part of the proceedings, and then the courts determine whether the information provided by the recounts justifies accepting the new vote totals or retaining the certified totals. For example, in a case similar to *Bush v Gore* because its final resolution also lay appropriately with a political branch, the Supreme Court allowed a state-run recount in a contested Senate election even though the Senate retained the ultimate authority whether to include the recounted ballots or not.[32]

The circumstances of the 2000 presidential election render Scalia's prediction especially contestable. After we watched the recounts in various Florida counties, observed the sometimes sloppy handling of the ballots, and listened to the arguments about dimpled and pregnant chads, many of us were left with a sense that a subsequent evaluation of the recounted ballots would be required. Certainly, some partisans would embrace any recount that put Gore ahead, just as some partisans accepted without hesitation the decision to stop counting punch card ballots when some would likely have shown objective and clear evidence of a vote not counted by the machines. But, for most of us, there were enough questions about the recount process to allow a further consideration of new vote totals. Moreover, a reasoned decision not to include all or some of the recounted ballots would have received significant political support. Certainly, the legitimacy of Bush's win would not have been cast in more doubt than it was by a process that allowed the Supreme Court to determine the winner.

Another disturbing aspect of the Court's enthusiastic intrusion into the counting process was that a recount might well have rendered the final decision unnecessary. So far, Governor Bush had won every count and recount. It is possible he would have continued to win after the recount that

31. *Bush v Gore*, 121 S Ct at 512 (Scalia concurring).

32. *Roudebush v Hartke*, 405 US 15 (1972). See also Samuel Issacharoff, Pamela S. Karlan, and Richard H. Pildes, *When Elections Go Bad: The Law of Democracy and the Presidential Election of 2000* 25–27 (2001) (discussing cases where recounts occurred and in some the results were not accepted, and cases where recounts were not conducted).

would have been supervised by Leon County Judge Lewis. Or Judge Lewis might have imposed standards that would have satisfied, or at least ameliorated, the equal protection concerns articulated by seven justices. Preliminary results of the media-funded recount suggest that a continued recount would have eliminated the need for the Court to issue a decision that selected the next president because Bush was likely to remain the winner.[33] We could have learned the answer much more quickly had the Court exercised restraint and worried less about political damage to Bush that was more speculative than real under the circumstances.

In short, the Court was not an unwilling party forced to participate in the 2000 election contest. It made choices to intervene at three different times. Had it made different choices in the decision to remand and the decision to stay the recount, it might have avoided rendering the controversial final decision that effectively selected George Bush as president. But, some argue, the decision to intervene, which opened the Court to charges of partisanship, should be seen as courageous because it risked the Court's reputation to avert a constitutional crisis. It is to such arguments—that the decision's positive effect on the stability of our democracy justifies the judicial intrusion into the presidential election process—that I turn next.

II

Even those who cannot be counted as supporters for the Court's reasoning in *Bush v Gore* have argued that the Court's intervention is nonetheless justified because it had ancillary benefits. First, some have argued that the Court's decision will propel election reform and that its role in spurring long-needed changes in the way we cast ballots is a beneficial side effect of the ruling.[34] The Court explicitly stated that "[a]fter the current counting, it is likely legislative bodies nationwide will examine ways to improve the mechanisms and machinery for voting."[35] That, of course, is the point. After the mess in Florida, election reform was going to be a salient item on the public agenda *whether or not* the Court became involved. In two of three states that have recently adopted comprehensive election reform, Mary-

33. John M. Broder, *Study Finds Some Ballots Unaccounted For,* NY Times A16 (Apr 5, 2001) (finding Bush would have won under most standards to discern voter intent had the recount of sixty counties ordered by the state supreme court continued).

34. See, for example, Samuel Issacharoff, *The Court's Legacy for Voting Rights,* NY Times A39 (Dec 14, 2000).

35. *Bush v Gore,* 121 S Ct at 529.

land and Oklahoma, election disasters convinced citizens to fund modern-
ization and standardization. In the third, California, an elected official with
a passion for improving the mechanisms of voting, Secretary of State Bill
Jones, has forcefully brought the issue to the public's attention.[36] Already
federal lawmakers have introduced bills to help fund improvements or to
offer expertise in ballot design and voting machinery.[37]

These efforts may or may not be successful.[38] Even though the issue is a
hot button one now, the obstacle course awaiting any legislative proposal in
the states or Congress is arduous. Disagreements about the right kind of reform may make action difficult even if all agree that change is necessary. Although he has initially appeared supportive of changes in election procedures, President Bush may decide not to back reform either because it
impermissibly intrudes on state sovereignty or because such efforts cast
doubt on the legitimacy of his election. In the end, states and localities may
not be willing to pay the cost of comprehensive reform by raising taxes,
floating bond issues, or redirecting resources from other priorities. The
Court's involvement makes little difference in this process, however, and
may actually undermine reform efforts. First, if legislators believe that the
courts will force election reform using the new equal protection right in
Bush v Gore, they may delay making difficult choices until they can blame an
activist judiciary for requiring expensive reforms. Second, even if legislatures develop comprehensive programs that make difficult trade-offs between accuracy and finality and consider the myriad other ways resources
can be spent to increase voter turnout, information, and political participation, the courts now have the green light of *Bush v Gore* to become involved. As was the case with campaign finance regulation, regulating all aspects of state and local elections is not a task for which courts are well
suited. At best, judicial involvement in this arena means nothing with respect to election reform; at worst, it will be counterproductive.

More serious for the country is the claim that the Court's involvement
was warranted solely because it solved a political crisis. Not only does this
line of argument overstate the seriousness of the election mess by elevating

36. See Siobhan Gorman, *Florida Times 50,* Natl J 3720 (Dec 2, 2000).

37. See Mark Murray, *Federal Help on the Way,* Natl J 3722 (Dec 2, 2000).

38. Indeed, recent developments suggest that the electoral reform movement on
Capitol Hill has already stalled. See Jackie Calmes, *Panel Meets, but Reform of Voting System
Is Going Nowhere Fast on Capitol Hill,* Wall St J A24 (Mar 28, 2001).

it to the level of "constitutional crisis," but also it overlooks potential negative long-term consequences for the Court and the political branches. First, there was no crisis, nor was one likely to arise. Unlike other instances in our history where the presidential election ended in a dispute, no armed forces were gathering. Nor was the country at a critical historical juncture, as it was in 1876, when it faced rebuilding part of the country in the wake of a civil war.[39] Instead, we watched as local and state officials tried to apply a rather confusing statutory structure to unanticipated events. We learned about the relationship of elected administrative officers like the secretary of state to the state courts and to the state legislature. We saw the interaction in a federal system of state and national entities. We listened as appellate justices at the state and national levels asked probing and difficult questions. To the extent that people were paying attention—and a good number of us were—we were also learning about how a stable democracy deals with problems that arise in elections.

Would a crisis have developed if the Court had exercised its discretion not to hear any aspect of *Bush v Gore?* We will never know, but I doubt it. It is possible that the elected and appointed officials in Florida would have resolved matters by December 12, the date that would have entitled Florida's electors to the safe harbor under federal statute, or by December 18, the date that the electors voted. If not, the appropriate forum for determining the outcome of this election was Congress, the politically accountable branch of government and the branch most likely to reflect the political judgment of America's citizens. Congress was prepared to deal with a dispute arising from the Florida election because of the submission of two slates of electors or some other controversy. In 1887, Congress passed an intricate, somewhat confusing, and not entirely complete set of rules of decision to use when faced with a contested electoral college vote.[40] The Electoral Count Act is designed to provide a framework to structure debate, deliberation, and decisionmaking to avoid the debacle of the Hayes-Tilden election of 1876. The framework is by no means perfect: its gaps might have undermined its effectiveness, there are questions about the constitutional-

39. For histories of this period, see Paul Leland Haworth, *The Hayes-Tilden Disputed Presidential Election of 1876* (1966); C. Vann Woodward, *Reunion and Reaction: The Compromise of 1877 and the End of Reconstruction* (1956).

40. See John W. Burgess, *The Law of the Electoral Count,* 3 Pol Sci Q 633 (1888) (describing act and deliberations).

ity of some of its provisions, and Congress might have ignored some of its requirements. However, it provided some order for the political process of counting the electoral college's votes. Congress decided to try to take this decision out of the "political cauldron"[41] evident in the 1876 experience through ex ante adoption of a structure, not through abdication to the unelected judiciary.

By trying to reduce the naked partisanship that characterized the Hayes-Tilden decision, Congress was not trying to depoliticize the decision. Electing a president is a political act, and it should be left to the people and their representatives. As Representative Cooper said in 1886, "[T]hese two assembled bodies, the Senate and the House of Representatives, have the right, and have the duty imposed upon them, to see to it that the votes counted are in fact the votes of the States."[42] Sometimes that process is unruly, often it is full of partisan statements and actions, but the system includes correctives for extremism. The passage of the Electoral Count Act is an example of a corrective; Congress was attempting to reduce partisan influences, but not to eliminate political influences. Other legislation provides for an orderly transfer of power and appointment of an interim president in the unlikely event that the congressional dispute could not have been resolved by January 20.[43]

Adopting a structure for deliberation and decisionmaking before it will be used and at a time when it is not clear what particular interests will benefit from certain procedural choices and what interests will be harmed is a strategy often relied on to reduce partisanship and opportunistic behavior.[44] One of the difficulties in 1876 was that Congress established the Election Commission after the election dispute had arisen and the stakes were clear and concrete. Each decision was suffused with partisanship because supporters of Hayes worked to advance his interests, as the supporters of Tilden worked to advance his. In the aftermath of that controversy, legislators wisely sought to avoid a repeat by ex ante specification of procedures

41. See 15 Cong Rec 5079 (June 12, 1884) (remarks of Representative Browne).

42. 18 Cong Rec 47 (Dec 8, 1886).

43. Presidential Succession Act, ch 264, § 1(a) to (f), 61 Stat 380 (1947) (3 USC § 17).

44. This is a strategy used in other contexts to good effect. See Michael A. Fitts, *Can Ignorance Be Bliss? Imperfect Information as a Positive Influence in Political Institutions*, 88 Mich L Rev 917 (1990) (discussing generally); Elizabeth Garrett, *Rethinking the Structures of Decisionmaking in the Federal Budget Process*, 35 Harv J Legis 387, 411–12 (1998) (discussing in the budget process context).

that would channel political behavior. As Senator Sherman explained in the debate concerning the Electoral Count Act: "[It] comes before us again at the beginning of an administration, when no party advantage can be derived from our decision, . . . and now, if ever, this matter ought to be settled upon some basis of principle."[45]

The electoral connection between the people and members of Congress provides another corrective. If some members of Congress had gotten out of hand, then voters could have sent a strong message when the lawmakers stood for election in 2002. Political pressure can be brought to bear through communications to legislators during congressional deliberations as the public watches elected officials on television. If those who feared a political crisis were drawing their conclusions from the often extreme behavior of legislators during another politically charged deliberation, the Clinton impeachment and trial, they may have reached the wrong conclusions. Not only did those proceedings not precipitate a crisis, or render the president politically impotent, but also some of the more extreme partisans faced tough reelection fights in part because of their actions.[46] It is possible that members of Congress had learned from the impeachment and would have behaved more reasonably.

Nonetheless, some of the rhetoric in the congressional debate would surely have appeared extreme and unreasonable. That is part of the political process, and through deliberation and discussion, those views are often rejected. The debate would not have resembled the formal interactions in the Supreme Court, and only a small part of the legislative discussion would have risen to the intellectual level of some of the repartee between justices and advocates. But the activity of the political branches is not supposed to resemble a law school classroom or a Supreme Court argument. The election of the president is a political act and should remain in that sphere when possible. The dismay that some commentators express when confronted with legislative debate and political wrangling is an unfortunate re-

45. 17 Cong Rec 815 (Jan 21, 1886).

46. See Thomas Hargrove, *Congressional Incumbents Get Lower Margins,* Scripps Howard News Service, <http://shns.scripps.com/cgi-bin/webed_show_story?pk=ELECT-PATTERNS-11-08-00> (Nov 8, 2000) ("Members of Congress who voted to hold impeachment hearings—the most bipartisan vote in the otherwise straight-party pattern of the impeachment process—had significantly lower re-election averages than did those who opposed Clinton's impeachment. Fifty-five percent of those in the House who voted to hold impeachment hearings were reelected with lower margins than in 1998.").

action. Not only does it have elements of elitism, but also it reinforces the increasing alienation of the people from our elected representatives.[47] In the academy, this attitude is part of the cynicism about elected officials, fed by public choice theorists who view legislators as maximizing personal gain in a crudely venal sense. All legislative behavior, according to this view, is rooted in relatively tangible forms of self-interest, such as the quest for money, fame, and power; these scholars typically ignore personal satisfaction from justified accomplishment or the promotion of ideological goals.

Of course, there is no reason to believe that we have avoided the political wrangling that would have accompanied any congressional determination in a disputed election. These debates have merely been postponed, perhaps until the first round of appellate court appointments or until President Bush sends to the Senate his first appointment to the Supreme Court.[48] These confirmation battles would have been intense and heated even without *Bush v Gore* and the Court's involvement in selecting the president.[49] Given the importance of the judiciary in policymaking and the ideological divide between the parties on key issues that will come before judges, partisan disagreement is not inappropriate. But its level and tone will be driven in no small measure by lingering resentment about the Court's role in the election.

To the extent that *Bush v Gore* and the sometimes grudging support for the opinion as our salvation from chaos feed the distrust of and distaste for decisionmaking by the legislative branch, the case has significant negative long-term consequences. It leads to an environment of low expectations for elected officials, in which we no longer hold them to an acceptable standard of responsiveness and reflective judgment or require them to enact and oversee wise policies. We leave that to the unelected judges who work in an institution ill-designed to craft comprehensive policies that can be modified and improved over time. Moreover, by requiring the justices to save us from a political "crisis," we ask the Court to make decisions that will

47. See, for example, John R. Hibbing and Elizabeth Theiss-Morse, *Congress as Public Enemy: Public Attitudes Toward American Political Institutions* (1995).

48. For an extreme reaction to the case, see Bruce Ackerman, *The Court Packs Itself,* Am Prospect 48 (Feb 12, 2001) (arguing that the Senate should refuse to confirm any Bush appointee to the Supreme Court).

49. See Michael J. Gerhardt, *The Federal Appointments Process* (2000) (describing increasingly partisan tone of confirmation process).

be characterized as partisan and may reduce judicial legitimacy, undermining the justices when they act within their proper sphere. The justices who served on the Election Commission in 1876—in particular, Justice Bradley—were widely excoriated for the role they played.[50] Although service on the commission was more obviously a foray into the political thicket, the experience should serve as a warning to the Court when it is tempted to exercise its discretion and accept a case like those involving the 2000 presidential election.[51] The Court's willingness to volunteer for this role is particularly questionable because the political mechanisms were in place in Congress to resolve any dispute that emerged after Florida had finished.

The lesson of *Bush v Gore* is that we do not need to be saved *from* politics; instead, the constitutional structure augmented by statutory procedures allows us to be saved *by* politics. Here, as in many areas of decisionmaking made challenging by pathologies in the process and collective action problems, Congress has constructed a framework, albeit a clumsy and partial one, to constrain opportunism and channel deliberation. If the decision of the legislature is unjustified or irrational, or if the behavior of politicians is inconsistent with the citizens' preferences, voters have recourse at the next election to make their views known forcefully. The turnover of recent Congresses, beginning with the transformation in the 104th Congress that resulted from the people's dissatisfaction with some of Clinton's policies, demonstrates that the electoral threat is not illusory. Even if it is not as robust a threat as some would like, it is a more effective one than any we possess when we believe that the Court has entered the political fray in an unseemly and counterproductive way. Here, as in a number of other political and electoral contexts, the judges would serve us better if they would leave the decision to Congress.

50. See Woodward, *Reunion and Reaction* at 165–74 (cited in note 39).

51. See *Bush v Gore*, 121 S Ct at 557 (Breyer dissenting). Michael Klarman predicts, however, that this decision will not have a serious, harmful effect on the Court's standing or legitimacy. See Michael J. Klarman, Bush v Gore *Through the Lens of Constitutional History*, Cal L Rev (forthcoming 2001).

3

Political Judgments

SAMUEL ISSACHAROFF

Without doubt, the partisan fires of the last presidential election still burn too fiercely for retrospective evaluations to have much chance of standing independent of their outcome-determinative quality. The still smoldering events of the Florida protest and contest phases continue to shape the positions taken by observers across the political spectrum. On the left, there are the sudden converts to state autonomy, unfettered local electoral discretion, the ability of local jurisdictions to proclaim a "do-over" in a national election, and the perfidy of the Electoral College. On the right, the former champions of states' rights have now embraced federalism in its original nationalist guise, have become infatuated with the Fourteenth Amendment, and have learned to love their federal courts as aggressive as they come.

Despite the odds against drawing a successful balance sheet at this point, there are observations that should be made, and that can be measured against standards independent of who won and who lost in Florida. The first point that may be lost amid the partisan ardor is that the legal system responded remarkably well to tremendous stress. For over a month, the United States underwent what in much of the world would have been characterized as a succession crisis following the end of an incumbent's reign. Strikingly, however, throughout this period, there was essentially no social

This essay draws heavily on my long-standing collaboration with Pamela Karlan and Richard Pildes. I also benefited from discussions with and comments by Richard Briffault, Michael Dorf, Cynthia Estlund, and Justin Nelson. All opinions expressed are of course mine alone.

unrest, no crisis of governance, no inability to maintain discipline in foreign affairs, no instability in financial markets, no crisis in consumer markets, no stockpiling of goods, and so forth. Instead, there was a captivating display of high-powered lawyering that seized the national spotlight and resolved what in much of human history would have been an invitation to disorder and despair.

Much may be argued about the excess of legal regulation of our society. But it was law and lawyering that allowed a resolution of an election whose margin of victory proved less than the margin of error in the electoral system overall. Undoubtedly, there will be many proposals for change of the more ossified electoral practices. But in the manner of the well-intentioned proposal to move first base back five feet—so as to avoid so many close calls at first—so too there will never be any mass electoral system that will completely escape the frailties of human design. At the end of the day, law and the popular faith in the legal process brought an orderly end to the election crisis.

The second point, however, is much less rosy. Although the legal system brought closure to the process, it did so at a price. Hastily concocted doctrines and resolutions brought the judiciary into the public's political scrutiny as rarely before. Particularly after *Bush v Gore*,[1] the question must be asked, did the Court accomplish anything more than the delivery of a resolution to the dispute that placed in office the candidate most in keeping with the Court's philosophical predilections? The fact that law was the instrumentality of resolving disputes does not of itself establish that the law was well utilized or that its principles were wisely applied.

Here there is simply no escaping the fact that the Supreme Court's foray into Election 2000 is the first time that the Court has pronounced a victor in any election, let alone the most dramatic election of all. Prior to *Bush v Gore,* the Court categorically eschewed reviewing the outcomes of elections. The Supreme Court was simply not in the business of providing solace to disappointed office-seekers; in Justice White's time-honored terms, "As our system has it, one candidate wins, the others lose."[2] Even when courts had to look at election outcomes to determine if the system had malfunctioned, they did so only over the long term to see if "the electoral system is arranged

---

1. 121 S Ct 525 (2000) (per curiam).

2. *Whitcomb v Chavis*, 403 US 124, 153 (1971) (considering the use of multimember legislative districts).

in a manner that will consistently degrade a voter's or a group of voters' influence on the political process as a whole,"[3] or if a minority group had encountered structural obstacles that allowed majority voters "*usually* to defeat the minority's preferred candidate."[4] And when called upon to evaluate tensions between state electoral processes and federal dates for assuming office, the Court showed tremendous solicitude for state practices, including recounts, that were an "integral part" of state practice and accordingly fell "within the ambit of the broad powers delegated to the States" by the Constitution.[5]

Certainly, events change, new legal issues require doctrine to be reformulated, and the facts of the cases just invoked do not precisely correspond to the events in Florida. But the general tenor of this case law imposes some burden of justification for the Court's unprecedented and swaggeringly confident intervention into Election 2000. In what follows, I will suggest that the Court may well have been justified in its desire to expand constitutional scrutiny to cover on-the-run, post hoc alterations of electoral practices, but that it failed in the preservation of an institutional reticence to intercede in the political thicket when other institutional actors were amply well positioned to address the claimed harm. For those keeping score at home, this puts me most in line with Justice Breyer's dissenting opinion, most notably his advocacy of "self-restraint" on the part of the Court.[6]

To make this assessment, it is necessary to go back to the still festering disputes over the Court's abandonment of the political question doctrine. Until the breakthrough reapportionment cases of the 1960s, the Court refused to immerse itself in any claim implicating the political process. In *Luther v Borden*,[7] the Court introduced a prudential bar on having courts adjudicate contested questions of electoral legitimacy and declined to en-

3. *Davis v Bandemer,* 478 US 109, 155 (1986) (holding that the district court's findings did not meet the threshold for showing vote dilution).

4. *Thornburg v Gingles,* 478 US 30, 31 (1986) (emphasis added) (considering the use of multimember districts in legislative apportionment).

5. *Roudebush v Hartke,* 405 US 15, 25 (1972) (lifting a lower federal court's injunction on a recount proceeding under state law).

6. *Bush v Gore,* 121 S Ct at 557–58 (Breyer dissenting), quoting *United States v Butler,* 297 US 1, 79 (1936) (Stone dissenting).

7. 48 US (7 Howard) 1 (1849) (addressing a "republican form of government" clause claim arising from the Dorr rebellion).

tertain a challenge between contending factions claiming to be the rightful governors of Rhode Island. As defined by Justice Frankfurter in invoking caution about entering "the political thicket," the "Constitution has left the performance of many duties in our governmental scheme to depend on the fidelity of the executive and legislative action and, ultimately, on the vigilance of the people in exercising their political rights."[8]

The Court evaded the political question straitjacket in 1962 in *Baker v Carr*,[9] but did so by denying the applicability of a truncated version of the political question doctrine[10] and by invoking curiously assumed "[j]udicial standards [that] are well developed and familiar."[11] *Baker* left to subsequent cases the task of providing guidance for how courts were to navigate the political shoals, most notably *Reynolds v Sims*[12] and the development of the one-person, one-vote doctrine. As I have argued elsewhere,[13] the Court in *Baker* never managed a cogent explanation of its abandonment of the political question doctrine or of how courts were to avoid being sullied by immersion into electoral disputes.

In retrospect, the successful evasion of the political question barrier to judicial review, most notably in the reapportionment context, required a

8. *Colegrove v Green*, 328 US 549, 556 (1946) (affirming the dismissal of an action to invalidate certain provisions of state law governing congressional districts).

9. 369 US 186 (1962) (relying on the Equal Protection Clause to invalidate a state's legislative apportionment scheme).

10. The Court's redefinition was:

Prominent on the surface of any case held to involve a political question is found a textually demonstrable constitutional commitment of the issue to a coordinate political department; or a lack of judicially discoverable and manageable standards for resolving it; or the impossibility of deciding without an initial policy determination of a kind clearly for nonjudicial discretion; or the impossibility of a court's undertaking independent resolution without expressing lack of the respect due coordinate branches of government; or an unusual need for unquestioning adherence to a political decision already made; or the potentiality of embarrassment from multifarious pronouncements by various departments on one question.

Id at 217.

11. Id at 226.

12. 377 US 533 (1964) (striking down a plan for apportionment not based on population).

13. See Samuel Issacharoff, *Judging Politics: The Elusive Quest for Judicial Review of Political Fairness*, 71 Tex L Rev 1643, 1647–55 (1993). See also Michael C. Dorf and Samuel Issacharoff, *Can Process Theory Constrain Courts?*, 72 U Colo L Rev (forthcoming 2001).

combination of factors.[14] First, and foremost, the Court needed to articulate a simple and judicially manageable standard for measuring the constitutional right at stake. This was a critical response to the challenge from Justice Harlan in *Reynolds* that "cases of this type are not amenable to the development of judicial standards."[15] Second, and equally critical, the Court needed clearly to explain why it should be the institutional actor to provide redress, in effect rising to answer Frankfurter's invocation in *Colegrove* of the executive, the legislature, and the people as the repositories of constitutional vindication.[16] This point is compellingly argued in *Baker* by Justice Clark, who clearly sets out why the courts were the only source of potential remedy for claims of systemic malapportionment:

> Although I find the Tennessee apportionment statute offends the Equal Protection Clause, I would not consider intervention by this Court into so delicate a field if there were any other relief available to the people of Tennessee. But the . . . majority of the voters have been caught up in a legislative strait jacket. Tennessee has an "informed, civically militant electorate" and "an aroused popular conscience," but it does not sear "the conscience of the people's representatives." This is because the legislative policy has riveted the present seats in the Assembly to their respective constituencies, and by the votes of their incumbents a reapportionment of any kind is prevented. The people have been rebuffed at the hands of the Assembly; they have tried the constitutional convention route, but since the call must originate in the Assembly it, too, has been fruitless. They have tried Tennessee courts with the same result, and Governors have fought the tide only to flounder. . . . We therefore must conclude that the people of Tennessee are stymied and without judicial intervention will be saddled with the present discrimination in the affairs of their state government.[17]

The question then becomes how does *Bush v Gore* measure up against this two-part template for successful avoidance of the Court being ensnared

---

14. I treat this theme more fully in an earlier critical assessment of the Court's willingness to entertain political gerrymandering claims in *Davis v Bandemer,* 478 US 109. See Issacharoff, 71 Tex L Rev 1643 (cited in note 13).

15. 377 US at 621 (Harlan dissenting).

16. 328 US at 556.

17. 369 US at 258–59 (Clark concurring) (footnotes omitted).

in the political thicket. Has the Court identified a clear constitutional principle and how it is that it shall be managed judicially? And, has the Court explained why the judiciary is the proper institutional actor to ford the turbulent political streams?

I. THE CONSTITUTIONAL INTEREST IN ELECTION PRACTICES

The first question to address is the nature of the constitutional harm identified in *Bush v Gore*. There are three different theories put forward by the Court in *Bush v Gore* and its immediate predecessor, *Bush v Palm Beach County Canvassing Board*.[18] As an initial matter, therefore, the political question inquiry requires addressing the clarity and robustness of the claimed federal constitutional interest.

A. ARTICLE II, SECTION I

The first claimed harm concerns the source of state law authority for regulating electoral disputes. This narrow issue turns on the peculiarity of presidential elections given the language of Article II, Section I of the Constitution, which provides that electors shall be appointed "in such Manner as the Legislature Thereof May Direct."[19] In *Bush v Palm Beach County Canvassing Board*, the Court vacated and remanded the Florida Supreme Court's reconfiguration of the Florida statutory protest and contest phases on the grounds that, "we are unclear as to the extent to which the Florida Supreme Court saw the Florida Constitution as circumscribing the legislature's authority under Art. II, § I, cl. 2."[20] This approach, which ultimately garnered only three votes in *Bush v Gore*, provides little basis for a robust approach to the problem of elections gone bad.[21]

18. 121 S Ct 471 (2000) (per curiam).

19. US Const Art II, § 1, cl 2.

20. 121 S Ct at 475.

21. In his essay in this volume, Richard Epstein makes a strong case for the proposition that the Florida Supreme Court created new rules of conduct for the election after-the-fact. From this he attempts to draw the conclusion that the Article II, Section 1 claim was in fact the decisive constitutional issue. See Richard A. Epstein, *"In such Manner as the Legislature Thereof May Direct": The Outcome in* Bush v Gore *Defended*, in this volume. As I will set out, there are two defects with this approach. First, it proves too much. If the problem is with after-the-fact alterations of electoral processes in a potentially outcome-determinative fashion, why should this principle be limited to presidential elections alone, subject to Article II, Section 1? Should not the protection of the integrity of the election

To begin with, the Court in *Bush v Palm Beach County Canvassing Board* and Rehnquist's concurrence in *Bush v Gore* place great emphasis on the distinction between the acts of the Florida legislature and the other sources of state law derived either from the state constitution or the principles of equity. Perhaps not since *Erie v Tompkins*[22] overruled *Swift v Tyson*[23] has a decision turned so heavily on the question of the source of state law.[24] *Bush v Palm Beach County Canvassing Board* suggests that the constitutional delegation of authority in Article II, Section 1 of the Constitution is an exclusive grant of authority to the state legislature to create the procedures for the election of the state's presidential electors.[25] The opinion further raises the possibility that no other state law (including the state constitution) may intercede absent an express delegation of authority from the legislature.[26] If so, the invocation of state constitutional law to cabin the acts of the state legislature would, by extension, violate the Supremacy Clause of the U.S. Constitution.

This formal rendition of the source of state law actually accomplishes very little. As matters stood after *Bush v Palm Beach County Canvassing Board*,

---

system correspond to a more central constitutional command? Second, the claim proves too little. The fact that the Florida Supreme Court recast the state electoral practices does not in itself mean that a violation of Article II, Section 1 was present. What if the Florida Supreme Court overturned a legislative enactment that limited the franchise to only men? Or only white citizens? Does anyone seriously claim that Article II, Section 1 would be an obstacle to enforcement of the federal constitutional protections of the Fifteenth and Nineteenth Amendments?

22. 304 US 64 (1938).

23. 41 US (16 Pet) 1 (1842).

24. *Swift* had drawn a sharp distinction between legislative enactments and decisional law of the state courts. For Justice Story, the former were true sources of law that federal courts under the Rules of Decision Act were obligated to follow in construing state law in diversity cases. The latter were merely interpretive guides that could be subsumed under the federal common law without doing violence to state law. Id at 9–11.

25. See 121 S Ct at 474. The Court relied for this proposition on its reading of *McPherson v Blacker*, 146 US 1 (1892). As discussed in *When Elections Go Bad*, however, *McPherson* established only that there could be judicial review of a claim of abridgment of legislative prerogatives in setting the mechanism for selecting a state's electors. See Samuel Issacharoff, Pamela S. Karlan, and Richard H. Pildes, *When Elections Go Bad: The Law of Democracy and the Presidential Election of 2000* 105 (Foundation 2001). Nothing in *McPherson* purports to limit the constitutional interest in presidential elections solely to Article II, Section 1.

26. *Bush v Palm Beach County Canvassing Board*, 121 S Ct at 474–75.

there still appeared room for the normal operation of judicial interpretation of statutes. *Bush v Palm Beach County Canvassing Board* did not entertain
the notion that the state legislative scheme would either be fully responsive
to any emergency that might arise, or that it would be entirely self-revealing
and consistent. In this sense, the Court rejected the more extreme argument advanced by the Bush campaign that *any* state judicial review or interpretation would violate the federal constitutional scheme.[27] *Bush v Palm
Beach County Canvassing Board* does, however, appear to contemplate that
state judicial review of presidential election disputes takes as its cue state
legislative enactments rather than state constitutional or common law authority.[28] What remains uncertain is the source of *remedial* authority of state
courts in the event of a problem in the administration of the state statutory
election system. Thus, the *Bush v Palm Beach County Canvassing Board* remand leaves unclear whether the Florida Supreme Court's recasting of the
statutory date for certification could stand if it were based on a conflict in
the state election code combined with the need for redress through emergency court action. The plurality opinion in *Bush v Gore* adds little to the rationale of the Court in *Bush v Palm Beach County Canvassing Board*.

Perhaps more problematic for this approach, the reliance on Article II,
Section 1 entails a curiously cabined view of the federal interest in presidential elections. In light of the expansion of federal oversight of state practices under the Fourteenth Amendment, the treatment of Article II (or the
Twelfth Amendment) as the sole source of constitutional concern in federal
elections is curious, and certainly cannot survive *Bush v Gore*. For example,
if a state legislature decided to enact a system of election of presidential
electors that was based on a county-unit voting system, or some other basis
that violated the requirements of one-person, one-vote, is it conceivable that
such a selection mechanism would be unaffected by the equipopulation requirement of the Fourteenth Amendment? Or could a state enact a system
of selecting electors that limited the franchise to men, in derogation of the
Nineteenth Amendment? To ask these questions is to answer them. It is simply inconceivable that any court would seriously entertain the proposition
that the selection of presidential electors stands apart from other constitutional provisions covering the right to vote, regardless of whether they are

27. See Brief For Petitioner, *Bush v Palm Beach County Canvassing Board*, No 00-836,
*36–37 (filed Nov 28, 2000) (available on Lexis at 2000 US Briefs 836).

28. 121 S Ct at 473–74.

in the form of the text of other provisions of the Constitution or exist in the extensive interpretive case law of the past century.

Once the scope of federal constitutional oversight of presidential elections is recognized as sweeping beyond Article II, the power of the Article II approach is significantly vitiated, even as a limitation on state courts. The objectionable opinion of the Florida Supreme Court did indeed rely on state constitutional doctrine as the basis for its equitable intervention into the first stages of Election 2000.[29] But the principles drawn from Florida constitutional law were at such a level of generality that they could as easily have been derived from the basic federal cases establishing the right to vote as a fundamental right[30]—indeed, the very cases the U.S. Supreme Court subsequently relied upon in crafting the equal protection doctrines of *Bush v Gore*. Moreover, in its own opinion on the remand from *Bush v Palm Beach County Canvassing Board*,[31] the Florida Supreme Court came to precisely the same ruling as it had initially,[32] but was duly chastened from ever mentioning its own state constitution. To the extent that the constitutional infirmity in Florida turned on the use of state constitutional law, the Supreme Court's intervention into the Florida election crisis makes little sense. It is hard to give much credence to a constitutional principle that treats state constitutional law ultimately as the law that dare not speak its name.

B. RETROSPECTIVE CHANGES IN STATE PROCEDURES

In the brief window between *Bush v Palm Beach County Canvassing Board* and *Bush v Gore*, it appeared that the Court was searching for a constitutional principle that would look with great skepticism on after-the-fact alterations of election procedures. Certainly the skeletal rendition of the facts in Florida provided ammunition for such a concern. It was clear, for example, that the Florida Supreme Court's exercise in statutory interpretation in *Palm Beach County Canvassing Board v Harris*[33] was mightily strained

29. See *Palm Beach County Canvassing Board v Harris*, 772 S2d 1220, 1228 (Fla Nov 21, 2000), vacd and remd as *Bush v Palm Beach County Canvassing Board*, 121 S Ct 471.

30. See, for example, *Reynolds*, 377 US at 561–62 (stating that "[u]ndoubtedly, the right of suffrage is a fundamental matter in a free and democratic society").

31. *Gore v Harris*, 772 S2d 1243 (Fla Dec 8, 2000), revd and remd as *Bush v Gore*, 121 S Ct 525.

32. *Gore v Harris*, 772 S2d at 1260–62.

33. 772 S2d 1220 (Fla Nov 21, 2000), vacd and remd as *Bush v Palm Beach County Canvassing Board*, 121 S Ct 471.

and that the claimed statutory conflict between the "may" and "shall" instructions to the Secretary of State could have been reconciled in a variety of ways that required less judicial rewriting of the Florida election code.[34] Similarly, there was serious reason for concern in Palm Beach County where prior county board rules on the counting of the now infamous dimpled chads were fairly clearly abrogated in the rush to accommodate claims

34. The more one examines the Florida statutes, the more inescapable seems the conclusion that they are inherently defective. Arguably the deadlines in Fla Stat Ann § 102.111 (the "shall" language) should not apply when a protest has been filed but has not been resolved. The protest statute specifically grants a right of protest, with a deadline for filing a protest five days after the election or before certification (at most seven days). There is no deadline for completion of the protest, but the very last subsection (10) of the statute requires that the Secretary of State respond within three days to a request by the county to verify election software. The existence of this deadline, on the Department of State no less, could indicate that the legislature contemplated that the protest phase could and probably would take at a minimum eight days, and in any case could permissibly last longer than the seven day "shall" deadline. Thus, one reading could be that the "shall" language applies to results that have not been protested. This is further supported by the fact that Section 101.5614(8) specifies that "write-in, absentee and manually counted results shall constitute the official returns." Fla Stat Ann § 101.5614(8) (West 2000). This is also quoted by the Florida Supreme Court. See *Palm Beach County Canvassing Board v Harris,* 772 S2d at 1235. Because the statutory provisions for manual recount are in the protest section, it follows that official returns cannot be calculated until the protest phase (at least when manual recounts occur) is complete. If they cannot be calculated, they cannot be certified, since Section 101.111 requires that the Canvassing Commission "shall" certify "official" results.

There is however the complication of the penalties provided in Section 102.112 and the "shall be ignored" clause in Section 102.111. However, the "shall" language of Section 102.111 applies to elections that could have been certified by the county and were not or were and were not sent to the Secretary of State, and the "may" language applies to those that could not have been certified because of a protest or other delay. Under this reading, the statutory scheme would appear to be best read to give the Secretary of State discretionary power to determine whether there would be a meaningful right to protest.

The next statutory difficulty is that the contest phase can begin only after the results are certified and thus on my reading after all manual recounts are complete. See Fla Stat Ann § 102.168 (West 2000). There are no statutory deadlines for the completion of the contest or the protest. The most aggressive step taken by the Florida Supreme Court was to manufacture from whole cloth its own deadline by relying on the safe harbor provision of 3 USC § 5 and the right to a meaningful contest. This is clearly without foundation. See *Palm Beach County Canvassing Board v Harris,* 772 S2d at 1237. Certainly, this appears nowhere in the statute and since this is not a statute specific to presidential elections, it

of voter error and defective voting machines in Election 2000.[35] Particularly in light of the peculiar claims for selected recounts under shifting procedures, the Florida scenario was ripe for claims that the integrity of the process was being compromised for partisan aims.[36]

The concurring opinion by Chief Justice Rehnquist attempted to construe these alterations of preexisting practices as the core of an Article II, Section 1 violation independent of the earlier reliance on the Florida state constitution. The difficulty in raising this concern to a constitutional principle under Article II, Section 1 is that it would appear to proscribe actions taken in nonpresidential elections and alterations undertaken after-the-fact by the state legislature itself. Perhaps accordingly, the Article II, Section 1 argument was rejected by six members of the Court and, instead, the question of fidelity to previously enacted electoral procedures was transferred into a reliance on 3 USC § 5 (1994). This now famous statutory provision forecloses congressional challenge to a state's designated electors so long as a "State shall have provided, by laws enacted prior to [election day], for its final determination of any controversy or contest concerning the appointment of . . . electors . . . by judicial or other methods. . . ."

It is entirely fair to read 3 USC § 5 as codifying an important principle of electoral democracy requiring the rules of engagement to be explicated ex ante and to be fairly immutable under the strain of electoral conflict. The basic premise is that election officials, who are most likely partisan figures, cannot be trusted to improvise electoral remedies once the impact of their decisions is known and the temptation toward self-serving behavior becomes irresistible. Such an approach would have the advantage of fitting in well within a theory of democratic governance that relies heavily on procedural precommitments to insure fairness.[37] It further has the advantage of

---

would not even come into play in the majority of elections held pursuant to it. The court cites no legislative history to support its conclusion that the legislature intended to comply with this deadline.

35. Jeffrey Toobin, *Miami Postcard: As Nasty As They Gotta Be,* New Yorker 70 (Nov 27, 2000).

36. Hence I do not really take issue with Judge Posner's claim in this symposium that the final effect of the Supreme Court's intervention may have been "rough justice." See Richard A. Posner, Bush v Gore: *Prolegomenon to an Assessment,* in this volume. Judge Posner leaves aside the question whether the outcome was "legal justice"—but it is that question that occupies me.

37. For a further explication of this thesis, with particular application to the redis-

actually corresponding to a previously developed line of election cases that identifies significant legal interests, both federal and state, that are implicated by manipulations of the rules of elections.[38]

There are two key drawbacks to the altered procedures standard for constitutional review. The first is that despite the apparent concern over such alterations in *Bush v Palm Beach County Canvassing Board,* the Court essentially abandoned this path in *Bush v Gore* in favor of a revitalized equal protection approach. The second difficulty is a managerial one for federal courts. Resting federal constitutional oversight on fidelity to preexisting election procedures necessarily involves an assessment of what prior procedures were and what alterations were actually made. Since the conduct of elections is basically entrusted to states, and since states in turn devolve responsibility to county level election officials, federal constitutional review of changed state election procedures would in turn require that every local and state election procedure be subject to federal judicial scrutiny. Such an approach would run counter to long-standing abstention doctrines that would have federal courts step clearly aside when matters of interpreting state law and procedures are inherent to federal questions.[39]

---

tricting context, see Issacharoff, 71 Tex L Rev at 1661 (cited in note 13). The concept of precommitment and the political theory of constitutions as precommitment strategies have, at this point, extensive pedigrees. On precommitment, see, for example, Jon Elster, *Ulysses and the Sirens: Studies in Rationality and Irrationality* 37–47 (Cambridge 1979) (discussing precommitment strategies). See also Thomas C. Schelling, *Enforcing Rules on Oneself,* 1 J L, Econ & Org 357 (1985). Other scholarly works apply precommitment theory to constitutions. See Jon Elster, *Intertemporal Choice and Political Thought,* in George Loewenstein and Jon Elster, eds, *Choice over Time* 35 (Russell Sage 1992); Stephen Holmes, *Precommitment and the Paradox of Democracy,* in Jon Elster and Rune Slagstad, eds, *Constitutionalism and Democracy* 195 (Cambridge 1988).

38. The clearest example is from the *Roe* line of cases in the Eleventh Circuit, dealing with after-the-fact alterations in counting procedures for absentee ballots in an Alabama local election. See *Roe v Alabama,* 43 F3d 574 (11th Cir 1995). A fuller discussion of the *Roe* cases and the constitutional principles underlying them can be found in Issacharoff, Karlan, and Pildes, *When Elections Go Bad* at 15–24 (cited in note 25).

39. These are the well-known *Pullman* and *Burford* abstention doctrines. The abstention doctrine developed in *Railroad Commission of Texas v Pullman Co,* 312 US 496, 501 (1941), emerges from concern that there should not be premature federal court intervention when ongoing state proceedings might obviate the need for the federal court to act. The abstention doctrine set forth in *Burford v Sun Oil Co,* 319 US 315, 332–34 (1943), is based on considerations of federalism and comity that require federal courts to resist disrupting the customary procedures of state law.

To some extent the groundwork for more invasive federal examination has already been laid. Already, for example, the Supreme Court in the redistricting context has recast the familiar principle that federal courts should *abstain* from cases requiring interpretation of state law to one that they should retain jurisdiction but *defer* judgment until the state law issue may be resolved,[40] perhaps by certification to the highest court of the state.[41] The Court may well have realized that the articulation of a central federal concern in the proper application of state procedures would set aside all federalism-based considerations of federal court abstention. A significant step in that direction can be found in the Eleventh Circuit's treatment of abstention in the direct federal court challenge to Election 2000:

> Our conclusion that abstention is inappropriate is strengthened by the fact that Plaintiffs allege a constitutional violation of their voting rights. In considering abstention, we must take into account the nature of the controversy and the importance of the right allegedly impaired. Our cases have held that voting rights cases are particularly inappropriate for abstention. In light of this precedent, the importance of the rights asserted by Plaintiffs counsels against our abstention in this case; although, as discussed below, we are mindful of the limited role of the federal courts in assessing a state's electoral process.[42]

The risk in this approach is the federalization of all election law, akin to the concern a generation ago that the recognition of a due process interest

40. See *Growe v Emison,* 507 US 25, 32 n 1 (1993):
We have referred to the *Pullman* doctrine as a form of "abstention." To bring out more clearly, however, the distinction between those circumstances that require dismissal of a suit and those that require postponing consideration of its merits, it would be preferable to speak of *Pullman* "deferral." *Pullman* deferral recognizes that federal courts should not prematurely resolve the constitutionality of a state statute.
(internal citations omitted).

41. In *Tunick v Safir,* 209 F3d 67, 73 (2d Cir 2000), Judge Calabresi seized upon a statement by the Supreme Court that "[c]ertification today covers territory once dominated by a deferral device called '*Pullman* abstention,'" *Arizonans for Official English v Arizona,* 520 US 43, 75 (2000). Judge Calabresi noted, "The teaching of *Arizonans,* therefore, is that we should consider certifying in more instances than had previously been thought appropriate, and do so even when the federal courts might think that the meaning of a state law is 'plain.'" *Tunick,* 209 F3d at 73.

42. *Siegel v LePore,* 234 F3d 1163, 1174 (11th Cir 2000) (citations omitted).

in employment would constitutionalize all public sector employment law.[43] Since all state procedures would trigger a constitutional voting rights concern, either all election challenges would be immediately reviewable in federal court, or they would linger forever unripe since matters of state law interpretation would inevitably be present. Perhaps because of the disruption that would be caused to the law of federal courts, the constitutionalization of altered procedures was another path not chosen by the Supreme Court.

C. THE NEW EQUAL PROTECTION

In the scramble to find a suitable constitutional principle on which to rest its distrust of the Florida events, the Court finally settled on a sweeping, but rather vague rendition of equal protection. According to the Court:

> The right to vote is protected in more than the initial allocation of the franchise. Equal protection applies as well to the manner of its exercise. Having once granted the right to vote on equal terms, the State may not, by later arbitrary and disparate treatment, value one person's vote over that of another.[44]

In so holding, the Court revived the fundamental rights line of cases from the 1960s, most notably *Reynolds* and *Harper v Virginia Board of Elections*,[45] that had essentially collapsed of its own weight decades ago. The demise of this equal protection approach was, in part, the result of the unsuccessful attempt to extend fundamental rights claims to everything from privacy to wealth distinctions. In part as well, the fundamental rights line of cases succumbed to the emergence of intent-based equal protection review after *Washington v Davis*.[46] But part of the blame must also lie with the amorphousness of the claimed fundamental right to vote. Take for example the core constitutional principle relied upon by the Court in *Reynolds* in formulating the one-person, one-vote rule of apportionment:

43. See *Bishop v Wood*, 426 US 341, 349–50 (1976) (Justice Stevens invoking the principle that the Constitution must not become the vehicle for federalizing all state employment decisions).

44. *Bush v Gore*, 121 S Ct at 530.

45. 383 US 663 (1966) (striking down the poll tax as an abridgment of the fundamental right to vote).

46. 426 US 229 (1976) (holding that the racially disproportionate impact of a written employment test, which was neutral on its face, did not warrant the conclusion that the test was a purposely discriminatory device).

[R]epresentative government is in essence self-government through the medium of elected representatives of the people, and each and every citizen has an inalienable right to full and effective participation in the political processes of his State's legislative bodies. Most citizens can achieve this participation only as qualified voters through the election of legislators to represent them. Full and effective participation by all citizens in state government requires, therefore, that each citizen have an equally effective voice in the election of members of his state legislature. Modern and viable state government needs, and the Constitution demands, no less.[47]

As evocative as the principle of "full and effective participation" might be, it remains unclear thirty-five years later what are the precise parameters of this claimed right.[48] When reduced to a manageable doctrine, such as the equipopulation rule of apportionment, courts have successfully been able to constrain the structural obstacles to participation that were present in cases such as *Baker* and *Reynolds*.[49] But how far does "fair and effective participation" extend into campaign finance, party access to ballots, minority representation, or any of the other issues that have dominated the law of the political process over the past decade?

What then is the scope of the Court's newfound equal protection jurisprudence? Certainly the claim that states have a responsibility to ensure equality of access to the franchise is welcome. Since the emergence of suspect classifications as the sole effective source of equal protection redress, and following the development of the post-1982 Voting Rights Act as the most powerful vehicle for judicial intervention in the political arena, there has been a strong incentive to recast all claims of partisan disadvantage in the judicial arena as claims for racial redress.[50] To the extent that *Bush v*

47. 377 US at 565.

48. For a general discussion of this topic, see Samuel Issacharoff, Pamela S. Karlan, and Richard H. Pildes, *The Law of Democracy: Legal Structure of the Political Process* 145–50 (Foundation 1998).

49. The disparities between the largest and smallest populations assigned to a legislative district were 23-to-1 in *Baker* and 41-to-1 in *Reynolds*. See Issacharoff, 71 Tex L Rev at 1652 (cited in note 13).

50. See Pamela S. Karlan, *All Over the Map: The Supreme Court's Voting Rights Trilogy,* 1993 S Ct Rev 245, 251 (noting that partisan groups "use plaintiffs protected by the [Voting Rights Act] as stalking horses"); Pamela S. Karlan, *The Rights To Vote: Some Pessimism About Formalism,* 71 Tex L Rev 1705, 1732 (1993) (stating that "the political parties will enlist at least some members of the relevant groups to advance their views").

Gore revitalizes a non-race-based standard of constitutional protection of rights in the political process, the resulting diminution in the need to dress up all claims of wrongdoing in racial garb could be quite welcome. But even so, the newly articulated equal protection doctrine is dramatically wide-reaching. The claimed wrong in Florida, the disparity in the standards for counting contested ballots, pales before other disparities in access to a meaningful vote, most notably the well-documented failure of voting machines used in one part, but not in another, of many states, Florida included. That clearly would fall under the Court's new injunction that states have an obligation "to avoid arbitrary and disparate treatment of the members" of the electorate.[51]

The difficulty in defining the scope of this new equal protection right is made all the worse by the Court's disingenuous limiting instruction. Without explanation or doctrinal mooring, the per curiam opinion suddenly pronounces, "Our consideration is limited to the present circumstances, for the problem of equal protection in election processes generally presents many complexities,"[52] as if by such incantation the Court could restrict the sweeping new equal protection doctrine to the peculiar facts of recount procedures—the classic "good for this train, and this train only" offer. But without any principled distinction between recounts and any number of other procedures that might result in "arbitrary and disparate treatment" of different parts of the electorate, the limiting instruction is either meaningless or reveals the new equal protection as a cynical vessel used to engage in result-oriented judging by decree.

II. THE INSTITUTIONAL ROLE OF COURTS

A. THE AVAILABILITY OF POLITICAL REDRESS

The second facet of the political question inquiry is not simply whether there are clear terms of legal engagement, but whether courts are the proper institutional actors to repair the perceived constitutional harm. In both *Bush v Palm Beach County Canvassing Board* and *Bush v Gore*, the Court invoked, as part of its rationale in overturning the Florida Supreme Court, the concerns for established procedural orderliness and for clear time frames set forth in the federal Electoral Count Act.[53] Unfortunately, the Court's invocation of 3 USC § 5 raises more questions than it answers.

---

51. *Bush v Gore*, 121 S Ct at 530.
52. Id at 532.
53. Electoral Count Act of 1887, 24 Stat 373, codified at 3 USC §§ 5–7, 15–18 (1994).

Initially, the Court held up this portion of the Electoral Count Act as setting forth the federal interest in procedural regularity in the conduct of elections. That invocation of the federal interest leaves untouched the remedial question of how a breach of the federal interest should be remedied. Going back to Justice Clark's response to the Frankfurter/Harlan dissents in *Baker* and *Reynolds,* the question must be asked whether, independent of the substantive federal interest, it is the courts that should act to provide a politically contentious remedy in an electoral dispute. The direct inquiry set out by Clark carefully considered all other potential actors and concluded that the Court must act only after assessing the failure of all other potential avenues of redress.[54]

Bush v Gore is entirely lacking in such analysis. The Court presumed that once it found the federal interest, its remedial obligations followed.[55] In this regard, the Court's reliance on the magic December 12 date for the safe harbor under 3 USC § 5 is particularly ironic. This statutory provision emerged from a rather deliberate congressional effort to provide for orderly resolution of presidential election controversies in the wake of the hastily-crafted Electoral Commission approach from 1877.[56] A review of this statute, however, reveals that it carefully reserved to the political branches the key role in resolving contested presidential elections.

If one looks beyond 3 USC § 5 and examines the statute as a whole, there is actually a coherent attempt made to place responsibility for resolving contested presidential elections in the domain of politics. Thus, for example, as bizarre as it may sound to contemporary court-accustomed observers, federal law actually anticipates a potential role for state legislatures: when a state "has failed to make a choice [of electors to the electoral college] on the day prescribed by law, the electors may be appointed on a subsequent day in such a manner as the legislature of such State may direct."[57] More directly, 3 USC § 15 expressly anticipates that there could even be rival sets of electors each claiming to represent their states—as occurred with the Florida, Louisiana, and South Carolina delegations in 1876. Resolution

54. See text accompanying note 17.

55. Indeed, the expansiveness of that assumption may explain why Justices Ginsburg and Stevens in dissent so categorically refused to entertain any potential violation of federal law in the Florida imbroglio.

56. The history of the Electoral Commission and its controversial role in resolving the 1876 Hayes-Tilden election is set forth in Issacharoff, Karlan, and Pildes, *When Elections Go Bad* at 96–98 (cited in note 25).

57. 3 USC § 2 (1994).

of such disputes is entrusted to independent determination by each branch of Congress—with a preference in case of a split between the House and Senate going to the delegation whose certificates of appointment bear the signature of the governor of their state of origin.[58]

Nor was this delegation of dispute resolution authority to the political branches an oversight. Rather this was a considered judgment of Congress responding to the lessons of the stormy 1876 presidential election and the need to devise procedures for resolving future contested designations of presidential electors. Congress clearly concluded that such decisions would have an inevitable political cast and should therefore be kept clearly confined within the political branches. As set forth in the opening speech by the sponsor of the Electoral Count Act, Senator Sherman, Congress actually contemplated *and rejected* a role for the Court akin to the role assumed in *Bush v Gore*:

> Another plan which has been proposed in the debates at different times, and I think also in the constitutional convention, was to allow questions of this kind to be certified at once to the Supreme Court for its decisions in case of a division between the two Houses. If the House should be one way and the Senate the other, then it was proposed to let the case be referred directly to the prompt and summary decision of the Supreme Court. But there is a feeling in this country that we ought not to mingle our great judicial tribunal with political questions, and therefore this proposition has not met with much favor. It would be a very grave fault indeed and a very serious objection to refer a political question in which the people of the country were aroused, about which their feelings were excited, to this great tribunal, which after all has to sit upon the life and property of all the people of the United States. It would tend to bring that court into public odium of one or the other of the two great parties. Therefore that plan may probably be rejected as an unwise provision. I believe, however, it is the provision made in other countries.[59]

In place of the Court, the statutory scheme envisioned a different set of actors. In Election 2000, that would have meant Florida's governor and its legislature and the newly elected members of Congress. Note well that all of the designated actors in this rendition of the drama would be partisan elected officials. Nothing in the statutory scheme envisions a role for courts, even if our conception of judicial involvement in the political arena

58. Id § 15.

59. Counting of Electoral Votes, 17 Cong Rec S 817–18 (Jan 21, 1886) (Sen Sherman).

is much more developed than it was over a century ago when the Electoral Count Act was first devised.

No doubt, this scenario would look to many modern observers like a pure power grab, a partisan circumvention of orderly legal processes. But why is it either surprising or alarming that an electoral deadlock should be resolved by political officials and bodies elected by the same voters? The root cause of the difficulties in Florida was that the election proved undecisive and given the particular distribution of votes nationwide, the Florida electoral resolution would in turn decide the national election. Justice Breyer well captures this point: "However awkward or difficult it may be for Congress to resolve difficult electoral disputes, Congress, being a political body, expresses the people's will far more accurately than does an unelected Court. And the people's will is what elections are about."[60]

In the heated rhetorical battle of Election 2000, no charge was bandied about with greater derision than the claim that one or another group of partisans was engaged in partisanship. But it was, after all, a partisan election that was at stake. It hardly seems an affront to democratic self-governance to channel the ultimate resolution of a true electoral deadlock into other democratically-elected branches of government. All the more, if the alternative were to have judges making ad hoc judgments that further state proceedings might "cast a cloud" on the "legitimacy" of a Bush election.[61] As expressed by Justice Breyer, "Given this detailed, comprehensive scheme for counting electoral votes, there is no reason to believe that federal law either foresees or requires resolution of such a political issue by this Court."[62]

B. THE MAJORITARIAN DILEMMA

Much of course has changed since the first breach of the political question wall in the 1960s. We have become properly accustomed to the role of courts in guarding against fundamental distortions of the political process,

60. *Bush v Gore*, 121 S Ct at 556 (Breyer dissenting).

61. *Bush v Gore*, 121 S Ct 512, 512 (2000) (application for stay) (Scalia concurring). Lest I be accused of rehashing partisan views of my own, let me make clear that the likely beneficiary of reserving matters to the political branches would have been Governor Bush. Were there to have been rival slates of electors, his would have carried certificates bearing the signature of the governor of Florida (conveniently his brother), his party commanded control in one house of Congress, his allies controlled the Florida legislature, and under any number of scenarios, some combination of these factors would have delivered the presidency to him.

62. *Bush v Gore*, 121 S Ct at 556 (Breyer dissenting).

particularly when the distortions serve to lock in incumbents by thwarting political competition,[63] or serve to lock out racial minorities.[64] Each of these interventions corresponds to a claim that the election system "is systematically malfunctioning," as formulated by John Hart Ely's pioneering work.[65] But neither of these forms of distortions was at work in the procedures by which state and federal elected representatives could have directed the ultimate outcome of the contested 2000 presidential election.

Comparing the Court's response to Election 2000 to prior interventions into the political arena actually illuminates an unexplored problem in *Bush v Gore*. Invariably, the process of judicial review in the electoral arena gives rise in a particularly acute form to the concern over the countermajoritarian difficulty. After all, every time a court strikes down an election statute, or every time it calls into question electoral processes, the unelected judiciary substitutes its judgment for that of the democratically elected branches.

There are two distinct theories that justify such judicial intervention into the political arena, and each turns on the incapacity for repair from within. The first is the *Carolene Products*[66] rationale that identifies the need for judicial intervention to protect the famously termed "discrete and insular minorities."[67] Of importance here is not simply that the political process might be infected by prejudice, but that there is reason to believe that the challenged state practices "restrict[ ] those political processes which can or-

63. For a discussion of the importance of protecting competition in the political arena, see Samuel Issacharoff and Richard H. Pildes, *Politics as Markets: Partisan Lockups of the Democratic Process,* 50 Stan L Rev 643 (1998).

64. See generally Issacharoff, Karlan, and Pildes, *The Law of Democracy* at 367–545 (cited in note 48).

65. John Hart Ely, *Democracy and Distrust* 103 (Harvard 1980). According to Ely:
Malfunction occurs when the *process* is undeserving of trust, when (1) the ins are choking off the channels of political change to ensure that they will stay in . . . and the outs will stay out, or (2) though no one is actually denied a voice or a vote, representatives beholden to an effective majority are systematically disadvantaging some minority out of simple hostility or a prejudiced refusal to recognize commonalities of interest, and thereby denying that minority the protection afforded other groups by a representative system. Obviously our elected representatives are the last persons we should trust with identification of either of these situations.
Id.

66. *United States v Carolene Products,* 304 US 144 (1938).

67. Id at 152 n 4.

dinarily be expected to bring about repeal of undesirable legislation."[68] In other words, the process is unable to engage in self-repair because of the particular outcast quality of the minority.

The second rationale both builds on *Carolene Products* and extends it to conditions in which the political process has become immune to competitive challenge to the status quo. In cases of such process failure, denoted primarily by the entrenchment or lockup of political power in the hands of an electorally unshakable group, the impetus for judicial intervention is greatest. The classic example goes back to the distortions of political power evident in the fact patterns of cases such as *Baker* and *Reynolds*. In each of these cases a maldistribution of political power because of malapportionment made it impossible for even a majority of voters to dislodge minority rural control over state legislatures.[69]

What emerges from these rationales, paradoxical as it may sound, is greater legitimacy to judicial intervention in the political process for countermajoritarian purposes than when the Court seeks to invoke the role of protector of majority preferences. The premise of both *Carolene Products* and the political process theories that followed is that intervention is required because an electoral lock on power has made the system unresponsive to permanent electoral minorities—even if the protected minority happens to be a numerical majority of the population, as in *Baker* and *Reynolds*. The unexplored flip-side of this rationale is that there is correspondingly less justification for judicial intervention into the political process for majoritarian aims. This rationale dovetails with the second part of the Court's response to the political question demand for abstention from election controversies. As formulated by Justice Clark in his concurrence in *Baker*, the predicate for judicial intervention had to be the absence of alternative institutional actors capable of repairing the claimed harm.[70] In the case of discrete and insular minorities, or in the case of locked-in political power structures, presumably no other actor could fit the bill because of the unresponsiveness of the governing coalition to the claims of injustice by those on the outs politically. But that rationale extends poorly to electoral ma-

68. Id.

69. The justification for judicial intervention based on the lockup of power through anticompetitive devices is developed at length in Issacharoff and Pildes, 50 Stan L Rev at 643 (cited in note 63).

70. 369 US at 258–59 (Clark concurring).

jorities, particularly those that control alternative political institutional actors. For such politically engaged majorities, the presumption should be quite the contrary and should begin with the premise that vindication lies in the political arena.

CONCLUSION

In dissent, Justice Breyer struck an important tone of judicial modesty. Invoking Alexander Bickel, who termed the proper level of judicial restraint the "passive virtues,"[71] Justice Breyer worried that in spite of significant federal concerns in the Florida events, the Court had been insufficiently attentive to the risk of "undermining respect for the judicial process" as a result of its headlong leap into the electoral battleground.[72] It is not that the Court *cannot* enter the domain of politics, but that there are often compelling reasons why it *should not*. The demise of the political question doctrine left the Court with a warrant to enter the political fray, albeit reluctantly, when the lines of constitutional engagement were sufficiently clear and when no other institutional actor could repair the damage. What emerges most clearly from *Bush v Gore* is that this Court appears seriously lacking in the appropriate spirit of reluctance.

71. Alexander M. Bickel, *The Least Dangerous Branch: The Supreme Court at the Bar of Politics* 111–98 (Yale 2d ed 1986).

72. *Bush v Gore*, 121 S Ct at 557 (Breyer dissenting).

4

The Newest Equal Protection

Regressive Doctrine on a Changeable Court

PAMELA S. KARLAN

I believe we are on an irreversible trend toward more freedom and democracy—
but that could change.
—*George W. Bush, May 22, 1998*[1]

Most of the scholarly commentary about *Bush v Gore*,[2] at least so far, has been quite scathing.[3] A common thread has been that the Court's equal protection analysis "had no basis in precedent."[4] I think that criticism misses the mark. Unfortunately for equal protection law, *Bush v Gore* is not an aberration. Rather, it is yet another manifestation of the newest model of

As with all my work in this field, I owe many of my insights to conversations with Sam Issacharoff, Rick Pildes, and Jim Blacksher. In addition, I thank Henry Weinstein, Mary Anne Case, and Viola Canales for countless hours of conversations on the issues raised in this chapter. A portion of this chapter appears, in a somewhat different form, in *Nothing Personal: The Evolution of the Newest Equal Protection from* Shaw v Reno *to* Bush v Gore, 79 NCL Rev (forthcoming 2001).

1. Quoted at <http://littlegeorgebush.com/quotes2.html> (visited Mar 5, 2001).

2. 121 S Ct 525 (2000).

3. See, for example, the contributions of Samuel Issacharoff and Cass Sunstein to this volume. See also Michael J. Klarman, Bush v Gore *Through the Lens of Constitutional History*, Cal L Rev (forthcoming 2001). And even those scholars who defend the Court's judgment—such as Richard Epstein and Richard Posner—do so without embracing fully its reasoning.

4. Cass Sunstein, *Order Without Law*, in this volume. See also, for example, David G. Savage, *The Vote Case Fallout*, 87 ABA J 32 (Feb 2001) (quoting Professor A.E. Dick Howard as saying, "This is a remarkable use of the equal protection clause. It is not consistent with anything they have done in the past 25 years.").

equal protection, a model laid out in the Court's decisions regarding race-conscious redistricting[5] and Congress's power to enforce the Fourteenth Amendment.[6] Ironically, George W. Bush's previous appearance before the Supreme Court came in a lawsuit that lay at the intersection of these two lines of cases: *Bush v Vera*,[7] the hotly divisive, intensely partisan challenge to Texas's 1991 congressional redistricting, in which the Court struck down the plan as an unconstitutional racial gerrymander, but was so equivocal on the question whether Congress had the power to pass the 1982 amendments to the Voting Rights Act that Justice O'Connor ended up concurring with herself.

Both *Bush v Vera* and *Bush v Gore* involve what I will call "structural" equal protection. In this newest model of equal protection, the Court deploys the equal protection clause not to protect the rights of an individual or a discrete group of individuals, particularly a group unable to protect itself through operation of the normal political processes, but rather to regulate the institutional arrangements within which politics is conducted. Neither *Bush v Vera* and the other *Shaw* cases nor *Bush v Gore* fully answers the question of when, and why, courts should intervene in the deeply messy process of partisan politics. And each adopts a distressingly narrow perspective within which to measure equality.

As Richard Pildes perceptively notes, the "image of democracy" that has informed the contemporary Supreme Court's interventions into the political arena—in contexts as diverse as blanket primaries, ballot access, and candidate debates—is a fear of too much democracy, of too robust and tumultuous a political system.[8] That image underlies the Court's *Shaw* jurisprudence decisions as well: the Court sees itself as the only institution fully competent to resolve the difficult questions raised by the role of race in American democracy. In the enforcement clause cases, the Court goes even further, seeing itself as the sole institution capable really of deciding what equality means generally. Forty years after the judiciary's first significant foray into the political thicket, we find ourselves ensnared in the political *Bushes*.

---

5. *Shaw v Reno*, 509 US 630 (1993); *Miller v Johnson*, 515 US 900 (1995); *Shaw v Hunt*, 517 US 899 (1996); *Bush v Vera*, 517 US 952 (1996); *Hunt v Cromartie*, 526 US 541 (1999).

6. See *Board of Trustees v Garrett*, 121 S Ct 955 (2001); *Kimel v Board of Regents*, 528 US 62 (2000).

7. 517 US 952 (1996).

8. See Richard H. Pildes, *Democracy and Disorder*, in this volume.

BEFORE *BUSH V GORE:* THE *SHAW* CASES AND THE EMERGENCE OF THE NEWEST EQUAL PROTECTION

In 1993, in *Shaw v Reno,* the Supreme Court recognized a new, "analytically distinct" equal protection claim.[9] Prior to *Shaw,* there were basically two types of voting rights injuries: disenfranchisement and dilution. Disenfranchisement involved outright denial of the ability to cast a ballot. Dilution, by contrast, occurred when the votes of some identifiable group counted for less than the votes of other voters. *Shaw* added a third type of equal protection claim:

> [A] plaintiff challenging a reapportionment statute under the Equal Protection Clause may state a claim by alleging that the legislation, though race-neutral on its face, rationally cannot be understood as anything other than an effort to separate voters into different districts on the basis of race, and that the separation lacks sufficient justification.[10]

Plaintiffs in *Shaw* cases need not prove either that they were denied the right to vote or that their votes were diluted. In fact, despite the Court's reliance on prior vote dilution and disenfranchisement decisions, the real character of a *Shaw* case is not a claim about voting rights at all. As I have explained elsewhere,[11] the right to vote embodies a nested constellation of concepts: participation—the entitlement to cast a ballot and have that ballot counted; aggregation—the choice among rules for tallying votes to determine election winners; and governance—the ability to have one's policy preferences enacted into law within the process of representative decisionmaking. *Shaw* plaintiffs are not advancing a claim under any of these concepts. Rather, they are pressing a claim involving what we might call "metagovernance," that is, a claim about the rules by which the democratic political processes are structured.[12] It is a claim that the very use of race in the process of redistricting is illegitimate.

But notice that this claim does not distinguish the plaintiffs from all other citizens of their state, or, indeed, of the United States. The claim that

9. *Shaw v Reno,* 509 US at 652.

10. Id at 649.

11. Pamela S. Karlan, *The Rights to Vote: Some Pessimism About Formalism,* 71 Tex L Rev 1705, 1708 (1992).

12. See Pamela S. Karlan, *All Over the Map: The Supreme Court's Voting Rights Trilogy,* 1993 Sup Ct Rev 245, 286.

race played too great a role in the redistricting process is a paradigmatic example of "a generally available grievance about government—claiming only harm to . . . every citizen's interest in proper application of the Constitution and laws, and seeking relief that no more directly and tangibly benefits [the plaintiffs] than it does the public at large."[13] *Shaw* plaintiffs are advancing a "shared individuated right to a Government that obeys the Constitution."[14]

Normally, this sort of interest does not confer Article III standing. Rather, it "gives support to the argument that the subject matter is committed to the surveillance of Congress, and ultimately to the political process," rather than to the judiciary.[15] With the notable exception of claims under the establishment clause, the Court's general response is that when everyone has been affected equally by a governmental decision, no one has standing: these are precisely the cases in which the political process can be trusted to handle individuals' claims.

As I have explained before, the Court's minimalist approach to standing in the *Shaw* cases conveys a critical message: these cases "really aren't individual rights lawsuits in the first place. Rather they concern the meaning of 'our system of representative democracy.' "[16] Judicial endorsement of a color-blind conception of democracy necessarily entails judicial repudiation of the vision of democracy expressed by the normal majoritarian political process. To review now-Chief Justice Rehnquist's youthful observation regarding the *White Primary Cases,* "To the extent that this decision advances the frontier of . . . 'social gain,' it pushes back the frontier of freedom of association and majority

13. *Lujan v Defenders of Wildlife,* 504 US 555, 573 (1992).

14. *Allen v Wright,* 468 US 737, 754 (1984).

15. *United States v Richardson,* 418 US 166, 179 (1974). As *Richardson* explained, in denying standing to a plaintiff who claimed that the budget secrecy statute he challenged prevented him from "properly fulfill[ing] his obligations as a member of the electorate in voting for candidates seeking national office," id at 176, to permit litigation of such a claim "would mean that the Founding Fathers intended to set up something in the nature of an Athenian democracy or a New England town meeting to oversee the conduct of the [challenged process] by means of lawsuits in federal courts. The Constitution created a representative Government with the representatives directly responsible to their constituents . . . ; that the Constitution does not afford a judicial remedy does not, of course, completely disable the citizen who is not satisfied with the 'ground rules' established by the Congress. . . . Lack of standing within the narrow confines of Art. III jurisdiction does not impair the right to assert his views in the political forum or at the polls." Id at 179.

16. Pamela S. Karlan, *Still Hazy After All These Years: Voting Rights in the Post-Shaw Era,* 26 Cumb L Rev 287, 296–97 (1996) (quoting *Shaw v Reno,* 509 US at 650).

rule. . . . [I]t does not do to push blindly through towards one constitutional goal without paying attention to other equally desirable values that are being trampled on in the process."[17] The redistricting plans that the Supreme Court has struck down were the product of a robust political process. They were enacted by fairly elected state legislatures and were approved by the executive branch of the federal government pursuant to the authority conferred by a congressionally enacted statute that rests on the consensus that the Fourteenth and Fifteenth Amendments are best enforced by taking race into account, rather than by claiming color-blindness.[18] "Self-government, whether direct or through representatives, begins by defining the scope of the community of the governed and thus of the governors as well"; "[j]udicial incursions in this area may interfere with those aspects of democratic self-government that are most essential to it."[19] The Voting Rights Act and the various political realities of contemporary redistricting define self-government in ways that take into account America's racial and ethnic diversity, its history of exclusion, and current realities of racial polarization.

The Supreme Court's *Shaw* decisions undermine not only the legitimacy of particular majority nonwhite congressional districts, but also the perceived legitimacy of the political branches generally. In the short run, the Supreme Court's expressed skepticism about the bona fides of the Department of Justice and the various state legislators who participated in redistricting may undermine the public's sense of confidence in the integrity of other governmental actors. In the longer run, the roadblocks the Court has thrown in the way of achieving effective desegregation of political office risk undermining the legitimacy of a monoracial government for a multiracial society.

DURING *BUSH V GORE*

For those of us who spent much of the 1990s preoccupied with *Shaw v Reno* and its progeny, *Bush v Gore* had an aspect of déjà vu all over again. It raised quite similar issues of standing, remedies, judicial respect for the

17. Memorandum from William H. Rehnquist to Justice Robert Jackson regarding *Terry v Adams,* 345 US 461 (1953), reprinted in Samuel Issacharoff, Pamela S. Karlan, and Richard H. Pildes, *The Law of Democracy: Legal Structure of the Political Process* 92–93 (1998).

18. For example, Section 2 of the Voting Rights Act expressly states that "the extent to which members of a protected class have been elected to office in the State or political subdivision is one circumstance that may be considered" in deciding whether the political processes are equally open to minority voters. 42 USC § 1973(b) (1994).

19. *Cabell v Chavez-Salido,* 454 US 432, 439–40 (1982).

states and the political branches, and the frame within which to assess equal protection claims.

The central question in *Bush v Gore* was the constitutionality of a Florida Supreme Court decision ordering a manual recount of certain ballots in the agonizingly close presidential election. The United States Supreme Court reversed. It held that "Florida's basic command . . . to consider the 'intent of the voter'"[20] in deciding which votes should be included in the recount total was "standardless"[21] and a violation of the equal protection clause "in the absence of specific standards to ensure its equal application."[22] The Court rested its holding in part on an acknowledgment that "the standards for accepting or rejecting contested ballots might vary not only from county to county but indeed within a single county from one recount team to another."[23] Thus, *who* examined a ballot might determine whether that ballot was counted. The Court gave a concrete example of this problem: "Broward County used a more forgiving standard than Palm Beach County, and uncovered almost three times as many new votes, a result markedly disproportionate to the difference in population between the counties."[24]

In addition, the Court found an equal protection violation in the different treatment accorded to "undervotes" (ballots on which machine tabulation had failed to detect a vote for president and which the Florida Supreme Court had ordered reexamined during the recount) and "overvotes" (ballots that the tabulating machines rejected because there was more than one vote cast for a presidential candidate):

> As a result [of this different treatment], the citizen whose ballot was not read by a machine because he failed to vote for a candidate in a way readable by a machine may still have his vote counted in a manual recount; on the other hand, the citizen who marks two candidates in a way discernable by the machine will not have the same opportunity to have his vote count, even if a manual examination of the ballot would reveal the requisite indicia of intent. Furthermore, the citizen who marks two candidates, only one of which is discernable by the machine, will have his vote counted even though it should have been read as an invalid ballot.[25]

20. *Bush v Gore*, 121 S Ct at 530.
21. Id at 529.
22. Id at 530.
23. Id at 531.
24. Id.
25. Id.

Given these problems, which rendered the recount as ordered unconstitutional, and its view that the problems could not be cured within the available time,[26] the Supreme Court "reverse[d] the judgment of the Supreme Court of Florida ordering a recount to proceed,"[27] effectively ending the election.

Just as in the *Shaw* cases, it is worth asking what the precise constitutional injury was and who suffered it. With respect to the problem of different standards for deciding a previously uncounted ballot's validity, there are two easily understandable potential injuries in fact. First, a voter whose ballot was not counted in the initial machine count, but whose ballot would be recovered under the "liberal" standard applied by, for example, Broward County or by an "inclusionary" counting team, might claim an injury if her ballot were to be rejected because she lived in a county like Palm Beach County that employed a more stringent standard or because she had her ballot examined by a counting team with a more "exclusionary" approach. To my mind, this allegation has the structure of a classic equal protection claim.[28] And it is a colorable claim. Surely, a state statute that made this sort of distinction in a formal manner would raise serious equal protection problems, since there is no easily identifiable justification for using different standards to count ballots depending on where they were cast.

Second, a voter whose preferred candidate received disproportionate support in "stringent" counties might claim that she (and her preferred candidate's other supporters) had less of an ability to elect the candidate of their choice than would a voter whose candidate's support was concentrated in "liberal" counties, since liberal-county-preferred candidates are more able to recapture votes through a manual recount. For example, suppose the counties with a liberal standard were disproportionately Democratic, while the counties with a stringent standard were disproportionately Republican. A Republican voter anywhere in the state might then suffer an

26. The question of the precise time available is beyond the scope of this commentary. Suffice it to say, the question whether the recount had to be completed by December 12—the date mentioned in the Supreme Court's *Bush v Gore* opinion, id at 533—or whether there was in fact more time is among the controversial aspects of the Supreme Court's decision.

27. Id.

28. I leave to one side here the question whether such different treatment would ultimately occur, given unified judicial review of the county-conducted manual recounts.

injury-in-fact because Republican voters would be less likely to have their ballots recovered during the recount process.

In either event, assuming for the sake of argument that the recaptured votes were legally cast in the first instance,[29] the equal protection claim *with respect to the recount standards*[30] inheres in voters who claim that their votes, or the votes of the bloc of which they are members, are less likely to be captured manually than other citizens' votes.

A somewhat different set of potential injuries-in-fact flows from the Florida Supreme Court's directive to recount undervotes, but not to recount overvotes. First, the citizen who cast an overvote but whose intent was clear is injured. Her overvote will not be reexamined in the manual recount process.[31] As a result, she is denied the opportunity to have her vote recovered that is accorded to citizens who cast undervotes. If overvoters and undervoters whose intentions are equally clearly discernable are similarly situated, and I have no reason to doubt that they are, they have been treated unequally. Second, if it could be shown that the supporters of a particular candidate were more likely than other voters to cast recoverable overvotes, then supporters of that candidate might suffer a cognizable injury, since their candidate's relative inability to recover votes in the recount process would make it less likely that their voting bloc would succeed. These two claims, of course, resemble the claims available to voters challenging the different standards for recapturing undervotes. But according to the Supreme Court, there is a third potential problem with the failure to reexamine overvotes: this might allow invalid votes to be counted, since "the citizen who marks two candidates, only one of which is discernable by the machine, will have his vote counted even though it should have been read as an invalid ballot."[32]

This third category is problematic and distinctive. It is problematic be-

29. Thus, I set aside the claims of some Republicans (1) that Democratic-controlled canvassing boards were treating ballots differently if the potentially recoverable vote was for Gore than if it was for Bush and (2) that the recovered votes were not legal votes as a matter of Florida law.

30. I highlight this phrase because it will turn out that there is another important potential equal protection claim ignored by the Supreme Court's decision.

31. This category turns out to have a significant, perhaps decisively significant, number of voters. See Mickey Kaus, *Election 2000: The Race Tightens Up!*, Slate magazine (Jan 28, 2001).

32. *Bush v Gore*, 121 S Ct at 531.

cause it does not in fact exist. The problem identified by the Supreme Court arises from a failure to reexamine *all* ballots and not from a failure to reexamine overvotes. By hypothesis, after all, this group of ballots is unidentifiable as overvotes: they were counted, improperly as it turned out, in the mechanical process. No amount of reexamining overvotes would identify this category.

More significant, this injury is distinctive because it concerns the only category of ballots identified by the Supreme Court as to which other voters are necessarily injured by their *inclusion* in the official count. The injury-in-fact occurs because voters who cast valid ballots have the value of their votes diluted by the inclusion of these invalid ballots.[33] With respect to each of the other injuries, by contrast, the injury is produced by the *exclusion* of valid votes.

One striking thing about the Supreme Court's opinion in *Bush v Gore* is that it does not distinguish these analytically different injuries. But its general tone seems to focus largely on the claims of individual excluded voters rather than on voters whose preferred candidate was potentially disadvantaged by the recount the Florida Supreme Court ordered. Perhaps this was a tactical decision by the majority, which sought to avoid having its decision appear partisan: to say that the injury was suffered only by Republican voters whose overall voting strength was diluted by the recount standard would have made explicit that this was a case about partisan outcomes rather than abstract principles.[34] But if the injuries the Supreme Court sees are the exclusion of valid undervotes by stringent counties and exclusionary counting teams and the exclusion of valid overvotes by an incomplete recount process, who has standing to raise these claims?

George W. Bush? Why? He is not an excluded voter himself. So unless he has third-party standing, he is not a proper champion of the excluded voters' claims. Moreover, unless and until the Supreme Court is prepared to say that his supporters are disproportionately likely not to have their votes recovered under the prescribed process—and the Court made no such finding—he is an especially unlikely candidate for third-party standing. It is hard to see George W. Bush as the champion of a claim by undervoters in

---

33. See *Roe v State of Alabama*, 43 F3d 574 (11th Cir 1995); Samuel Issacharoff, Pamela S. Karlan, and Richard H. Pildes, *When Elections Go Bad: The Law of Democracy and the Presidential Election of 2000* 17 (Foundation 2001).

34. See id at 3.

overwhelmingly Democratic Palm Beach County that they are being denied equal protection because their votes would have been included under the more liberal Broward County standard. Indeed, Bush's third-party complaint in *Gore v Harris*—the source of his intervention in the case which the Supreme Court decided as *Bush v Gore*—alleged, among other things, that the standard used in Broward County was partisan, inconsistent, and unfair. The relief he sought was a declaration that "the illegal votes counted in Broward County under the new rules established after the election should be excluded under the Due Process Clause and 3 U.S.C. § 5."[35] Nothing in that proposed remedy vindicates the rights of excluded voters in Palm Beach County or elsewhere except in the brute realist sense that they might be content to have their votes excluded if that means that a disproportionate number of votes by the other guy's supporters get excluded as well.

I examined the pleadings filed by the other parties in *Gore v Harris* to see what they claimed their injuries to be.[36] There were three groups of voters who intervened. It turns out that none of them claimed an injury for which the United States Supreme Court's opinion provided appropriate relief. Stephen Cruce, Teresa Cruce, Terry Kelly, and Jeanette K. Seymour were registered voters who lived in West Florida.[37] Among other claims, the Cruce plaintiffs alleged a host of acts of misconduct by election officials in various counties, ranging from the improper exclusion of military absentee ballots or votes cast for Bush to the illegal inclusion of ballots that did not manifest a voter's clear intent. The nature of some of their arguments was somewhat opaque to me.[38] In any event, however, they distinguished them-

35. *Gore v Harris*, Third-Party Complaint of Defendants George W. Bush and Dick Cheney ¶ 40 (filed 12/2/2000), available at <http://election2000.stanford.edu> in the *Gore v Harris* section.

36. Intervenor John E. Thrasher sought to participate in his capacity as an elector pledged to George W. Bush, and his argument centered on the questions whether Gore had standing to contest the election in the first place and whether the Florida Supreme Court's recount order violated Article II, Section 1 of the Constitution. See Presidential Elector, John E. Thrasher's Motion to Intervene (filed 12/1/2000), available at <http://election2000.stanford.edu> in the *Gore v Harris* section. Thus, I do not discuss his arguments in the text.

37. Motion to Intervene in Election Contest by Stephen Cruce, Teresa Cruce, Terry Kelly, and Jeannette K. Seymour (filed 11/27/2000), available at <http://election2000.stanford.edu> in the *Gore v Harris* section.

38. By the time the case reached the United States Supreme Court, the Cruce intervenors' key claim seemed to be that the core problem with the recount ordered by the

selves from the candidate-parties (Bush, Gore, Cheney, and Lieberman) in the following terms:

> [Our] view of the 2000 presidential election in Florida comes from a statewide perspective, and [our] concerns lean toward the legitimacy and constitutionality of the election process, more than to [our] own preference of who ought to win.[39]

Put this way, their injury looks exactly like the real objection advanced by the *Shaw* plaintiffs: a "shared individuated right to a Government that obeys the Constitution."[40] There is nothing about their situation that distinguishes them from every other voter in Florida. They are not raising participation-based or aggregation-centered interests.[41] They are not claiming that the actual outcome of the election process does not reflect their choice among the candidates. Rather, they are raising metagovernance claims.

The other voters did raise more individuated claims. Matt Butler, a voter in Collier County, voted for George W. Bush. He intervened:

> to protect the integrity and value of his vote and those of other Florida voters in the same position. Matt Butler voted in a county which used

---

Florida Supreme Court was that it potentially denied voters who chose not to cast a vote in the presidential election their right against compelled speech. See Brief for Respondent/Intervenors Stephen Cruce, Teresa Cruce, Terry Kelly, and Jeannette K. Seymour in Support of Petitioners in *Bush v Gore* (filed 12/10/2000), available at <http://election2000.stanford.edu> in the *Bush v Gore* section, at 10–13. But none of the Cruce intervenors was denied that right: two of them did not vote at all and claimed that the *denial* of their right to vote was the injury they had suffered, and the other two just as clearly chose not to exercise their right not to vote, since they did cast votes for president.

39. Id at 3.

40. *Allen v Wright*, 468 US 737, 754 (1984).

41. In their motion to intervene, the Cruce intervenors did allege that "[d]ue to the news media's unreasonable interference with Florida's election, those citizens . . . who cast their votes in Central Time Zone counties suffered a debasement and dilution of their votes because, at that time, they reasonably expected their individual votes would be supported and strengthened by votes from their fellow voters of similar political views from those same counties. Instead, the strength of the vote from Panhandle counties for a particular candidate was diluted and debased." Cruce Motion to Intervene, ¶ 8(d) (cited in note 37). But there is no conceivable remedy for such an injury—even if the First Amendment does not bar liability altogether. They alleged no aggregation-based injury with regard to ballots actually cast.

punch cards and a vote tabulating machine. No ballots in that county
have been manually recounted or examined by hand. Matt Butler has no
way of knowing for sure whether or not his vote was in fact counted by
the machine; indeed there exists over three thousand ballots cast in
Collier County which did not register any vote for a Presidential candidate.

... He is gravely concerned that the Presidential votes in a few Florida
counties specifically selected by Gore are being given special treatment,
by being manually examined for "voter intent" as to the vote (if any) for
a Presidential candidate (and thereafter being counted for a candidate),
as opposed to those ballots otherwise not tallied as to any Presidential
vote by a machine count because no clear evidence of any Presidential
vote was machine-detected. This results in a subjective process to which
no ballots in Collier County, or in any other of the approximately sixty-
three counties not selected by Gore, were or are being treated.[42]

In a similar vein, voters Glenda Carr, Lonnette Harrell, Terry Richardson, Gary Shuler, Keith Temple, and Mark Thomas intervened to seek a declaratory judgment striking down those portions of the Florida election
code that allowed a candidate to pick the counties in which he would seek
a manual recount. They claimed that this selection device would allow a
candidate to seek recounts in only those counties where he would be likely
to pick up votes. This ability to pick and choose, "without consideration of
other counties which have discredited or 'undervoted' ballots," violated the
rights of voters in those counties whose returns were not reexamined.[43]

Butler and the Carr intervenors raise a plausible injury-in-fact that

42. Intervenor Matt Butler's Response to Plaintiffs' Memorandum in Opposition to
Motions to Intervene at 2–3 (filed 12/1/2000), available at <http://election2000.stan-
ford.edu> in the *Gore v Harris* section.

43. See Emergency Petition for Declaratory Judgment That the Florida Statutory
Scheme for a Manual Recount Is Unconstitutional and Motion to Dismiss the Complaint
to Contest Election at 3–4 (filed 11/29/2000), available at <http://election2000.stan-
ford.edu> in the *Gore v Harris* section. See also Motion for Order Allowing Intervention
¶ 4 (filed 11/30/2000) (arguing for intervention because "all votes manually recounted
in the counties unfairly selected by the Gore-Lieberman candidacy destroy[] their right
to due process and equal protection of the law, and because the statutory scheme for manual recounting allows the losing candidates to intentionally and unfairly skew the election
results thereby diminishing the weight of Petitioners'/Intervenors' right to vote.").

sounds in equal protection. But what is the appropriate remedy for their claims? To my mind, the most sensible remedy obviously is to reexamine ballots in their counties as well. The equal protection right of individual voters to participate can really be vindicated only by *expanding* the scope of the prescribed recount. The only equal protection right that can be vindicated by abolishing recounts altogether is a group-based aggregation interest that depends on the partisan composition of the unrecovered pool, precisely the issue the Supreme Court seemed to want to avoid, by couching its discussion in individualistic, atomistic terms. As I have pointed out elsewhere, equal protection rights generally are expansive, rather than restrictive:

> The general assumption in contemporary equal protection law, which seems to play out most of the time, is that faced with a finding of unconstitutionality, the state will remedy the inequality by providing the benefit to the previously excluded group (that is, by "leveling up") rather than by depriving the previously included group ("leveling down"). The few examples in ordinary equal protection of leveling down—the closing of the schools in Prince Edward County, Virginia, or the swimming pools in Jackson, Mississippi—stand out precisely because of their rarity.[44]

But that conventional equal protection remedy is not what the Supreme Court ordered. Instead,

> *Bush II* is essentially a leveling down case: since Florida could not conduct a manual recount that comported with the Supreme Court's definition of equal protection within the constricted time period, the Court held essentially that *none* of the as-yet uncounted votes should be included. From the tactical perspective of candidate Bush, this was of course an acceptable solution. But which *voters* had cognizable interests that were vindicated by the Court's decision? Is there any voter who is better off than she was before in a sense that the legal system can or should recognize?[45]

My answer to that rhetorical question from our casebook on the election is basically "no": whatever interest the Supreme Court's decision vindicated, it was *not* the interest of an identifiable individual voter. Rather, it was a per-

44. Pamela S. Karlan, *Race, Rights and Remedies in Criminal Adjudication,* 96 Mich L Rev 2001, 2027 (1998).

45. Issacharoff, Karlan, and Pildes, *When Elections Go Bad* at 169–70 (cited in note 33).

ceived systemic interest in having recounts conducted according to a uniform standard or not at all. It was structural equal protection, just as the *Shaw* cases have been.

The second substantial similarity between *Shaw* and *Bush v Gore* has to do with the excessively narrow frame within which the Supreme Court assesses equality. In the *Shaw* cases, the Court focuses on the claims of individual voters to the exclusion of claims about race-conscious districting's contributions to the achievement of effective political equality for minority communities. In *Bush v Gore,* the problem lies in the Court's myopic focus on potential unequal treatment in the manual recount process. The per curiam opinion acknowledged that one purpose of the manual recount process was to vindicate a right to vote that might not be adequately protected by the machine count,[46] but it never really confronted the magnitude of the inequalities produced in the first instance by Florida's use of different voting technologies in different parts of the state. The Broward County recount discerned votes on about 20 percent of the undervoted ballots, while the Palm Beach County recount, using a more stringent standard, recovered votes on about 10 percent of the undervoted ballots.[47] But as noted political scientist Henry Brady points out, while the disparity between the Broward and Palm Beach standards is troubling,

> it pales in comparison with the difference in the undervotes from using the Accuvote optical scanning devices versus the older punch card systems. The Accuvote devices (used in 16 Florida counties) have an undervote rate of about three per thousand. . . . The punch card systems (used in 24 counties) have an undervote rate of about fifteen per thousand. . . .
>
> But that is not all. Different voting machines lead to different numbers of total overvotes (those ballots where the tabulating machine detects two or more votes for the same office). The overvote rate for the Accuvote devices is about three to four per thousand. . . . The overvote rate for the punch card machines is about 25 per thousand. . . .
>
> By any reckoning, the machine variability in undervotes and overvotes exceeds the variability due to different standards by factors of ten to twenty. Far more mischief, it seems, can be created by poor methods of recording and tabulating votes than by manual recounts.[48]

46. See *Bush v Gore,* 121 S Ct at 530.
47. Henry E. Brady, *Equal Protection for Votes* (Dec 11, 2000) (on file with author).
48. Id.

To my mind, it simply will not do for the Supreme Court, in light of these huge disparities, to ignore the larger equal protection problem. That is why, to my mind, the most outrageous passage in *Bush v Gore* is the following:

> The recount process, in its features here described, is inconsistent with the minimum procedures necessary to protect the fundamental right of each voter in the special instance of a statewide recount under the authority of a single state judicial officer. Our consideration is limited to the present circumstances, for the problem of equal protection in election processes generally presents many complexities.
>
> The question before the Court is not whether local entities, in the exercise of their expertise, may develop different systems for implementing elections. Instead, we are presented with a situation where a state court with the power to assure uniformity has ordered a statewide recount with minimal procedural safeguards.[49]

A Court that believes that the real problem in Florida was the disparities in the manual recount standards, rather than the disparities in a voter's overall chance of casting a ballot that is actually counted for the candidate for whom he intended to vote, has strained at a gnat only to swallow an elephant.

Moreover, it has done so in a way that will continue to disadvantage the already disadvantaged. There is credible evidence that systems that disproportionately reject votes both have a racially disparate impact[50] and are more often used in the populous jurisdictions in which minority voters are concentrated.[51] Thus, the newest equal protection once again vindicates the interests of middle-class, politically potent voters, while ignoring the interests of the clause's original beneficiaries.

Finally, *Bush v Gore*, like the *Shaw* cases and the enforcement clause cases, manifests the United States Supreme Court's general disdain for the other branches and levels of government. It is hard to see the United States Supreme Court's opinions as anything other than contemptuous and suspicious of the Florida Supreme Court. Moreover, the Supreme Court seemed to think that neither the Florida legislature, using its powers under

---

49. *Bush v Gore*, 121 S Ct at 532.

50. See *Roberts v Wamser,* 679 F Supp 1513 (ED Mo 1987), revd on other grounds, 883 F2d 617 (8th Cir 1989).

51. See Brady, *Equal Protection* (cited in note 47).

Article II of the federal Constitution,[52] nor the United States Congress, using its powers under the Electoral Count Act,[53] was capable of policing the Florida election process. Once again, as it did in the *Shaw* cases, the Court intervened to short-circuit the normal, albeit potentially contentious and messy, process of self-government. And once again, the Court's decision left in its wake weakened institutions.

AFTER: DOES *BUSH V GORE* HAVE LEGS?

As I have already mentioned, the Supreme Court went out of its way to restrict *Bush v Gore*'s identification of yet another new, analytically distinct equal protection claim to its facts. But the 2000 election has already prompted a spate of proposed federal legislation that would regulate how state and local governments conduct elections, not to mention a deluge of lawsuits challenging various states' patchwork election systems as violations of the equal protection clause.

So this question arises: does *Bush v Gore* shed any light on Congress's power to regulate elections pursuant to its enforcement authority under Section 5 of the Fourteenth Amendment?[54] The Fourteenth Amendment's due process and equal protection clauses are the primary constitutional provisions protecting the right to vote. In a series of cases in the 1960s, the Supreme Court recognized that voting is a "fundamental" liberty interest and thus that restrictions on the franchise trigger strict scrutiny.[55]

There are two sorts of practices Congress might regulate using its en-

52. Article II, Section 1, Clause 2 confers on state legislatures the authority to select the manner in which a state's electors are appointed.

53. 3 USC §§ 1–5 (1994).

54. Congress also has power under the elections clause of Article I, Section 4 to "at any time . . . make or alter" a state's regulation of the time, place, or manner of holding elections for members of Congress. For reasons I explain elsewhere, this power is essentially plenary with respect to congressional elections, and the spillover effect may also result in congressionally mandated standards governing other elections—either for president or for state and local offices. See Pamela S. Karlan, *Congressional Authority to Regulate Elections and Election Technology* 2–5 (Mar 5, 2001) (on file with author).

55. See, for example, *Burson v Freeman*, 504 US 191, 213 (1992) (Kennedy concurring) ("Voting is one of the most fundamental and cherished liberties in our democratic system of government."); *Harper v Virginia Board of Elections*, 383 US 663, 670 (1966) ("Where fundamental rights and liberties are asserted under the Equal Protection Clause, classifications which might invade or restrain them must be closely scrutinized and carefully confined.").

forcement clause powers, and they raise different questions. First, Congress might provide special remedies for violations of the self-executing prohibitions of Section 1 of the Fourteenth Amendment. For example, Congress has provided for the award of attorneys' fees in cases where plaintiffs establish a violation of their constitutional right to vote.[56] Such provisions, which modify the traditional "American rule" that each party bears its own litigation costs, clearly make it easier for plaintiffs to vindicate their rights.

With respect to this first category, however, Congress does not itself prohibit any practices that are not already prohibited by the equal protection or due process clauses. It leaves up to the judiciary the decision whether a particular practice in a particular jurisdiction violates the Constitution.

The problem Congress has found with this sort of solution in the past is that litigation is costly, slow, and piecemeal. It is largely reactive, rather than proactive.

So with respect to protecting voting rights more generally, Congress has used its Section 5 enforcement power to deter or remedy constitutional violations by outlawing conduct without a prior judicial finding that the conduct violates the self-executing prohibitions of the equal protection or due process clause. The paradigmatic example here has to do with literacy tests. In *Lassiter v Northhampton County Board of Elections*,[57] the Supreme Court rejected the claim that fairly administered literacy tests violate the equal protection clause. Yet in *Katzenbach v Morgan*[58] and *Oregon v Mitchell*,[59] the Court upheld a congressional ban on literacy tests—including the very literacy test upheld in *Lassiter*[60]—as an appropriate use of Congress's enforcement power. The question then becomes how far beyond simply outlawing practices that violate the Fourteenth Amendment itself Congress can go.

The central decision in the Supreme Court's contemporary construction of Section 5's enforcement power is *City of Boerne v Flores*.[61] In *Boerne*, the Court struck down a provision of the Religious Freedom Restoration Act of 1993 (RFRA) that prohibited state and local governments from "substan-

56. See 42 USC §§ 1973*l*(e), 1988 (1994).

57. 360 US 45 (1959).

58. 384 US 641 (1966).

59. 400 US 112 (1970).

60. See Pamela S. Karlan, *Two Section Twos and Two Sections Fives: Voting Rights and Remedies After* Flores, 39 Wm & Mary L Rev 725, 728 n 17 (1998).

61. 521 US 507 (1997).

tially burdening" a person's exercise of religion even if the burden resulted from a rule of general applicability—that is, a rule that was not intended to burden religious free exercise—unless the government could demonstrate that the burden "(1) is in furtherance of a compelling governmental interest; and (2) is the least restrictive means of furthering that . . . interest."[62]

The federal government defended RFRA as an appropriate use of Congress's enforcement power under Section 5 of the Fourteenth Amendment. It argued that Congress's "decision to dispense with proof of deliberate or overt discrimination and instead concentrate on a law's effects accords with the settled understanding that § 5 includes the power to enact legislation designed to prevent as well as remedy constitutional violations."[63]

The Court, in an opinion by Justice Kennedy, disagreed. While it acknowledged that "[l]egislation which deters or remedies constitutional violations can fall within the sweep of Congress' enforcement power even if in the process it prohibits conduct which is not itself unconstitutional and intrudes into 'legislative spheres of autonomy previously reserved to the States,'" it declared that "[t]here must be a congruence and proportionality between the injury to be prevented or remedied and the means adopted to that end."[64]

With respect to RFRA, the Court found no such congruity: the record before Congress did not indicate a pervasive practice of intentional discrimination against religious free exercise that would justify the prophylactic step of prohibiting conduct with a discriminatory impact absent a finding of purposeful discrimination. Given that failure, the Court saw Congress's action as an attempt to redefine the substantive scope of First and Fourteenth Amendment protections, rather than an appropriate remedial response. The Court has followed *Boerne*'s analysis in several later cases construing Congress's authority under Section 5 to abrogate states' sovereign immunity under the Eleventh Amendment.[65]

---

62. 42 USC § 2000bb-1 (1994).

63. *Boerne*, 521 US at 517.

64. Id at 518, 520 (quoting *Fitzpatrick v Bitzer*, 427 US 445, 455(1976)).

65. See *Board of Trustees v Garrett*, 121 S Ct 955 (2001) (equal protection); *Kimel v Florida Board of Regents*, 528 US 62 (2000) (equal protection); *College Savings Bank v Florida Prepaid Postsecondary Education Expense Board*, 527 US 627 (1999) (due process). The Court also followed *Boerne*'s analysis in *United States v Morrison*, 529 US 598 (2000), where it invalidated a provision of the Violence against Women Act that provided for a private cause of action against individuals who engaged in gender-motivated violence as beyond Congress's equal protection clause enforcement power.

The "congruence and proportionality" requirement of *Boerne* requires asking, first, what practices violate Section 1 of the Fourteenth Amendment and, second, whether a congressional enactment that goes beyond banning simply those practices is nonetheless an acceptable response to the overall situation because such "overinclusive" legislation is appropriate to deter or remedy constitutional violations.

The first question is complicated in important ways with respect to the constitutional injury identified in *Bush v Gore*. Prior to *Bush v Gore*, there were no judicial decisions of which I am aware that held that a state's re-count procedures violated the Constitution.[66] *Bush v Gore* both raises the possibility that a jurisdiction's failure to set objective standards for tallying and recounting ballots or to treat votes uniformly regardless of where they are cast may violate the equal protection clause and seems to hedge the robustness of that holding in other circumstances. Moreover, although the opinion at one point uses language about voting being a "fundamental" right[67]—the kind of right whose denial or abridgement normally triggers strict scrutiny, under which a state practice can be sustained only if it is necessary to the achievement of a compelling governmental interest—most of its analysis seems to rest not on traditional strict scrutiny forms of analysis, but rather on a perception that Florida's scheme was simply arbitrary and therefore ran afoul of garden-variety rationality review.

This latter issue is important in light of the Court's more recent opinion in *Garrett*. There the Court struck down Congress's use of the enforcement clause to render states liable to suit for money damages for discriminating in their employment practices against the disabled. The Court's analysis seems to rest on the following syllogism: the disabled are not a suspect or quasi-suspect class; therefore, discrimination against them is unconstitutional only if it fails rationality review because it is arbitrary or capricious; the congressional findings that undergirded the Americans with Disabilities Act (ADA) may suffice to show that states have treated the disabled differently in a variety of ways, but this does not show that the differential treat-

66. For more extensive discussion of *Boerne*'s potential relevance to voting issues, see Karlan, *Two Section Twos and Two Sections Fives* at 728–29 (cited in note 60); Douglas Laycock, *Conceptual Gulfs in* City of Boerne v Flores, 39 Wm & Mary L Rev 743, 749–52 (1998); John Matthew Guard, Comment, *"Impotent Figureheads"? State Sovereignty, Federalism, and the Constitutionality of Section 2 of the Voting Rights Act After* Lopez v. Monterey County *and* City of Boerne v Flores, 74 Tul L Rev 329 (1999).

67. 121 S Ct at 529.

ment was arbitrary; without a basis for seeing a serious risk of *unconstitutionally* arbitrary differential treatment, Congress exceeded its powers because there was no Section 1 violation to which the Section 5 enforcement mechanism could be proportional and congruent.

The reason this is important in figuring out Congress's power to proscribe or prescribe particular election practices using its enforcement power is that it matters whether only *arbitrary* differential treatment of voters violates the equal protection clause or whether states will be held to some higher standard—for example, showing that differential treatment was necessary or substantially related to some weighty government interest. Under the former scenario, it may be hard for Congress to build the empirical record through hearings showing that there is a substantial risk of unconstitutional state and local behavior that nationwide standards or practices are necessary to avoid. And this may be particularly true if one gives much weight to the concurrence in *Garrett* by Justice Kennedy, joined by Justice O'Connor, which seems to suggest that Congress must have before it not merely a record of practices that *it* thinks are arbitrarily discriminatory, but rather a sufficient record of judicial *findings* of unconstitutionality to justify prophylactic legislation.

In any event, one thing seems clear about the enforcement clause power. The Supreme Court has been looking quite closely at the evidentiary record before Congress when Congress makes its decision about how to regulate the states. So if Congress intends to use its enforcement clause powers, it should anticipate building a record designed to show substantial and pervasive constitutional violations.

On the other hand, even if there is no federal constitutional right to vote in presidential elections,[68] there clearly *is* a federal constitutional right to vote in congressional elections (albeit one dependent in part on state laws about voter eligibility). Thus, despite the apparent attractiveness of relying on *Bush v Gore*'s newly delineated equal protection principle as the source of congressional enforcement power, it might make more sense to rely on congressional power to avoid and deter violations of the preexisting fundamental right to vote. Suppose, for example, that Congress were to have evidence showing that there is substantial ballot spoilage due to particular voting methods or technologies. This might justify congressional intervention under the equal protection clause (in its fundamental rights strand) or the due process clause (in either its procedural or substantive dimensions).

68. See id.

The most notable thing about the newest equal protection and the enforcement clause, however, is the Court's repeatedly articulated skepticism of Congress's motives and its competence. The last time the Court expressly upheld Congress's use of its enforcement power to go beyond the self-executing prohibitions of the due process and equal protection clauses seems to have been in *City of Rome v United States*,[69] decided more than twenty years ago. Given the Court's general attitude, it is hardly surprising that it declined to leave the question of who Florida's electors should be to Congress to resolve under the Electoral Count Act.

CONCLUSION

Both the *Shaw* cases and *Bush v Gore* reenlist equal protection in the service of less, rather than greater, equality and democracy. And both the enforcement clause cases and *Bush v Gore* reflect a Court that sees itself, rather than the political process the reapportionment revolution did so much to democratize, as the only guarantor of a free and open process. George W. was right: the irreversible trend toward more freedom and democracy has changed. Or as Robert Frost more poetically observed: "[T]he trouble with a total revolution . . . [i]s that it brings the same class up on top."[70]

69. 446 US 156 (1980).

70. Robert Frost, *A Semi-revolution,* in *The Poetry of Robert Frost* 363 (Edward Connery Lathen, ed 1969).

5

Two-and-a-Half Cheers for *Bush v Gore*

MICHAEL W. MCCONNELL

By Inauguration Day, 2001, press recounts indicated that George W. Bush almost certainly would have won the election in Florida even if Vice President Gore had gotten everything his lawyers asked for in court. Gore asked for inclusion of the certified recounts in Broward County (567 votes), inclusion of the late recount in Palm Beach County (176 votes[1]), and inclusion of a partial recount of all ballots in the most heavily Democratic areas of Miami-Dade County (168 votes).[2] That left him 193 votes short of victory (disregarding the Bush campaign's legal objections to many of these results, and ignoring an uncertain number of still-uncounted foreign absentee ballots). Gore's hopes, therefore, were pinned on his remaining demand: for a manual recount of the so-called "undervotes" in the remaining sections of Miami-Dade County.[3] On January 15, the Associated Press reported that an examination of all 10,600 "undervotes" in Miami-Dade County, conducted by newspaper reporters paired

1. Some reports put this number at 215, but apparently were not correct. See Stuart Taylor, Jr., *Why the Florida Recount was Egregiously One-Sided*, Natl J 3932 (Dec 23, 2000) (noting how the 176 number, not 215, was correct).

2. I put aside claims involving Nassau, Seminole, and Martin Counties that were rejected on the merits and not revived by the Florida Supreme Court.

3. "Undervote" was the word used by the Gore legal team for ballots in which voters failed to mark their ballots in such a way as to be readable by the counting machines. Some of these were deliberate decisions not to cast a ballot for president. Some presumably reflected voter confusion or problems with the voting machinery. "Overvote" was the term used for ballots in which voters marked more than one candidate for president.

with county elections staff, produced a net gain of six votes for Bush.[4] That means Gore lost.

Paradoxically, Gore's only chance of victory in a recount would have required rejection of his legal position. In the United States Supreme Court, Gore's lawyer David Boies specifically stated that there was no legal basis for counting "overvotes,"[5] and the Gore lawyers never sought recounts in more heavily Republican areas.[6] But a press recount in Lake County, which went for Bush, suggests that the richest source of additional votes for Gore would have been the "overvotes" in Republican-dominated counties using optical scanning vote systems.[7] It is unclear whether these votes would have been numerous enough to overcome Bush's advantage.[8] In any event, Gore did not ask that they be counted, and the Florida Supreme Court did not require it.

Thus, we can now say with some confidence not only that Bush won under the law as interpreted by the United States Supreme Court, but he

4. _Review Shows Bush Gained 6 Votes in Miami-Dade County,_ Fla Times Union B3 (Jan 16, 2001). This means that Gore not only would not have gained votes from the recount in the remaining precincts in Miami-Dade, but that he was not entitled to the 168 votes the Florida Supreme Court certified on the basis of the partial recount. See _Gore v Harris,_ 772 S2d 1243, 1262 (Fla Dec 8, 2000) (requiring that the results of the partial Miami-Dade recount be included in the final tally of votes), revd and remd as _Bush v Gore,_ 121 S Ct 525 (2000) (per curiam).

5. Transcript of Oral Argument, _Bush v Gore,_ No 00-949, *62–63 (Dec 11, 2000) (available on Lexis at 2000 US Trans Lexis 80).

6. Indeed, in _Gore v Harris,_ Gore's lawyers presented as one of the grounds for appeal the trial court's ruling that "in a contest proceeding in a statewide election a court must review all the ballots cast throughout the state, not just the contested ballots." _Gore v Harris,_ 772 S2d at 1252.

7. See David Damron, Ramsey Campbell, and Roger Roy, _Gore Would Have Gained Votes in GOP Stronghold: "Overvotes" Counted Elsewhere,_ Orlando Sentinel A1 (Dec 19, 2000). It turns out that significant numbers of Democratic voters (a net 130 votes out of more than 6,000 discarded ballots in a heavily Republican county) both darkened the circle for Gore on the ballot and wrote his name as a write-in. Machines registered these as spoiled ballots.

8. Ballots containing this error were already counted in some Florida counties. See _Gore v Harris,_ 773 S2d 524, 535 n 26 (Fla Dec 22, 2000) (Pariente concurring). Moreover, according to press recounts, Bush gained votes in other counties. See Alan Scher Zagier, _Bush Easily Tops Gore in Collier Hand Recount,_ Naples Daily News (Jan 20, 2001), available online at <http://naplesnews.com/01/01/naples/d579324a.htm> (visited Jan 25, 2001) (reporting net gain of 226 votes for Bush in Collier County).

would have won even if Gore had prevailed in his Florida contest action. But this knowledge has not quelled criticism of the way the election was handled. Many Americans believe that Gore somehow would have prevailed if only the United States Supreme Court had allowed the Florida courts to continue the vote-counting process. Of course, many other Americans believe just as passionately that the United States Supreme Court prevented the Florida courts from fabricating enough votes to swing the election in Gore's favor.

Anger at the Court was fueled by the apparently partisan breakdown of the vote regarding the proper remedy. The five justices who voted to end the recounting process were all appointed by Republican presidents, and are regarded as the most conservative members of the Court. To cynical eyes, that rendered their votes in favor of the Bush legal position suspect. Of course, the charge of partisanship can be hurled with equal force in both directions: the justices who voted in favor of the Gore legal position were the most "liberal" of the Court, and may have had their reasons for preferring a Gore victory. In many eyes, the whole affair exposed the Court as an untrustworthy institution. In the words of Justice John Paul Stevens: "Although we may never know with complete certainty the identity of the winner of this year's presidential election, the identity of the loser is perfectly clear. It is the Nation's confidence in the judge as an impartial guardian of the rule of law."[9]

As one who thinks that the judiciary has played an overly large role in American public life over the past few decades, often cloaking the judges' own opinions in a thin veneer of law, I am inclined to think that a dose of realism about the human frailties of the judiciary is not entirely unwelcome. But I fear that rather than stimulating serious reflection on the role of the Court, *Bush v Gore*[10] may exacerbate the already corrosive cynicism about public institutions and undermine public faith in the rule of law itself. Before we leap to conclusions about the outcome of *Bush v Gore,* based on nothing but the pattern of votes, we need to take a closer look at what the Court did.

Litigation over the election came in two rounds. In both rounds, state or local election officials made certain decisions, which were challenged in court either by the Gore campaign or by Democratic-majority county

9. *Bush v Gore,* 121 S Ct at 542 (Stevens dissenting).

10. 121 S Ct 525 (2000) (per curiam).

boards. In the trial courts, those decisions were upheld by local state court judges (all of them Democrats). In the Florida Supreme Court, which is composed entirely of Democratic appointees, Gore's lawyers found a more sympathetic ear. On grounds that seemed dubious at best and disingenuous at worst, the Florida court ruled each time in favor of Gore. That put the U.S. Supreme Court in an awkward position. It could either allow a state court to decide the national presidential election through what appeared to be one-sided interpretations of the law, or render a decision that would call its own position, above politics, into question.

I believe the Court deserves two-and-a-half cheers for its performance. But the half cheer it forfeited, by failing to produce a bipartisan consensus on the remand issue, continues to cast long shadows both on the Court and on the Bush presidency.

The Court's first, unanimous ruling was masterful.[11] It reminded the Florida Supreme Court that its decisions were subject to review on federal grounds and—in effect—warned the court that its handiwork in the first round of litigation was not sufficiently attentive to the law.[12] At the same time, the Court decided nothing of practical consequence, and certainly could not be accused of doing anything that swayed the electoral outcome. Unfortunately, the Florida Supreme Court did not take the hint. In the second round, the Florida court—this time split 4–3—again rendered a decision reversing a lower court decision on grounds that seemed difficult to square with the law.[13] This time, it was more difficult for the Supreme Court to correct the error without appearing to determine the ultimate outcome. The Court nonetheless came close. Seven of the justices—including Justice Stephen Breyer, a Clinton appointee and former staffer to Senator Edward Kennedy, and Justice David Souter, a Bush Senior appointee but a regular member of the liberal faction on the Court—agreed with the five conservatives that the terms under which the Florida court ordered the statewide manual recount were unconstitutional. Justice Souter called the recounting procedure "wholly arbitrary,"[14] and Justice Breyer declared it implicated "principles of fundamental fairness."[15] In light of the 7–2 vote, the

---

11. See *Bush v Palm Beach County Canvassing Board,* 121 S Ct 471 (2000) (per curiam).

12. Id at 473–75.

13. See *Gore v Harris,* 772 S2d at 1243.

14. *Bush v Gore,* 121 S Ct at 545 (Souter dissenting).

15. Id at 551 (Breyer dissenting).

Court's judgment cannot plausibly be attributed to base partisan motives. As discussed below, the Fourteenth Amendment holding, while not very clearly explained in the hastily prepared opinion, was both sensible and persuasive. This part of the opinion was the most important, and the Court—especially Breyer and Souter—deserve far more credit than they have received for achieving a bipartisan near-consensus on so contentious a question.

But the Court split on remedy. Five justices believed that there was not sufficient time for a remand—a decision they attributed to state law—while two justices maintained that the case should be remanded to the Florida courts to try, if they could, to complete a recount in compliance with con-stitutional standards. For reasons I will explain below, I think the decision to halt the recount was incorrect as a matter of law (though the question is closer than the Court's critics like to think). But perhaps more important even than law, in this case of high constitutional moment, was the ques-tionable judicial statesmanship of this part of the ruling. The 5–4 split cre-ated the appearance—whether or not justified—that the Court voted its politics instead of the law. And it deprived the new president—whichever man it would be—of the public assurance that the results were won in the ballot box and not in the courtroom. In effect, the Court accepted the Florida Supreme Court's premise that a manual recount was necessary, but then invoked a questionable reading of state law to say that no such recount could even be attempted. That is an unsettling conclusion. If the five jus-tices in the majority had joined with Justices Souter and Breyer, and re-manded to the Florida courts to conduct a recount under strict constitu-tional standards, the near unanimity of the decision would have been vastly reassuring to the American people. And whichever candidate had won would enter office with far greater public confidence in the legitimacy of his election.

I. THE LEGAL ISSUES

Opponents of the Supreme Court's decision in *Bush v Gore* have focused principally on the unseemliness of resolving a presidential election by a split vote in the Supreme Court. It is not obvious why resolving it by a split vote in the state supreme court would be an improvement, and it is not ob-vious why the split character of the vote impugns the majority position rather than the dissent. For the criticism to make sense, therefore, there must be an assumption not only that the Court was split, but that the majority was wrong. That requires a more detailed examination of the issues. The electoral controversy turned, in the first instance, on state law. Lurking behind the state law, however, are certain principles of federal constitutional law, found in Article II and the Fourteenth Amendment. I will turn first to those principles, then to the two phases of litigation in the Florida courts and the U.S. Supreme Court, then to the question of remedy. I will conclude with some comments on the paradoxically self-defeating character of much of the litigation.

II. THE FEDERAL CONSTITUTIONAL OVERLAY

Article II, Section 1, Clause 2 of the U.S. Constitution provides: "Each State shall appoint, in such Manner as the Legislature Thereof May Direct, a Number of Electors." By specifying "the Legislature" as the source of state law, this Clause departs from the usual principle of federal constitutional law, which allows the people of each state to determine for themselves how to allocate power among their state governing institutions. This puts the federal court in the awkward and unusual posture of having to determine for itself whether a state court's "interpretation" of state law is an authentic reading of the legislative will.

There is no relevant legislative history explaining why the framers of the Constitution made this departure. There are, however, two apparent functional justifications. First, the provision ensures that the manner of selecting electors will be chosen by the most democratic branch of the state government. The selection of presidential electors need not be directly democratic; the legislature could select the electors itself, or even delegate that authority to a more limited body (subject to whatever limits the Republican Form of Government Clause[16] may impose). But by vesting the authority to choose the mode of selection in the most democratic branch, the framers gave that decision a democratic bias.

Second—and more relevant for our purposes—legislatures, in contrast to courts and executive officials, must enact their rules in advance of any particular controversy. A legislative code is enacted behind a veil of ignorance; no one knows (for sure) which rules will benefit which candidates. To use examples from Election 2000, no one could have guessed in advance which candidate would favor strict enforcement of vote-counting deadlines, no one could have guessed which candidate would benefit from counting

16. US Const Art IV, § 4.

ambiguous chads and dimples as votes, and no one could have guessed how the choice between optical scanning and punchcard voting systems would affect the relative positions of the candidates. To be sure, this veil of ignorance is only partially opaque: it is sometimes possible to make an educated guess about the probable partisan consequences of particular electoral rules. For example, favorable rules for recognizing absentee ballots from abroad could be expected to benefit Republicans, and easy registration of voters could be expected to benefit Democrats. Partisan calculation therefore can play a role. By requiring the manner of selection of electors to be specified in advance by the legislature, however, the Constitution limits the ability of political actors to rig the rules in favor of their candidate.

Courts and executive officials making judgments after the fact operate behind no such veil of ignorance. The officials counting dimpled chads in Broward County knew precisely which candidate would be advantaged by what rule—and indeed, how many votes they needed to discover to put their favored candidate over the top. (By all appearances, they changed standards until they found the one that would produce the desired results.) The members of the Florida Supreme Court knew (or at least thought they knew) which candidate would gain if they extended the vote-counting deadline. They knew this because one candidate was asking for the extension and the other was opposing it. And the U.S. Supreme Court knew who would be elected president if the manual recount were put to an end. Under such circumstances, there is inevitably the danger that a rule will be adopted because it will produce a particular result, and then rationalized on other grounds.

I do not claim that all decisions made under such circumstances are unfair. But when decisionmakers face a set of interpretive options, each of which is plausible in the abstract but has predictable effects on the electoral outcome—a matter as to which no decisionmaker is neutral—it would not be surprising to find that their judgment is affected. And even if it is not, there will be no way to prove it to the disappointed faction.

Thus, there is wisdom in the provision of Article II, which places authority to set electoral rules in the institution least able to manipulate the rules to favor a particular candidate. Justice Ginsburg is correct that, in ordinary cases, federal courts must defer to state courts with regard to interpretations of state law.[17] But in this unique context, there is a constitutionally-based

---

17. *Bush v Gore*, 121 S Ct at 549 (Ginsburg dissenting).

federal interest in ensuring that state executive and judicial branches adhere to the rules for selecting electors established by the legislature, and do not use their interpretive and enforcement powers to change the rules after the fact. (I strongly suspect that, if a state supreme court composed entirely of Republican appointees had rendered crucial decisions of dubious legal validity, which had delivered the state to Bush, Justices Stevens and Ginsburg, and many others who complained of Supreme Court meddling, would have seen the necessity of federal court review.)

The second relevant federal constitutional principle is that of equal protection and due process of law.[18] As a matter of original meaning, it is highly questionable that the Fourteenth Amendment was intended to apply to voting rights.[19] And there was something to be said for Justice Frankfurter's argument that federal courts should avoid these unanswerable political questions altogether.[20] The reaction to _Bush v Gore_ (praise by Republicans, denunciation by Democrats) lends weight to Frankfurter's prediction that courts could not enter the political thicket and still maintain their apolitical character, or the appearance of it. But those are old arguments, long rejected by the Court. The right to vote has been recognized as a fundamental right, and strict scrutiny is applied to ensure that every citizen within the jurisdiction is treated precisely equally with regard to that right.[21]

This principle has never been applied in the context of a presidential election before, nor has the Supreme Court addressed the problem of differing voting systems and methods of vote counting. But the logic of the voting rights cases strongly supports the view that a state must use a consistent protocol for counting votes—or, at least, that it may not be arbitrary in its recognition of legal votes. Seven justices agreed with that principle in _Bush v Gore_. Were it not for the partisan context in which the issue was first addressed, I do not believe that it would be considered controversial. There is something fundamentally wrong with a system in which one voter's ballot is recognized when the chad is merely dimpled, but an identical ballot by a

18. US Const Amend XIV, § 1.

19. _Reynolds v Sims,_ 377 US 533, 593–611 (1964) (Harlan dissenting) (thoroughly discussing the history and language of the Fourteenth Amendment, concluding it does not apply to state voting rights); Michael W. McConnell, _The Redistricting Cases: Original Mistakes and Current Consequences,_ 24 Harv J L & Pub Pol 103, 110 (2000).

20. _Baker v Carr,_ 369 US 186, 266–68 (1962) (Frankfurter dissenting).

21. See, for example, _Dunn v Blumstein,_ 405 US 330, 336–37 (1972); _Kramer v Union Free School District,_ 395 US 621, 626–27 (1969).

voter in the same jurisdiction is not recognized. The problem was particularly egregious in the context of Election 2000 in Florida because of the correlation between partisan affiliation and vote-counting rules. The Democrats were advocating a loose standard for recognition of legal votes, as in Broward County, while the Republicans were advocating a strict standard. The predictable result of a standardless recount, therefore, was to skew the results, as officials in Democratic areas applied the loose standard and officials in Republican areas applied the strict standard.[22] If such a thing happened in an ordinary election—for town clerk, for example—most lawyers, law professors, and judges would treat this as an obvious equal protection (or due process) violation. With this constitutional backdrop, let us look at the various legal controversies in *Bush v Gore*.

III. ROUND ONE

The first round of litigation centered on two issues: whether to permit a manual recount of the votes, and whether to enforce statutory deadlines for vote counting. The Bush campaign argued that manual recounts were not authorized by Florida law except in cases where there was "an error in the vote tabulation."[23] According to Bush, the undervotes at issue in Florida were attributable to the failure of individual voters to comply with voting instructions, rather than to an error in the vote tabulation. The voting machines were not designed to register votes where the chad had not been removed from the ballot card, and thus their failure to do so could not be described as an error. This position found support in an interpretive ruling by the Secretary of State, and later was endorsed by Chief Justice Rehnquist in his concurring opinion in *Bush v Gore*.[24]

The Florida Supreme Court rejected this argument.[25] While the question was close, I think this conclusion was within the bounds of reasonable interpretation. The Florida Election Code provides that in conducting a manual recount, the counting team's duty is "to determine a voter's intent in casting a ballot."[26] Since a ballot cast in full compliance with the voting

---

22. See Taylor, Natl J at 3933 (cited in note 1).

23. Fla Stat Ann § 102.166(5) (West 2000).

24. 121 S Ct at 537 (Rehnquist concurring).

25. See *Palm Beach County Canvassing Board v Harris*, 772 S2d 1220, 1228 (Fla Nov 21, 2000) (holding that plain language of Section 102.166(5) was contrary to the Secretary of State's interpretation), vacd and remd as *Bush v Palm Beach County Canvassing Board*, 121 S Ct 471 (2000) (per curiam).

26. Fla Stat Ann § 102.166(7)(b). Oddly, the Florida Supreme Court did not cite this

instructions is highly unlikely ever to raise questions about voter intent, this suggests that manual recounts are expected to include some ballots that were not in compliance with the instructions. This does not necessarily mean that dimples should be counted—they had never been counted in previous Florida elections—but it does provide support for the Florida court's conclusion that manual recounts should include some ballots that were rejected by the machines.

That leaves the question of deadlines. In some elections, it does not matter (much) how long the vote-counting process takes. If the county sheriff's term begins a few weeks late, who cares? Election of a president is different. To begin with, in order to prevent gamesmanship among the states, the Constitution empowers Congress to set a uniform date for presidential elections, and requires Congress to set a uniform date on which the electors must meet and vote.[27] In 2000, election day was November 7, and the date on which the electors voted was December 18. Any process of counting, recounting, and judicial review must fit within that time frame. Moreover, the practicalities of selecting the president-elect of the world's greatest power militate in favor of a prompt resolution. A smooth transition to a new administration takes time, and uncertainty about who is to be the next president is profoundly unsettling to the nation, and to the world. There is inevitably a balance between time to check and recheck the results and the need for a prompt and definitive resolution; but in this context tight deadlines are rational and must be observed. (Behind a veil of ignorance, I hazard the guess that Democrats, no less than Republicans, would favor a system with tight deadlines for counting presidential ballots. Deadlines become controversial only when it is evident which candidate might gain from having more time for recounting.)

Florida state law explicitly sets a deadline of seven days after the election for county canvassing boards to count the votes and report the results.[28] A

---

provision of the Election Code, instead referring to a different section, which addressed the problem of preparing duplicate ballots when the original was damaged and unreadable. *Gore v Harris*, 772 S2d 1243, 1256 (Fla Dec 8, 2000) (citing Fla Stat § 101.5614(5) (2000)), revd and remd as *Bush v Gore*, 121 S Ct 525. This contributed to the impression that the state supreme court was playing games with the statute. The court also cited Section 101.5614(6), which provides that a ballot must be counted for other offices even when the vote on one office is not clear.

27. US Const Art II, § 1, cl 4 ("The Congress may determine the Time of chusing the Electors, and the Day on which they shall give their Votes; which Day shall be the same throughout the United States.").

28. Fla Stat Ann §§ 102.111, 102.112 (West 2000).

recent amendment allowed the Secretary of State to waive this deadline, but that decision is left to her discretion,[29] and she has determined that waivers are appropriate only in very limited circumstances. Her decision was upheld by the circuit court[30] (in an opinion by a Democratic judge, if that matters), but it was overturned by the Florida Supreme Court in *Palm Beach County Canvassing Board v Harris*.[31] In an opinion that was long on words but short on clarity, the Florida court extended the deadline for reporting and certification from November 14 to November 26.[32]

On certiorari to the United States Supreme Court, the Bush campaign made a powerful argument that this decision was contrary to the plain language of the Florida electoral code, and hence in violation of Article II, which vests the legislature—not the courts—with authority to determine the manner for choosing electors. The trouble, however, was that by the time the case got to the High Court, the new deadline had already passed, Governor Bush had been certified the winner, and the legal conflict had moved on to a new phase, rendering *Palm Beach County Canvassing Board v Harris* all but moot. As already noted, the Supreme Court vacated the decision and remanded to the Florida court for clarification of its legal basis.[33] This was a powerful warning to the state court that the U.S. Supreme Court was keeping a close eye on its proceedings, and was prepared to intervene if it appeared that the state court were twisting or distorting state law.

The Supreme Court focused on language in the state court opinion that suggested it was relying on state constitutional law—rather than state statutory law—for its decision.[34] In my opinion, the more substantive problem was not that the Florida court consulted its state constitution in rendering the decision, but that it disregarded the plain language of the statute and substituted a new deadline entirely of its own making. This was obviously not "interpretation." From its denunciation of "hyper-technical reliance

29. Id § 102.112(1).

30. *McDermott v Harris*, 2000 WL 1714590, *1 (Fla Cir Ct Nov 17), revd as *Palm Beach County Canvassing Board v Harris*, 772 S2d 1220, vacd and remd as *Bush v Palm Beach County Canvassing Board*, 121 S Ct 471.

31. 772 S2d 1220, 1228–29 (Fla Nov 21, 2000), vacd and remd as *Bush v Palm Beach County Canvassing Board*, 121 S Ct 471.

32. *Palm Beach County Canvassing Board v Harris*, 772 S2d at 1240.

33. *Bush v Palm Beach County Canvassing Board*, 121 S Ct at 475.

34. Id at 473–74.

upon statutory provisions"[35] to its fabrication of new deadlines out of whole cloth,[36] the court demonstrated that it would not be bound by the legislature's handiwork. The state court's claim that it was reconciling inconsistent provisions in the statute[37] was specious. To be sure, one statute said that the Secretary of State "shall" ignore late-filed returns,[38] and another statute said she "may" ignore late-filed returns.[39] But that provides no support for interpreting the law to say that she "shall not" ignore them, or to authorize the court to create its own deadline. Nor was the court correct to say that the seven-day deadline conflicted, as a practical matter, with the provision allowing a candidate to request a recount as late as five days after the election.[40] Presumably, a candidate takes a risk if he waits the full five days (how big a risk this is, I will address in a moment). But to call this a "conflict" is like saying a Monday morning deadline for a student research paper "conflicts" with allowing the student to wait until Sunday night to begin work.

More importantly, the state court ripped the deadline issue out of its broader context. The deadline (as I read the statute) is not absolute. It is merely the deadline for completing the pre-certification, or "protest," phase. During this phase, the county canvassing boards have discretion to decide whether to conduct manual recounts. At the end of this phase—seven days after the election—the counties must report to the Secretary of State, who certifies the results. Certification, however, is not the end of the road. After certification, candidates may file election "contests," in which they challenge the decisions of the county boards, including their mistakes in vote counting and their failure to conduct recounts, so long as those decisions involved "rejection of a number of legal votes sufficient to change or place in doubt the result of the election."[41]

The Florida Supreme Court defended its deadline extension on the argument that failing to recognize votes for purposes of certification is tantamount to "disenfranchis[ing]" the voters.[42] This, the court said, is "unrea-

35. _Palm Beach County Canvassing Board v Harris_, 772 S2d at 1227.

36. Id at 1240.

37. Id at 1231–36.

38. Fla Stat Ann § 102.111.

39. Id § 102.112.

40. See _Palm Beach County Canvassing Board v Harris_, 772 S2d at 1231–33.

41. Fla Stat Ann § 102.168(3)(c) (West 2000).

42. _Palm Beach County Canvassing Board v Harris_, 772 S2d at 1237–38.

sonable, unnecessary, and violates longstanding law."[43] So it might be, if certification were the final step in the process. But it is not. Certification is simply the legal step that leads to the "contest" phase, during which disappointed candidates can challenge the results. By postponing certification to November 26, the state court did not prevent "disenfranchisement"; it simply shortened the "contest" phase by more than a week.[44]

Ironically, in its second decision, discussed more fully below, the Florida Supreme Court adopted an interpretation of the "contest" phase that empowered circuit courts to conduct recounts on their own authority, de novo, without regard to the decisions of the county boards.[45] Under this interpretation of the statutes, the certification of the results by the county boards and the secretary have no legal consequence, except to serve as "evidence,"[46] on a par with the parties' submissions. This made the court's earlier decision to extend the deadline truly perverse. The court added twelve days to a phase that had no real legal significance, while shortening the time for obtaining genuine legal relief. If, as the court held in *Gore v Harris*,[47] the state court in the "contest" phase can order manual recounts any time it believes they might affect the result, then it certainly does not "disenfranchise" voters to put a quick end to the pre-certification phase of the proceeding.

In my opinion, the court got it wrong both times. In *Palm Beach County Canvassing Board v Harris,* the court overstated the importance of certification, and in *Gore v Harris,* the court understated its importance. Properly interpreted, the pre-certification phase is one in which county officials, under the supervision of the secretary, perform the initial vote count, exercising discretion in such matters as whether to conduct manual recounts. The post-certification phase is styled a "contest" of the certified result, and is in the nature of judicial review of an administrative decision. As in most instances of judicial review of administrative decisions, the administrative decision enjoys a presumption of validity,[48] which the contestant can over-

43. Id.

44. Later, in *Gore v Harris,* the court ruled that the Secretary had to accept county recount results, even when they arrived after the new deadline set by the court. 772 S2d at 1262. Thus, in effect, the court eliminated the deadline altogether.

45. Id at 1252.

46. Id.

47. 772 S2d 1243 (Fla Dec 8, 2000), revd and remd as *Bush v Gore,* 121 S Ct 525.

48. See *Krivanek v Take Back Tampa Political Committee,* 625 S2d 840, 844–45 (Fla 1993) ("[T]he judgment of officials duly charged with carrying out the election process should

come by a showing that it was an abuse of discretion or contrary to law. This is an intermediate position between *Palm Beach County Canvassing Board v Harris,* which assumed that the certified results were conclusive, and *Gore v Harris,* which treated them as legally irrelevant.

At the time, *Palm Beach County Canvassing Board v Harris* looked like a devastating blow to Bush. It gave more time to the county canvassing boards in certain Democratic counties—all dominated by Democratic officials—to "find" just enough votes to put Gore over the top, and it shortened the time that the disappointed candidate—probably Bush—would have to challenge these decisions in court. The most likely scenario was that the Democratic boards would deliver the necessary votes, and that the clock would run out precisely at the point when Republicans were challenging judgment calls that were made by political bodies loaded against them. The Florida courts would then choose between disregarding Republican protests (or treating them summarily) and risking Florida's representation in the electoral college. It looked very bad for Bush.

As it turned out, the decision injured Gore instead of Bush. Palm Beach County could not complete its recount even under the new deadline, and Miami-Dade (after a slow beginning) did not even try. (My suspicion at the time[49]—now corroborated by events—was that the experienced politicians conducting the Miami-Dade recount realized from the partial recount that Bush, not Gore, would benefit from completing the recount, and thus decided not to bother.) Thus, when the new deadline passed, Bush remained in the lead; it was Gore, not Bush, who was in the position of contesting the certified results; and it was Gore, not Bush, who needed more time at the end. If the contest period had not been shortened by over a week, and all else had remained the same, there might have been time to conduct a constitutionally proper recount after the

---

be presumed correct if reasonable and not in derogation of the law."); *Boardman v Esteva,* 323 S2d 259, 268 n 5 (Fla 1975) (agreeing with the trial court's observation that "[t]he election process . . . is committed to the executive branch of government through duly designated officials all charged with specific duties. . . . [Their] judgments are entitled to be regarded by the courts as presumptively correct."); *Broward County Canvassing Board v Hogan,* 607 S2d 508, 510 (Fla Dist Ct App 1992) ("The statutes clearly leave the decision to conduct a manual recount within the discretion of the board.").

49. See Alan Brinkley and Michael McConnell, *Dialogue: What Now?,* Slate magazine (Nov 28, 2000), available online at <http://slate.msn.com/dialogues/00-11-15/dialogues.asp?iMsg=16> (visited Feb 22, 2001).

final decision in *Bush v Gore*. Like a boomerang, Gore's strategy had reversed its course and smitten its creator.

IV. ROUND TWO

The second round of litigation occurred after certification. On November 26, the new deadline set by the Florida Supreme Court, Secretary Harris certified the electoral result, finding Bush to be ahead of Gore by 537 votes. This result was affirmed by the state trial court, essentially on the ground that Gore had failed to show any abuse of discretion.[50] In the Florida Supreme Court, a 4–3 majority held that Gore was entitled to the relief he had requested: inclusion of results of a late recount in Palm Beach and a partial recount in Miami-Dade, and an order requiring a recount in the rest of Miami-Dade.[51] The court also ordered a statewide recount of all "undervotes," which neither party had requested.[52] The court declined to set any standard (beyond the "intent of the voter") to guide the recount.[53] Moreover, without stating any reasons, the court rejected Bush's challenges to the recounts in Broward and Volusia Counties, and to the results of the partial recount in Miami-Dade, all of which relied on an expansive definition of what properly counts as a legal vote.

There were multiple problems with this ruling. To begin with, the court treated the contests as de novo proceedings.[54] This replaced a process in which local governing bodies were the principal vote-counting authorities,[55] subject to supervision by the Secretary of State and judicial review, under an abuse of discretion standard,[56] with a process in which the courts themselves conduct the vote counting in close elections. That seems a significant change in the law. Moreover, the court brushed aside a set of statutory safeguards for manual recounts, including the requirement that "all ballots" be included in any manual recount,[57] that recounting be conducted by bipartisan panels

---

50. *Gore v Harris*, 2000 WL 1790621, *4 (Fla Cir Ct Dec 3), revd and remd as *Gore v Harris*, 772 S2d 1243 (Fla Dec 8, 2000), revd as *Bush v Gore*, 121 S Ct 525.

51. *Gore v Harris*, 772 S2d at 1262.

52. Id.

53. Id at 1252.

54. Id at 1252, 1260.

55. Fla Stat Ann §§ 102.131, 102.141(2) (West 2000).

56. Id § 97.012(1) (authority of Secretary of State); id § 102.168(1) (judicial review in contest proceedings). On the abuse of discretion standard, see cases cited in note 48.

57. Id § 102.166(5)(c).

"when possible,"[58] and that any disagreements regarding voter intent be resolved by the county canvassing boards,[59] subject to judicial review.[60] Under the court-ordered recount, only undervotes would be counted,[61] the panels were to be composed of anyone the court could find to do the job,[62] party observers would be prohibited from lodging oral objections during the vote-counting process,[63] and no written record would be kept of decisions regarding particular ballots, thus rendering appeals virtually impossible.[64] That seems a significant change in the law. Perhaps most strikingly, the court held that the recount should be statewide, and conducted under the supervision of a single circuit judge.[65] Neither Bush nor Gore requested this statewide recount, and it is hard to see how the appellate court had the authority to order it. Contest proceedings take the form of legal challenges to the decisions of county canvassing boards, which are denominated the defendants in the contest actions.[66] How could the Florida Supreme Court order review of the certified results from counties whose results had not been contested, and which were not parties to the litigation?

Any of this could have been the basis for a persuasive finding of an Article II violation. But the Article II argument attracted only three votes on the U.S. Supreme Court,[67] and I shall address it no further.

58. Id § 102.166(7)(a).

59. Id § 102.166(7)(b).

60. Id § 102.168(3)(e). To be sure, these statutory safeguards pertain to manual recounts ordered by county canvassing boards during the protest phase, and not (expressly) to recounts ordered by circuit courts in the contest phase. But the only statutory authorization for manual recounts appears in the code sections pertaining to the protest phase. There is no reason to assume that the safeguards for manual recounts were intended to disappear in the post-certification period. The more likely interpretation is that the court in a contest phase is limited to hearing "contests" to the certified results, and if the court concludes that the county board should have conducted a manual recount, it should order such relief—in accordance with the statutory procedures for manual recounts specified in Sections 102.166(5)(c) and 102.166(7).

61. See *Gore v Harris*, 2000 WL 1811188, *24 (Fla Cir Ct Dec 8) (Lewis).

62. See id at *25.

63. See id.

64. See id.

65. See *Gore v Harris*, 772 S2d at 1261–62.

66. Fla Stat Ann § 102.168(4). See *Gore v Harris*, 772 S2d 524, 532 (Fla Dec 22, 2000) (Pariente concurring) (pointing out that there is no procedure in Florida law for obtaining a statewide manual recount).

67. See *Bush v Gore*, 121 S Ct at 533–39 (Rehnquist concurring).

The key problem with the decision turned out to be the court's failure to specify a consistent and uniform standard for recognition of legal votes. With some vote counters recognizing dimpled chads, and other vote counters following more restrictive principles, there was no way that the state-ordered recount could produce a fair and accurate result. Moreover, by certifying the results from Palm Beach as well as Broward and Volusia Counties, the court effectively ensured that the statewide recount would reflect very different vote-counting standards. Palm Beach treated a "dimpled chad" as a legal vote only if there were extrinsic evidence that this was the voter's intent (for example, if there were similar dimples for other offices on the ballot).[68] By contrast, in a series of 2–1 party-line votes, the Broward County Board recognized dimples as votes without regard to extrinsic evidence of voter intent, producing, on average, more than three times as many votes per 100 disputed ballots as were recognized in Palm Beach.[69] In addition, the Florida Supreme Court certified the results of the partial recount in Miami-Dade, based on an examination of *all* the ballots in the most heavily Democratic precincts,[70] even though the recount in the more Republican areas would include only the undervotes. Gore gained 490 more votes in Broward and Miami-Dade than he would have gained from application of the Palm Beach standard.[71] That could easily have been the margin of victory, if the statewide recount had found a few hundred more. Remarkably, the Florida court did not even mention Bush's challenges to these votes—let alone explain why they were being rejected.

It was no surprise, therefore, that the United States Supreme Court stepped in. The per curiam opinion described the recount as "inconsistent with the minimum procedures necessary to protect the fundamental right of each voter."[72] Justice Souter, who voted to deny the petition for certiorari

68. See Tina Cassidy, *Election 2000/Court Date: Democrats Plan Legal Challenge of Tallies in 3 Counties*, Boston Globe A10 (Nov 27, 2000).

69. See Mike Williams, *Florida Certifies Bush Win but Court Battles Continue*, Atlanta J & Const 1A (Nov 27, 2000).

70. The 135 precincts included in the recount (out of 614 precincts in the county) registered a 74 percent vote for Gore. The county as a whole went for Gore 53 percent to 47 percent. See John Fund, *The Myth of Miami* (Nov 26, 2000), available online at <http://www.opinionjournal.com/diary/?id=65000686> (visited Feb 22, 2001).

71. For the derivation of these numbers, see Taylor, Natl J at 3932–33 (cited in note 1).

72. *Bush v Gore*, 121 S Ct at 532.

and disagreed vehemently with the majority on all other issues, conceded that this disparity in vote-counting standards, which he described as "wholly arbitrary," was "a meritorious argument for relief."[73] He stated that he could "conceive of no legitimate state interest served by these differing treatments of the expressions of voters' fundamental rights."[74] He "would therefore remand the case to the courts of Florida with instructions to establish uniform standards for evaluating the several types of ballots that have prompted differing treatments."[75] Justice Breyer, who like Justice Souter disagreed with the decision to grant certiorari and with the remainder of the Court's decision, concluded that the lack of uniform vote-counting standards "does implicate principles of fundamental fairness."[76] He went out of his way to note that an "appropriate remedy" would not only entail "the adoption of a uniform standard" but also new recounts in Broward, Volusia, Palm Beach, and Miami-Dade Counties "whether or not previously recounted."[77] This was evidently a response to Bush's argument that the recounts in these counties had been improperly conducted.

Were it not for the press of time, and the majority's decision not to allow the state courts to conduct a recount under proper constitutional standards, I do not believe this holding would strike many observers as controversial. It may be true that the Equal Protection Clause typically protects against discrimination against identifiable groups, but as recently as last year, the Court summarily affirmed the principle that it also protects against "irrational and wholly arbitrary" state action, even where the plaintiff does not allege that the unequal treatment was on account of "membership in a class or group."[78] And in cases involving fundamental rights, such as the right to vote, the Court applies strict scrutiny to all disparities, without regard to whether the disparities reflect discrimination against any protected group.[79] Minor and unsystematic variances from precise population equality for legislative districts injure no identifiable

---

73. Id at 545 (Souter dissenting).

74. Id.

75. Id.

76. Id at 551 (Breyer dissenting).

77. Id.

78. *Village of Willowbrook v Olech*, 120 S Ct 1073, 1074–75 (2000).

79. See Laurence H. Tribe, *American Constitutional Law* § 16-7 at 1454 (Foundation 2d ed 1988).

group, but nonetheless violate the Equal Protection Clause.[80] Similarly, to treat one voter's ballot as a legal vote, and another voter's identical ballot as spoiled, in the same jurisdiction, for no conceivable public purpose, certainly states a plausible equal protection claim.

Even Justice Stevens, joined by Justice Ginsburg in dissent, acknowledged that "the use of differing substandards for determining voter intent in different counties employing similar voting systems may raise serious concerns."[81] They declined to find a constitutional violation, however, on the ground that "[t]hose concerns are alleviated—if not eliminated—by the fact that a single impartial magistrate will ultimately adjudicate all objections arising from the recount process."[82] That assurance rings hollow in the circumstances of this case, where Leon County Circuit Judge Terry Lewis announced that he would not set or enforce a uniform standard, where partisan observers were not permitted to voice objections as disputed ballots were counted, where vote counters maintained no written records of the disposition of disputed ballots, on which an appeal to Judge Lewis might be based, and where the pace of events would scarcely allow him to exercise review over some sixty thousand ballots.[83]

Critics make a slippery slope argument: that if different standards for vote counting are unconstitutional, this would render the use of different voting systems by different counties unconstitutional.[84] I think not, for two reasons. First, the Equal Protection Clause requires equality of treatment within a jurisdiction, but not between jurisdictions.[85] Florida law delegates

---

80. See *Karcher v Daggett*, 462 US 725, 744 (1983). Of course, it could be said that the injured "group" is residents of the larger districts. But that is analytically analogous to saying that voters with uncounted votes were the injured group in *Bush v Gore*.

81. *Bush v Gore*, 121 S Ct at 541 (Stevens dissenting).

82. Id.

83. *Gore v Harris*, 2000 WL 1811188 at *24–26.

84. See, for example, *Bush v Gore*, 121 S Ct at 541 (Stevens dissenting).

85. This is the implicit, and convincing, explanation for the holdings of *San Antonio Independent School District v Rodriguez*, 411 US 1, 55 (1973) (ruling that a state's use of property taxation for school funding did not violate the Equal Protection Clause), and *Milliken v Bradley*, 418 US 717, 745 (1974) (ruling that district court could not impose a multidistrict remedy in a single district de jure school segregation situation). The ostensible explanation in *Rodriguez*—that education is not a fundamental right and poverty is not a suspect class—is unconvincing. 411 US at 17–18. I cannot believe a court would hold there is no violation if a school district deliberately provided a less valuable education to poor children.

authority over elections to counties, and there is no constitutional problem if different counties adopt different voting systems. The constitutional issue arose in this election because the Florida Supreme Court (in my opinion erroneously, as a matter of state law) consolidated statewide vote-counting authority in a single jurisdiction, Leon County Circuit Court, without requiring a uniform standard for vote counting within that jurisdiction. Second, there are some aspects of the administration of elections that cannot be remedied after the fact without conducting a revote, which is a drastic remedy never required in the absence of intentional fraud or other extraordinary circumstances. If the use of different voting machines by different counties raises a constitutional issue, it must be challenged before the election, when it could be remedied. Protocols for vote counting are an entirely different matter, since differences can easily be remedied by institution of a uniform standard.

But even if these slippery slope arguments were more persuasive, they would not carry the day because the bottom of the slippery slope is not particularly unattractive. Why *not* require every state to adopt a uniform vote-counting system? Every voting system has its flaws, but in ordinary cases the effects are randomly distributed. The problem in Florida arose because the optical scanning system is predominantly used in more Republican areas, while the punchcard system is predominantly used in more Democratic areas. Thus, the errors were not randomly distributed. We may not know the perfect voting system, but we could solve most of the problem by requiring that the same system be used throughout the state. Then the random errors would not matter.

V. THE REMEDY

On the merits, then, the Court's 7–2 decision to reverse the Florida Supreme Court's decision was well founded. But the same cannot be said of the decision not to allow the lower court to attempt a recount under constitutionally appropriate standards. Had the Court majority accepted the Article II theory that the Florida court misread Florida law in ordering a manual recount to correct individual voter error rather than errors in vote tabulation, it would have been logical to stop the recounting process.[86] But

---

86. *Bush v Gore*, 121 S Ct at 537–38 (Rehnquist concurring). Most other Article II errors identified by the concurring Justices could, in theory, have been corrected on remand.

there were only three votes for that theory of the case. Having rested the decision on the standardless character of the recount ordered by the state court, the logical outcome was to remand under proper constitutional standards.

The per curiam opinion explained its conclusion about the remand as follows:

> The Supreme Court of Florida has said that the legislature intended the State's electors to "participat[e] fully in the federal electoral process," as provided in 3 U.S.C. § 5. [772] So. 2d, at —, 2000 WL 1800752 (slip op. at 27); see also *Palm Beach Canvassing Bd. v. Harris,* [772] So. 2d [1220], —, 2000 WL 1725434, *13 (Fla. 2000). That statute, in turn, requires that any controversy or contest that is designed to lead to a conclusive selection of electors be completed by December 12. . . . Because it is evident that any recount seeking to meet the December 12 date will be unconstitutional for the reasons we have discussed, we reverse the judgment of the Supreme Court of Florida ordering a recount to proceed.[87]

Sympathetic as I am to the nation's need for a resolution to the election imbroglio, I do not find that explanation very persuasive. As a matter of federal law, the December 12 date is not a strict deadline, but merely a "safe harbor" date insulating electors chosen by that date from congressional challenge. No doubt the Florida legislature hoped to take advantage of that safe harbor, but it passed no statute embodying that intention. Nor do the two cited Florida Supreme Court opinions supply any authoritative pronouncement that December 12 is the absolute deadline for state law purposes. The first citation, to *Gore v Harris,* seems to be in error.[88] The "see also" citation, to *Palm Beach County Canvassing Board v Harris,* comes closer, but is far from unambiguous.[89]

87. *Bush v Gore,* 121 S Ct at 533.

88. Nothing on that page, or surrounding pages, seems relevant. See, for example, *Gore v Harris,* 772 S2d at 1248 (commenting on 3 USC § 5 but not describing it as an absolute deadline).

89. In this passage, the Florida court observes that it would be appropriate for the Secretary of State to disregard late-filed returns if they are "so late that their inclusion will . . . preclud[e] Florida voters from participating fully in the federal electoral process," and drops a footnote to 3 USC §§ 1–10. *Palm Beach County Canvassing Board v Harris,* 772 S2d at 1237 n 55. This *could* be taken as a reference to the safe harbor rule of 3 USC § 5, but that would be a stretch.

It might still be true that December 12 is the deadline under state law. Language in support of that conclusion can be found in _Palm Beach County Canvassing Board v Harris_,[90] the Florida Supreme Court's decision on remand from _Bush v Gore_. This decision was handed down on December 11, the day of oral argument in _Bush v Gore_, and must not have come to the justices' attention. In footnote 17, the Florida Supreme Court explained that a reasonable time to complete a manual recount would depend on the election, and stated:

> In the case of the presidential election, the determination of reasonableness must be circumscribed by the provisions of 3 U.S.C. § 5, which sets December 12, 2000, as the date for final determination of any state's dispute concerning its electors in order for that determination to be given conclusive effect in Congress.[91]

Moreover, in footnote 22, the court referred to December 12 as "the outside deadline."[92] These passages may not justify the Supreme Court's decision, since the Court did not rely on them, but they indicate that the Court may have reached the right result for the wrong reason. If the Florida Supreme Court was prepared to recognize December 12 as "the outside deadline," then the same ultimate outcome would have been reached even if the High Court had remanded for further proceedings.

Some commentators have defended the decision to halt the recount on the ground that a continued recount would have produced a constitutional crisis. That was a serious possibility, and may help to explain, even if not to justify, the Court's decision. But I am skeptical. Let us canvass the possible outcomes, in order of their potential for provoking a crisis. First, as now appears most probable, Bush could have won the recount, perhaps by a wider margin. That would have put all reasonable doubts about the election to rest. Second, as appeared most likely at that juncture, there might not have been time enough to conduct a recount under fair and consistent standards, with opportunity for appeals, by the federal constitutional deadline of December 18.[93] From Gore's point of view, that would have been no im-

90. 772 S2d 1273 (Fla Dec 11, 2000) (per curiam).

91. Id at 1286 n 17.

92. Id at 1290 n 22. (I thank Professor James Blumstein for bringing these footnotes to my attention.)

93. In her dissenting opinion in _Bush v Gore_, Justice Ginsburg suggested that there is no federal deadline short of January 6, the date on which Congress meets to count the

provement over the actual decision, except for a few days' more grief. But it would have deflected attention—and responsibility—from the Supreme Court, which acted as expeditiously as humanly possible,[94] to the process in Florida.

Third, if Gore had won a full and fair recount, then Congress would have been required to choose between two competing slates of electors. The worst scenario, I suppose, is that even after receiving instructions from the Supreme Court regarding constitutionally appropriate vote-counting standards, the Florida court had conducted a recount in an unfair fashion. Either of these scenarios would indeed have produced a constitutional confrontation. A good case can be made, however, that the Constitution and laws have designated Congress—not the Court—as the arbiter of such a conflict. I do not assume that all members of Congress would necessarily vote the party line. Whether following politically contentious—but legal— procedures would constitute a constitutional crisis is not obvious, and might well depend on how Congress rose to the occasion.

VI. HINDSIGHT

In retrospect, one of the most remarkable features of the Election 2000 controversy was the consistent way in which lawyers misjudged their clients' best interests. I have already discussed the fact that Gore's lawyers asked for the extension of the certification deadline, only to be injured by the concomitant shrinkage of the contest period. But Gore's lawyers' miscalculations went far beyond that. They attempted to gain an advantage by con-

---

electoral votes. 121 S Ct at 550. With due respect, I think that is plainly incorrect. Article II, § 1, cl 4 empowers Congress to determine the day on which the electors meet to give their votes, and states that this "Day *shall* be the same throughout the United States" (emphasis added). December 18 was so designated by statute. It would be unconstitutional for Congress to allow the electors from a single state to give their votes on a later date. I am aware that in the 1960 presidential election, Congress recognized electors from the state of Hawaii who had been chosen after this deadline. That should not be treated as a precedent. In that election, the votes of Hawaii were not necessary to the result, and on the suggestion of the losing candidate, Vice President Richard Nixon, in his capacity as President of the Senate, were recognized as a courtesy.

94. Some attribute the timing problem to the Supreme Court's grant of a stay on December 9. But this is a red herring. The recount then underway was constitutionally defective, and would have had to be done over, if the stay had not been granted. See *Bush v Gore*, 121 S Ct at 551 (Breyer dissenting).

fining their recount requests to a few heavily Democratic counties in south Florida. They did not request a statewide recount, presumably because they assumed that recounts produce more votes, that the new votes would go to the candidates in proportion to their support in the county, and thus that recounts outside the Democratic strongholds would benefit Bush. They did not request recounts of the "overvotes," presumably because these would be more numerous in counties with optical scanning systems, which tended to be Republican. They did not seek a uniform standard for vote counting, presumably because they benefited from a subjective standard, which maximized their votes in Democrat-controlled Broward and Volusia Counties, while not swelling Bush votes elsewhere.

These tactics were, in hindsight, a mistake. First, by confining their requests in this fashion, they fostered the cynical impression—probably true—that they were less interested in a full and fair result than in winning. That was bad for their public relations campaign. Second, by failing to request a statewide recount, they postponed the day on which the Florida courts would ultimately decide that such a recount would be necessary, until it was too late. Third, their failure to seek uniform standards laid the groundwork for the equal protection problem, which ultimately invalidated their recount. Most ironically, we now know that the selective recounts they sought would not have been enough to put Vice President Gore over the top. Their only hope of winning, it now turns out, was to recount the overvotes in predominantly Republican parts of the state—just what they were trying to avoid.

The Bush legal strategy was more coherent. His lawyers and publicists had a theme, and they stuck to it: Bush won the machine count, and any attempt to supplement it by manual recounting was just an invitation to human error or abuse. Whatever the merits of this position, I do not think they won the public relations battle on this point. Too many people were persuaded by the Democratic claims that votes were not counted. Thus, in the end, when the recount was aborted, many millions of Americans were persuaded that President-elect Bush's victory was not legitimate. Now we know that, if the Bush campaign had simply agreed to a limited recount of the contested counties under a fair and uniform standard, the whole affair could have been concluded more quickly, and Bush would have emerged as the undisputed winner. Indeed, in Miami-Dade County, he would even have picked up votes from the recount.

What is the moral of this story? Perhaps that even in the midst of partisan confrontation, it is sometimes best not to pursue what appears, at the moment, to be to your candidate's maximum advantage. If Gore's position had been a little fairer, he might have obtained the recount he thought he deserved. If Bush's position had been a little more accommodating, he might have obtained a more secure mantle of leadership. The nation might have gained, as well, by the spectacle of the two candidates yielding a little, and recognizing at least a part of the justice in the other side's position. That would have been good practice for the coming four years.

6

Suspicion, or the New Prince

FRANK I. MICHELMAN

I. SUSPICION?

We of the civilized nations sometimes convict people of offenses we strongly suspect them to have committed, even when we are not absolutely certain of guilt. We think it barbarous, though, to make a separate offense out of "being suspicious," here in the sense of behaving in a way that calls down suspicion upon oneself.[1] Is that so? Is it barbarous ever to see suspiciousness of behavior as itself a breach of good order?

A great many Americans suspect that a certain five justices of the United States Supreme Court, or some of them, acted reprehensibly in *Bush v Gore*.[2] The suspicion is that these justices, who cast judicial votes in that case to terminate the process of the year 2000 presidential election, were prompted to their actions by a prior personal preference for a Bush vic-

---

Thanks to Heather Gerken, Andrew Kaufman, Richard Posner, and L. Michael Seidman for helpful comments and suggestions.

1. See John H. Langbein, *Torture and the Law of Proof: Europe and England in the Ancien Régime* 47–48 (Chicago 1977) (absolving seventeenth-century Roman-canon law of accusations of the "barbarous practice" of punishing people not found guilty of anything else for "being suspicious"). See also *Rex v Haddock*, Misl Cas C Law 31 (Herbert, ed 1927) (Frog), reprinted in A. James Casner and W. Barton Leach, *Cases and Text on Property* 31 n 2 (Little, Brown 2d ed 1969):

> [C]itizens who take it upon themselves to do unusual actions which attract the attention of the police should be careful to bring these actions into one of the recognized categories of crimes and offenses, for it is intolerable that the police should be put to the pains of inventing reasons for finding them undesirable.

2. 121 S Ct 525 (2000) (per curiam).

tory. The feeling is that they would not have done the same had the positions of the political parties and their nominees been reversed in an otherwise identical case—had it been Gore not Bush whom a Democratic Secretary Harris sought to declare victorious, Bush not Gore seeking recounts from Republican-appointed judges on the state supreme bench, and so forth.

The suspicion is not baseless. It springs initially from the observation that the justices who cast the pro-Bush votes include all and only the five who are commonly identified as composing the conservative wing of an ideologically polarized Court, and it is girded by certain additional observations: the apparent novelty, contentiousness, and narrowness of the legal grounds supplied for the pro-Bush votes by those who cast them; the apparent difficulty of mapping the judicial votes cast, or the legal issues with respect to which they were cast, onto any cognizable grid of constitutional principles and ideals, or competing sets of them, that independently might explain the Court's division over these issues; and the refusal of the conservatives to heed their liberal colleagues' calls for abstention of the Court from substantial involvement in the election controversy when another branch of government was constitutionally available to resolve it—that branch having the clear institutional advantage, with the choice of a president hanging in the balance, of direct accountability to the electorate. In part, my purpose here is to see whether these grounds of suspicion are true or false, apt or inapt. In part, it is to ask "so what if they are true and apt?"

In the eyes of the public, and surely in the justices' eyes as well, the current membership of the United States Supreme Court is ideologically polarized. Not for the first time in American history, the Supreme Court today appears split into identifiably "conservative" and "liberal" wings of opinion, outlook, and sensibility. On the basis of such categorizations, we, and probably they, form our expectations of how the justices severally will vote when the Court divides over a wide range of matters. In practice, lawyers make tactical use of these perceptions, and doubtless justices do too, not to mention presidents and senators engaged in selecting new justices—although, of course, there are occasional surprises. No justice currently sitting is considered nonaligned. While not all are perceived as equally purist or predictable, and sometimes a justice's particular track record suggests in advance that he or she may break the usual ranks in a particular sort of case, each is perceived, by us and doubtless by them, to belong basically to one or the other wing.[3]

Acting at the insistence of a bare majority of the justices, a Supreme Court exactly split into the familiar, identifiably ideological wings threw itself aggressively and decisively into the year 2000 presidential election. As the justices fully knew it would do, the Court's action secured for the Republican candidate a victory then otherwise far from certain—a victory that either might not have been his at all or might have been his but severely compromised. Had the judicial recount proceeded to completion in Florida, Bush might or might not have been the winner judicially declared. Had he not been, the election would have had a materially different outcome from the one vouchsafed to the country by the ministry of the Supreme Court.[4] Either Bush would not now be President, or he'd be President with however compromised a mandate would have issued from an election decided in Congress and maybe brokered by Congress, on whatever special terms of power-sharing, express or implied, would have been the price. Out of uncertainty's jaws, then, the conservative majority's action drew a clean win for the candidate whom any judicial conservative could fairly be supposed to prefer, other things being in their minds more-or-less equal.

3. It may not be entirely clear what draws together, into identifiably "conservative" and "liberal" packages, the sets of positions a justice tends to take on matters as varied as religious establishment and religious freedom, states' rights and the extent of congressional powers to enact social and economic legislation, the scope and status of non-"enumerated" so-called fundamental rights of persons (including but not limited to abortion), the scope and strictness of constitutional protection for private property holdings against redistributive or regulatory acts of government, the scope and strictness of the Constitution's broadly-speaking procedural safeguards respecting criminal law enforcement, and the constitutional-legal status of so-called benign race-conscious legislation. Consider Robin West, *Progressive and Conservative Constitutionalism*, 88 Mich L Rev 641 (1990). See also J.M. Balkin, *Some Realism About Pluralism: Legal Realist Approaches to the First Amendment*, 1990 Duke L J 375, 383 (on "ideological drift"). Maybe ideological polarization of the bench is traceable to some underlying, deep-rooted cleavage of temperament. Explaining its origins is not, however, our business here. It's enough for my purposes that its existence as fact is axiomatic in American political culture.

4. See *Bush v Gore*, 121 S Ct 512 (2000) (application for stay) (Scalia concurring) (stating that "[t]he counting of votes that are of questionable legality does . . . threaten irreparable harm to . . . [Bush] . . . by casting a cloud upon what he claims to be the legitimacy of his election").

It is the stark fact of the five-to-four split in *Bush v Gore* that anchors my reflections here. I mean, of course, this particular split, in which an identifiably conservative-leaning majority, over the protest of an identifiably liberal-leaning minority, decides a legal case involving a presidential election on terms that effectively award an otherwise uncertain victory to the candidate that any judicial conservative obviously would tend to prefer. It is hard to say whether the fact that should mainly interest us is that the Court did in fact split along the familiar ideological divide, over legal issues that do not seem readily to map onto it,[5] or rather is that the majority saw fit to proceed once it saw that such would be the case. Let it be both.

This fact, or these facts, raises several questions worthy of consideration. *First,* is what happened remarkable in the slightest degree? *Second,* does its having happened give fair reason to suspect anything wrong about any justice's conduct? Given the actual division of the subjective views of conservative and liberal justices, respectively, regarding the legal issues raised by the *Bush* petitioners, what honest or good faith alternative, if any, did any justice have to acting as he or she in fact did act?

Here I must interrupt my list of questions to mention that an obvious alternative for the Court was abstention, meaning either refusal of review or dismissal of review once granted without decision on the merits. That leads to further questions: *Third,* how strong and clear were the reasons for abstention? Strong enough to fuel suspicion of ideologically self-serving motives on the part of a conservative majority that would not yield to them? *Fourth,* what apt or honorable explanations might there be for the majority's conduct, and are they compelling enough to dispel suspicion? *Fifth,* so what?

In what follows, I'll try to keep the focus from time to time on one or another of the questions in my list. Clean separation will not always, however, be possible.

II. IDEOLOGY?

There is nothing inherently untoward about a polarized Supreme Court, by which I mean a Court whose members line up repeatedly and often predictably in opposing wings having stable memberships. To find something amiss in that would be to eject ideology from constitutional adjudication in a way that can only be called wrongheaded in light of our country's long ex-

5. See Part II.

perience with this form of public decisionmaking. Justices arrive at the Court already honestly divided over sundry major issues of constitutional-legal principle, policy, and preference. Notwithstanding the futile and embarrassing protestations to the contrary of some judges and judicial candidates, knowledgeable, grownup Americans accept the ideological difference as unavoidable fact consistent with the public-spirited good faith of a judge, and we don't, therefore, normally feel betrayed or aggrieved by its manifestations.[6] We think that there *are* such things in good people's heads as "constitutional ideals."[7] We think those things can vary, within limits, among reasonable, good faith American jurists. What less, then, should we expect of a judge than that she keep her adjudications in line with her own honest best understanding of the Constitution's aims, values, and meanings?

Accepting all of that, let me now ask you: Was it, accordingly, predictable that the Court would split as it did, right along the familiar conservative/liberal divide, over the particular legal issues raised by the parties in *Bush v Gore?* I want you to answer, for now, on impulse and not after anguished pondering.

If you said "yes," then let me be quick to point out that the division was *not* readily predictable from any liberal/conservative alignment of constitutional ideals, of the kind I have just been describing and condoning. Taking one by one the issues of law that crucially divided the majority from the dissenters in *Bush v Gore*, it seems that ideological alignment either doesn't predict a vote at all or that it predicts the opposite of the votes cast by conservatives.

Does the use of the word "legislature" in Article II, Section 1, Clause 2 of the Constitution mean any of the following: that a state court is in any degree barred from adjudicating claims under the state's general election code, insofar as applied to elections of presidential electors? or that the state court's statutory-interpretative practice is, in that context, required to be any different from the same court's established, accepted, general practice of statutory interpretation, including its interpretations of the same election code as applied to all other elections? or that the state court's applications of state election law are, in such cases, required to proceed in disregard of the state's constitution or that these interpretations and applications are subject to a stepped-up, unusual kind and degree of federal judicial scrutiny?

In response to these questions, three and only three justices concluded

---

6. See David A. Strauss, Bush v Gore: *What Were They Thinking?*, in this volume.

7. See text accompanying note 23.

that Article II, Section 1, Clause 2 required the national Supreme Court, in this case, to substitute its state statutory interpretations for those of the state's own high court.[8] Those three were exactly the three we'd normally have expected, on ideological grounds, to be the last and not the first to find such a claim persuasive. Their action in this instance was not predictable from their known prior stock of constitutional principles and ideals.[9]

Fairly read, do the Florida Supreme Court's opinions in the election cases[10] decide, as a matter of state law, that meeting the "safe harbor" date specified by federal statute is a hard-and-fast requirement of the Florida statutory election code as applied to elections of presidential electors?

Four liberals said "no."[11] Five conservatives said "yes."[12] Whichever to

8. The silence here of Justices O'Connor and Kennedy is fully consistent with suspicion that they acted in *Bush v Gore* (a) as judicial conservatives and (b) out of preference for a Bush presidency. They stood ready to assert other grounds in support of an order terminating the election controversy in Bush's favor. They may have wished not to compromise or complicate the general conservative stance in favor of maximum respect for the dignities of the states including their judicial branches, see, for example, *Teague v Lane*, 489 US 288, 310 (1989). And they may have wished to give their action as much protective cover of apparent nonpartisanship as could be mustered, witness their threadbare claim—ignoring the solid opposition of four justices to any intervention by the Court at all—of a seven-justice majority in favor of a decision for Bush (but for an insinuatedly minor disagreement over remedy). See *Bush v Gore*, 121 S Ct at 533.

9. Once the (unpredictable) decision is made that Article II requires a sharp deviation from the usual stance of extreme deference to state judiciaries construing state law, *then* it may become fairly predictable that some of the Court's most conservative members—being also the ones most hostile to relatively freewheeling modes of legal interpretation—will be quickest to find excessive liberality in a state court's treatment of a state statutory election code. See Richard A. Posner, *Florida 2000: A Legal and Statistical Analysis of the Election Deadlock and the Ensuing Litigation*, 2000 S Ct Rev 1.

10. *Gore v Harris*, 772 S2d 1243 (Fla Dec 8, 2000), revd and remd as *Bush v Gore*, 121 S Ct 525; *Palm Beach County Canvassing Board v Harris*, 772 S2d 1220 (Fla Nov 21, 2000), vacd and remd as *Bush v Palm Beach County Canvassing Board*, 121 S Ct 471 (2000) (per curiam).

11. *Bush v Gore*, 121 S Ct at 541 (Stevens, joined by Ginsburg and Breyer, dissenting); id at 543 (Souter, joined by Breyer, Ginsburg, and Stevens, dissenting); id at 553 (Breyer, joined by Stevens, Ginsburg, and Souter, dissenting).

12. Id at 533 (per curiam). No legal deadline posed a need for federal judges thus to preclude Florida's high court from speaking for itself on this matter. As Professor McConnell notes, if—but only if—the *Bush* majority was right about the Florida court's understanding, an open remand would certainly have led to the same result as the one secured by the U.S. Supreme Court's actual order. See Michael W. McConnell,

you seems the better response, how could you hope to predict any judge's answer from his or her membership in one or the other of the Supreme Court's ideological wings, lacking information about the concrete electoral outcomes hanging in the balance?

Does the Fourteenth Amendment's Equal Protection Clause require use of a standard more specific than manifest intent of the voter to govern evaluation of contested election ballots by sub-referees reporting to a single supervising judge?

The liberals divided over this one, while the conservatives uniformly answered yes. So far as I am aware, in no case prior to *Bush v Gore* has the Court recognized a claim to unequal protection of voting rights in which there was on the state's part no explicit or implicit act of what the jargon calls "classification"—that is, ex ante division of a population of actual or would-be voters into groups (defined by race, party, place of residence, wealth, or financial capability) to whose members the state accords differentially advantageous treatment within the general voting scheme.[13] This hitherto apparently crucial element of classification is missing from the *Bush v Gore* equal protection theory, in which the complaint is that identical-looking ballots cast by sundry atomized individuals might be treated differently by different counters in the same or different places, although always in a fair-minded manner and randomly with respect to voter interest or partisan alignment.[14]

I do not here contend that the doctrinal novelty on which the *Bush v Gore*

Two-and-a-Half Cheers for Bush v Gore, in this volume. In that event, the Florida court itself would soon have ordered all recounts terminated, retroactively, as of midnight, December 12. Secretary Harris forthwith would have recertified a Bush victory to Governor Jeb Bush, who forthwith would have certified the Bush electors to the federal authorities in Washington. The Governor's certificate would have been signed and arrived after the safe harbor day. So what? What chance was there that a Bush slate would have undergone a challenge on January 5? For all that was practically at stake, there was no compelling reason for the *Bush v Gore* majority to cram an unspoken holding down the throat of the Florida court.

13. See *Bush v Gore*, 121 S Ct at 531 ("The idea that one group can be granted greater voting strength than another is hostile to the one-man, one-vote basis of our representative government."), quoting *Moore v Ogilvie*, 394 US 814, 819 (1969); Richard A. Epstein, *"In such Manner as the Legislature Thereof May Direct": The Outcome in* Bush v Gore *Defended*, in this volume; Cass R. Sunstein, *Order Without Law*, in this volume.

14. See *Bush v Gore*, 121 S Ct at 530–31; Part IV.

majority based its intervention is normatively wrong. My point is only that as legal doctrine it is novel, newly minted on the occasion of this case, hitherto—I daresay—widely unsuspected by bar and bench, and furthermore that it is perceived as problematic from birth by the very majority that authored it.[15] After all, it's not particularly to the Court's conservative ideological wing that you would normally look for a somewhat daring doctrinal innovation on behalf of voting rights. Conservative activism on behalf of individual rights claims has been confined to property rights and rights against ("reverse") racial classification. The current conservatives have displayed no special tenderness for voting rights.[16]

Back, now, to my question about the predictability of the Court's five-to-four split along the familiar ideological boundary. If your impulse-answer to my question was that the split was predictable, you must impulsively have found it so—this is what I have been arguing—on the basis of something other than any justice's known commitment to any cognizable set of "conservative" or "liberal" constitutional principles or ideals. On the basis of what, then, if not your assumptions about the election-outcome preferences of known-conservative as opposed to known-liberal judges? I don't mean you'd have to be thinking that any justice *calculatedly* or even consciously chose sides on the crucial legal issues with a view to achieving a preferred electoral outcome. In retrospect, though, you'd have to be saying at least this: that justices who could and should have been alert to the danger of bias from motives extraneous to the legal merits—on even the most expansive understanding of the legal merits—and who could and should, furthermore, have been alert to the near-certainty that that is exactly how a sizeable fraction of the country would view their action later given the ac-

15. Allowing that equal protection's application to "election processes generally" presents "many complexities," the Court took care to confine committed application of its new doctrine to the "special instance" of "a statewide recount under the authority of a single state judicial officer." *Bush v Gore*, 121 S Ct at 532. Regardless of whether the Court's "limiting instruction" proves durable, see Samuel Issacharoff, *Political Judgments*, in this volume, there can be no doubt that it was issued.

16. Racial gerrymandering cases, see, for example, *Miller v Johnson*, 515 US 900 (1995); *Shaw v Reno*, 509 US 630 (1993), are not to the contrary, being obviously contained within the same conservative commitment against race-conscious government action that is reflected in countless cases not involving voting. See, for example, *Adarand Constructors, Inc v Pena*, 515 US 200 (1995); *City of Richmond v J.A. Croson Co*, 488 US 469 (1989).

tual lineup of the votes and the transparent contestability of the grounds, went ahead anyway rather than leave the matter to Congress.

III. ABSTENTION?

To me, as to many,[17] the majority's action was surprising. Abstention—or dismissal—is the course that, from the beginning, I fully expected the Court to take, at least in the event that the members found themselves without clear and compelling grounds for decisive intervention, commanding agreement from some majority other than that particular (predictable?) majority of five.[18] We cannot fault judges for giving an ear to what petitioning parties in a case of this magnitude have to say, or for having their own preliminary looks at the legal issues the parties raise. But preliminary looking is one thing and decisive intervention is another.

It is not as if the Court lacked a proper, honorable alternative to decisive intervention. The majority's woebegone plea to the contrary—"[w]hen contending parties invoke the process of the courts . . . it becomes our unsought responsibility to resolve the federal and constitutional issues the judicial system has been forced to confront"[19]—cannot be sincere. Why is certiorari jurisdiction discretionary, then? What is a political question?[20]

There were obvious considerations of principle, arguing powerfully for the Supreme Court's abstention in *Bush v Gore*. The first is a procedural consideration of gut fairness that Bush partisans have directed loudly against the actions of the Supreme Court of Florida, but which seems to apply as well to those of the Supreme Court of the United States. The second is an institutional consideration of profound significance to the understanding of Americans regarding the question of who governs in this country.

Speaking first, then, to those who take exception when rule deciders de-

17. See, for example, Strauss, page 187 in this volume (cited in note 6).

18. Lacking credibility myself as a shill for the passive virtues in the face of human rights claims, see Alexander Bickel, *The Least Dangerous Branch: The Supreme Court at the Bar of Politics* 111–98 (Yale 2d ed 1986), I can't press to extremes the case for abstention. Had the *Bush* petitioners presented the Court with a case involving some evident, grave unfairness, which clearly applicable and pre-established legal grounds gave it some way to correct rather than re-enact, I would not be writing this. The point is, they didn't. There is such a thing as going too far.

19. *Bush v Gore*, 121 S Ct at 533.

20. See Issacharoff, pages 58–60 in this volume (cited in note 15).

cide the rules after matters have proceeded so far that the decision obviously determines an outcome to which the deciders are perceived to be not indifferent; why not on that ground protest the action of the ideologically identifiable majority in *Bush v Gore*? That majority intervened aggressively, decisively, and knowingly to resolve a presidential election in favor of the contestant who had named two of them as the judicial models by which he would select future justices. It did so on the basis of a hitherto undeclared and unsuspected doctrine of constitutional law,[21] which it drew with a remarkable precision expressly meant to leave its authors unfettered in any future case that any of them are remotely likely to see in their lifetimes.[22]

Passing now to the question of who governs here, the issues generally perceived to divide judicial liberals and conservatives are ones in which the supposedly self-governing people of this country take a great interest. The Court—that is, its temporally prevailing majorities—to greater and lesser degrees decides these matters for the country. Some members go so far as to claim for themselves the role of "speak[ing] before all others" for the "constitutional ideals" of the country.[23] Shall a current ideological majority of a Court claiming such powers assume further for itself, then, unnecessarily and gratuitously, a crucial role in deciding whether relative conservatives or relative liberals are to be in control of its own near-term succession? What could be more grossly at odds than that with the divided powers, checks and balances spirit of American constitutional invention?

It is not as if some court had to preside over the election, and the choice was between which of the two high courts it would be, Florida's or the nation's. Had the national court kept out of the way, the Florida judiciary and

21. See text accompanying notes 13–16.

22. See note 15; John Yoo, *In Defense of the Court's Legitimacy*, in this volume, pages 229–30. Compare Antonin Scalia:

> I had always thought that the common-law approach had at least one thing to be said for it: it was the course of judicial restraint, "making" as little law as possible in order to decide the case at hand. I have come to doubt whether that is true. For when, in writing for the majority of the Court, I adopt a general rule, and say, "This is the basis of our decision," I not only constrain lower courts, I constrain myself as well. If the next case should have such different facts that my political or policy preferences regarding the outcome are quite the opposite, I will be unable to indulge those preferences; I have committed myself to the governing principle.

Antonin Scalia, *The Rule of Law as a Law of Rules,* 56 U Chi L Rev 1175, 1179 (1989).

23. *Planned Parenthood of Southeastern Pennsylvania v Casey,* 505 US 833, 868 (1992) (O'Connor, Kennedy, and Souter).

legislature would have done whatever they were going to do. In due course, a contested Florida election would have landed on Congress's doorstep.[24] In the latter event, whatever claims of electoral rights and wrongs were put to the Court could have been put to Congress and doubtless would have been, very loudly and publicly. That includes voting right claims. In the course of resolving the election, Congress or some part of it might or might not have arrived at something like a holding on a voting rights or equal protection claim, whether pressed by opponents or proponents of the state court's recount.[25] Had it done so, the Court, on a suitable future occasion, could have given that holding such value as a precedent as it saw fit.

In a comparison between the five-member, ideologically identifiable judicial majority that decided *Bush v Gore* and whatever partisan-political majority, coalition, or machination would have decided the election in Congress, individual members of either might claim lack of interest in any dimension of the outcome save getting the matter resolved according to law, or abstract fairness, or procedural justice. Members of neither could do so with much credibility. Senators and representatives have partisanly self-serving reasons to wish their party in control of the federal executive. Justices of an ideologically charged and divided Court have ideologically self-serving reasons to wish their ideological allies in a position to control the coming composition of the Court. The glaring difference, of course, is that senators and representatives caring to retain their offices would have had to face the judgments of voters on their manner of settling the election. In the circumstances of this case, that is a tremendous advantage of institutional competency or fitness. Whatever benefit may be claimed in other settings for the

24. The Constitution does not in so many words assign to Congress, any more than it does to the Supreme Court, a responsibility to resolve disputes over the presidential elector election outcomes. The Twelfth Amendment's provision for electoral vote counting "in the presence" of the House and Senate is somewhat suggestive, however, as is the choice of the House and Senate as the forums for resolving failures of any candidate to achieve electoral-vote majorities. Presumably it was, in part, on the basis of these textual intimations that various Congresses enacted, and various Presidents signed, the bills now regulating the electoral process in 3 USC §§ 1–15 (1994).

25. The Court itself affirms that Congress in its own house may reach its own conclusions in matters of constitutional right. See *City of Boerne v Flores,* 521 US 507, 535 (1997) (Kennedy) (stating that "[w]hen Congress acts within its sphere of power and responsibilities, it has not just the right but the duty to make its own informed judgment on the meaning and force of the Constitution").

independence of the judiciary, this is one setting—the choosing not only of a political chief executive but of a maker of future members of the judiciary—in which insulation from the voters seems just about disqualifying.

All told, then, the *Bush v Gore* majority pressed ahead in apparent disregard for some obvious and weighty institutional counterindications. In doing so, they may have caused injury to public confidence either in the Court's supposed special guardianship of the rule of law or in the capacity of Congress to carry the burden of political leadership in conditions of constitutional stress.[26] On those grounds, many judge them to have acted extremely badly.

What, then, of the *Bush v Gore* dissenters? They, no doubt, had reasons parallel to those of the majority for preferring an opposite electoral outcome and hence for preferring an opposite legal outcome in *Bush v Gore,* meaning any outcome that would have left the events in Florida to run their course unmolested by the federal judiciary. Still one cannot reprobate with an even hand, neater though it might be to do so. The dissenters get an exemption because they all maintain that the Court should have denied or dismissed the writs of certiorari in the election cases.[27] Granted, the exemption may just be a matter of the dissenters' moral luck.[28] We cannot know whether their abstemiousness was a matter of principle or rather was an accidental effect of the fact (assuming it was a fact—I don't know their wishes regarding the presidential election of 2000) that it was their Gore getting oxed by the Court's intervention.

In sum, the Court, and the majority as its steward, had both glaringly obvious and publicly respectable reasons of principle for keeping itself free of substantial, much less decisive, involvement in the election controversy. Doing so would have cost the justices some accusations of cowardice or shirking, but they could have relied confidently on armies of legal publicists and pundits to explain to the country the good grounds for their action,

26. See Gerald Gunther, *Judicial Hegemony and Legislative Autonomy: The* Nixon *Case and the Impeachment Process,* 22 UCLA L Rev 30, 30 (1974) (stating "[i]t seems to me that some of the added strength of the Court has been achieved—unnecessarily, unfortunately, and unwisely—at the expense of the most emaciated and deserving of the three branches, the legislature").

27. *Bush v Palm Beach County Canvassing Board,* 121 S Ct 510 (2000); *Bush v Palm Beach County Canvassing Board,* 121 S Ct 471 (2000) (per curiam); *Bush v Gore,* 121 S Ct 512 (2000) (application for stay); *Bush v Gore,* 121 S Ct 525.

28. See Thomas Nagel, *Mortal Questions* 24–38 (Cambridge 1979).

just as I am doing here, alas counterfactually.[29] Other things being equal, the case for abstention seems solid so far.

IV. OUTRAGE IN FLORIDA?

Suspicion and the grounds for it, as I sketched them near the beginning, are now before us. Are there reassuring explanations for the majority's conduct that we have yet to consider?

We want and expect judges to correct outrageous injustice, don't we, even at the cost of smashing a few dishes? Suppose, in November–December, 2000, a justice is told by a petitioning party that monstrous injustices are in the course of perpetration in Florida—two of them, one macro, one micro: on the micro level, a denial to an indefinite number of voters of the constitutionally protected, fundamental human right to have one's vote counted equally with those of others; on a macro level, an injustice to candidate Bush and his political supporters (or consider it, if you prefer, an injustice to the country), consisting of the Florida Supreme Court's illegal swiping from them of a legitimate electoral victory.[30]

Consider first the claim of micro-injustice, the individual rights claim on which the majority in fact based its intervention. A due regard for the "equal dignity owed to each voter," says the Court, prevents states from valuing any person's vote over any other's.[31] Assuming there had been a petitioning party with clear and genuine standing to raise such a complaint to which the Court's new equal protection wrinkle is supposed to be responsive, of exactly what maltreatment would she have complained? The bottom line answer is: the chance that her ballot, in the event it fell into a batch submitted to recount, would undergo appraisal by an intent-of-the-voter standard, honestly applied by whoever would be applying it. True, her ballot stands possibly to be rejected by the official who happens to be the one to pick it up, whereas it might have been accepted if another official had

29. Had the Court preferred the assurance or the dignity of speaking these good grounds for itself, it easily could have done so. It could have granted the writ, denied the stay, ordered argument as to why the matter should not be classed as a political question unfit for judicial resolution, and then disposed of it accordingly ("case dismissed") with a full, explanatory opinion, maybe even including a gesture of confidence in Congress, the Constitution, and the country looking on.

30. David Strauss disapprovingly explains the decision as prompted by a perception of this sort of macro-injustice. See Strauss, page 203 in this volume (cited in note 6).

31. *Bush v Gore,* 121 S Ct at 529–30.

been the one to pick it up first, because of differing rules of thumb in use by the two, each of them reasonably and impartially adopted and applied. These are eventualities about which our voter will never know, and it is not clear why she has any reason to care about them, either, given that the anticipated vagaries of ballot appraisal are utterly random with respect to partisan voter interest.

On the record before the Court in *Bush v Gore,* there was nothing going on more oppressive or nefarious than that. In *Bush v Gore,* to go by the doctrinal proposition there declared, the majority intervened not on behalf of would-be Gore voters whose votes were being weeded out by biased Republican counters, or would-be Bush voters whose votes were being weeded out by biased Democratic counters. All they found legally wrong was that the intent-of-the-voter standard—they thought unnecessarily—allows different honest counters, or groups of them, to make different dispositions of identical ballots, on a basis that is utterly random with respect to voter interest.[32] No one's equal dignity is impugned by this practice, and only Humpty Dumpty would describe it as valuing one person's vote over another's.[33] Is this a human rights emergency? I would like you even to put a name to the human right undergoing violation here.[34]

Remember, the issue for the moment is not whether the best theory of electoral administration, or the best theory of political justice, requires a strict by-the-numbers rule for the hand counting of contested punchcard ballots. It is whether higher duties of protection of the fundamental rights of persons compelled the Supreme Court's intervention in this case, against otherwise compelling reasons to the contrary. Why should we not be suspect when conservative justices suddenly forget their own characteristic insistence that the Supreme Court "need not . . . inject itself into every field of human activity where irrationality and oppression may theo-

32. Id at 529–32.

33. See note 13.

34. How about the right to associate freely and equally with others in securing the election of your candidate of choice? That would make the Court's equal protection ruling into a newfangled protection against vote dilution—a hard thing to foist on the justices who elsewhere have concluded that vote dilution claims are far too lost in political theory to be justiciable. See *Holder v Hall,* 512 US 874, 892–94 & n 1 (1994) (Thomas, joined by Scalia, concurring) (maintaining that it is error to read either Section 2 of the Voting Rights Act or the Equal Protection Clause to cover dilution claims because such claims are beyond the proper adjudicative capacities of courts).

retically occur"[35]—in a case, of all cases, where a presidential election hangs in the balance?

What of the claimed macro-injustice? The per curiam opinion in *Bush v Gore*—the only one to draw support from a majority of the Court—makes no reference to any such thing, being grounded solely on the proposition of an individual right to an equally counted and weighted vote. But we can't on that account dismiss the macro-injustice claim, because what we're trying to do just now is to see whether the *Bush v Gore* majority had an honorable or commendable ground for its action, which we should allow may not necessarily mean a ground it could prudently mention in public. Still, questions do come to mind. It's not just a given, after all, that the alleged macro-injustice —a subversion of the election by a reckless or larcenous Florida Supreme Court—was in fact occurring. The judicial minority in *Bush v Gore* did not think that it was, rather finding the Florida court to be acting within the bounds of a nonpartisan legal reason.[36] With the matter in that posture, why not leave it—it was a *presidential election,* for crying out loud—to Congress?

V. SALVATION?

A justice might lack confidence that Congress could manage the election imbroglio fairly, or without inflicting grave harm on the country. He or she might believe that members of Congress lack the temerity to withstand public pressure to hand the presidency to Gore, in case the Florida court's recount gave Gore the larger number of votes, in disregard of legitimate complaints about that recount from the Bush side; or that they otherwise lack motivation or skill to conduct the election *dénouement* in a manner likely to sustain public confidence in the basic decency, fairness, or good sense of the outcome; or that a congressional resolution would be so long delayed as to jeopardize national security interests or the preservation of governmental order; or that the country's general welfare cannot risk four years of a presidency scarred and weakened from birth by protracted partisan-political infighting required to create it. We easily may imagine a justice convinced beyond doubt, on grounds such as these, that the nation desperately needs a *clean* termination *now* to the year 2000 election.

35. *Cruzan v Director, Missouri Department of Health,* 497 US 261, 300–301 (1990) (Scalia concurring). Justice Scalia went on immediately to add "and if it tries to do so it will destroy itself," id, a point on which I don't insist.

36. *Bush v Gore,* 121 S Ct at 546–49 (Ginsburg, joined by Stevens, Souter, and Breyer, dissenting).

Believing that only the Supreme Court can give the country what it needs, our justice would be caught in a paradox.[37] The Court's unique ability to produce a clean termination depends on the country's habit of unquestioning obedience to its rulings, and that habit, in the view of our justice,[38] depends on the country's belief that whatever the Court rules, it rules for reasons of law. If the Court stands openly before the country in the posture of a regent, assuming dictatorial powers to tide us over an interregnal gap, the country will not heed it and the salvational project will fail. Thus, as our justices see matters, the Court—the governmental chamber expected beyond all others never to act for reasons other than the very ones it announces—cannot accomplish its national salvational end by saying up front that national salvation, not the law, is its reason for acting as it does.

Reasons having the form of plausible legal grounds will, therefore, have to be produced by the Court to explain its actions, regardless of whether one or another justice believes them to be true and adequate legal grounds. The Court, moreover, will have to do the best it can to frame these *faux-*legal reasons extremely narrowly with a view to minimizing any risk of wreckage to the full body of constitutional-legal doctrine. And the Court, finally, if it's going to undertake this clean-termination project at all, will have to undertake it on behalf of the candidate who leads in the official vote tally at the instant of the Court's decisive intervention, which must not be much longer delayed. That means candidate Bush, as it happens. So the justice we're imagining doesn't choose Bush because she likes Bush better than Gore. He or she would have done the same for Gore—for the country, really—had the positions been reversed.

That is a possible account of what happened in *Bush v Gore*. It is not without its own problems of credibility, but one might believe it. If it occurs to you to wonder why five conservative justices would see matters in the way I've just described, while four liberal justices would not, you should attend carefully to Professor Pildes's explanation of why indeed they might.[39] If Pildes does not persuade you, you ought still to be willing to allow that it

---

37. Compare Louis M. Seidman, *This Essay is Brilliant / This Essay is Stupid: Positive and Negative Self-Reference in Constitutional Practice and Theory,* 46 UCLA L Rev 501, 522–24 (1998) (writing of "the trap of self-knowledge that makes contradiction inevitable").

38. As in the view of Professor Yoo. See Yoo, pages 225–26 in this volume (cited in note 22).

39. See Richard H. Pildes, *Democracy and Disorder,* in this volume.

might, after all, in this instance be the conservatives who are having the moral luck.[40]

Insofar as you think members of the *Bush v Gore* majority may have acted on a basis something like what I've just sketched, suspicion for you is at an end—suspicion, I mean, that the majority justices were prompted to the actions they took by prior personal preference for a Bush victory. Repugnance, however, may still be going strong, for you possibly may think—as I tend to—that intentional judicial conduct of the kind I've just been sketching would have been arrogant, rash, miscalculated, even profoundly anticonstitutional and even bearing in mind that the Constitution is not a suicide pact. Of course, the conduct could have been all those things and still not shameless or depraved. The justices of the *Bush v Gore* majority might be imagined as Machiavelli's new prince, a ruler and savior prepared to sacrifice all to save the imperiled republic—probity, reputation, even the salvation of an honored place in history.[41]

Princes for judges. Is that what Americans want? Would that be keeping the faith?

I mean these questions in earnest. The answers, alas, are not obvious.[42]

40. See note 28 and accompanying text.

41. See Sebastian De Grazia, *Machiavelli in Hell* 217–40 (Princeton 1989). Compare Posner, 2000 S Ct Rev at 54 (cited in note 9) ("Judges unwilling to sacrifice some of their prestige for the greater good of the nation might be thought selfish.").

42. For my further consideration of these questions, see Frank I. Michelman, *Machiavelli in Robes? The Court in the Election,* Colin Thomas Ruagh O'Fallon Lecture at the University of Oregon (Apr 9, 2001). For starters, chew on the following. A Gallup Poll found that fully one-half of respondents to a survey taken December 15–17, 2000, believed the justices' votes were "influenced by their personal political views." Yet of the respondents who disagreed with the decision (49 percent), almost two-thirds (32 vs 17 percent) "accepted" it. The poll is reported at <http://www.cnn.com/2000/ALLPOLITICS/stories/12/18/cnn.poll/index.html> (visited Feb 25, 2001).

7

Democracy and Disorder

RICHARD H. PILDES

Some initial questions on constitutional cases involving democratic politics before the deluge of *Bush v Gore:*[1]

When judges see a "blanket" political primary, in which voters can pick and choose, office by office, which party's primary they want to vote in—the Republican primary for governor, the Democratic primary for Secretary of State, the Libertarian primary for treasurer—do judges see a crazyquilt process that threatens to undermine the integrity of political parties and democracy itself?[2] Or do judges view such novel political structures as stages in an ongoing trial-and-error process, a "progressive inclusion of the entire electorate in the process of selecting their public officials"[3]—starting with the early twentieth-century requirement that party candidates be selected through democratic election in the first place—in an effort, whether sensible or not, to encourage voter participation and to make government more responsive?

Democracy and Disorder © 2001 by Richard H. Pildes. For formative conversations and comments, I thank David Golove, Larry Kramer, and Sam Issacharoff. Others embarrassingly numerous to list have provided helpful comments, most of which I have not been able to respond to here. This essay also reflects ideas developed in the context of work on Samuel Issacharoff, Pamela S. Karlan, and Richard H. Pildes, *When Elections Go Bad: The Law of Democracy and the Presidential Election of 2000* (Foundation 2001), and Samuel Issacharoff, Pamela S. Karlan, and Richard H. Pildes, *The Law of Democracy: Legal Structure of the Political Process* (Foundation 1998).

1. 121 S Ct 525 (2000) (per curiam).

2. *California Democratic Party v Jones,* 120 S Ct 2402, 2410 (2000) ("[A] single election in which the party nominee is selected by nonparty members could be enough to destroy the party.").

3. Id at 2421 (Stevens dissenting).

When judges confront "fusion candidacies"—in which major and minor parties are permitted jointly to endorse the same candidate—do judges see the specter of "the destabilizing effects of party splintering and excessive factionalism"?[4] Or do judges see a vibrant, robustly competitive political sphere, akin to the economic sphere, in which third parties, like competing producers, exert healthy pressure on major parties to take neglected ideas and interests into account?[5]

When judges review the exclusion of ballot-qualified candidates from publicly sponsored campaign debates, do they immediately spy "the prospect of cacophony"[6] and therefore easily defer to judgments of others as to which candidates should be included and excluded? Or instead of such potential disorder, do judges see sufficient value in more open debates as to demand clear, objective standards, specified in advance, before public authorities can make judgments about the inclusion and exclusion of potential candidates?[7]

All these are recent, defining moments in the current Supreme Court's confrontation with issues of democratic politics. In each, the Supreme Court was also divided—twice by 6–3, once by 7–2. But in each case, the five justices who effectively ended *Bush v Gore,* the lawsuit, and hence Bush v Gore, the campaign, were in the majority. In each case, the Court overturned a federal court of appeals, including an en banc court of appeals, that had analyzed the issues differently. Among the dissenting voices, the one constant, perhaps surprisingly, was that Justice Stevens was the chief spokesman and Justice Ginsburg his constant companion.

Bush v Gore is the most dramatic moment in a constitutionalization of the democratic process that has been afoot for nearly forty years, ever since *Baker v Carr*[8] dramatically lowered the "political question" barrier to judicial oversight of politics. More recently, that constitutionalization has increased in pace, as issues like the status of political parties, the regulation of campaign finance, the role of race and partisanship in drawing election districts—and now, the counting of individual ballots—have been transformed into grist for the constitutional mill. As part of my own effort to ex-

4. *Timmons v Twin Cities Area New Party,* 520 US 351, 367 (1997).

5. Id at 381–82 (Stevens dissenting) (stating that "the entire electorate . . . will benefit from robust competition in ideas and governmental policies").

6. *Arkansas Educational Television Comm'n v Forbes,* 523 US 666, 681 (1998).

7. Id at 683–95 (Stevens dissenting).

8. 369 US 186 (1962).

plore this emerging constitutional law of democratic politics as a systematic whole, I want to assess *Bush v Gore* in this larger context. And I want to do so less in terms of doctrinal analysis (there will be time enough for that) or partisan politics (was the decision an act of political will or of legal judgment?) and more as a matter of what we might call judicial culture.

By judicial culture, I mean the empirical assumptions, historical interpretations, and normative ideals of democracy that seem to inform and influence the current constitutional law of democracy. Suffice it to say, when judges are as divided among themselves as in the cases I have described— within the Supreme Court as well as between that Court and the lower courts—it might be useful to assume that the formal sources of legal judgment are sufficiently open-textured as not to compel directly a uniquely determinate conclusion. At that point, the implicit understandings of democracy with which all judges necessarily work—whether American democracy is fragile or secure, whether it functioned better or worse at some (partially hypothesized) moment in the past, whether democracy means order and structure or chaos and tumult—have the greatest latitude to operate. Unlike *Bush v Gore*, the cases I describe have no obvious partisan consequences in terms of the fortunes of the Democratic or Republican Parties or their candidates. Yet it is of considerable moment, I believe, that certain justices consistently gravitate toward the same side of these cases—the five-member Bush majority that terminated the Florida recount on one side, Justices Stevens and Ginsburg on the other. Just as interesting is that Justice Souter, who occupied a sort of middle ground in *Bush v Gore,* is the justice sometimes in dissent, sometimes in the majority, in these signal cases. Whatever role analytical considerations and partisan politics might have played in *Bush v Gore,* there is another dimension—the cultural one—potentially at work. By looking for larger patterns in the Court's recent democracy cases, I want to explore that cultural terrain.

I. IMAGES OF DEMOCRACY AND *BUSH V GORE*

At least two key moments, one concrete, the other envisioned, can be seen as tests of the *Bush v Gore* Court's cultural vision of democratic politics. The former is the image of individual, elected, three-member county canvassing boards voting on individual ballots under diverse standards. I will say nothing about that here. For it is the envisioned moment, far more than the concrete one, that offered the most dramatic test of how the justices (how we all) imagine democracy. Judicial responses to this anticipated moment, I believe, get at the deepest and most essential foundations of not just *Bush v Gore*, but at the current Court's jurisprudence of democratic politics more generally. That moment was the prospect of the result had the Court not terminated the election dispute near midnight on December twelfth. That hour, of course, was purportedly the final moment for Florida's electoral votes to find a congressional "safe harbor," according to the Electoral Count Act of 1887[9]—although it should be noted, but appears not to have been, that from the time this 1887 Act was adopted, serious constitutional questions have existed as to whether Congress has any power at all to threaten state electors, particularly a single slate of electors, with loss of an immunity that Congress might have no power to violate in any event.[10]

Had seven justices agreed, not just that a recount had to be conducted under constitutionally required standards, but also further agreed to a remand that permitted such a process, the specter would have arisen of the ultimate resolution emerging from a political struggle within Congress over a possibly competing slate of Florida electors. This was a prospect, of course, not a certainty (perhaps the Florida Supreme Court, already divided four to three beforehand, would not have pushed to the next stage, or perhaps a constitutional statewide recount process would have confirmed the two rounds of machine counts and the contest would have dissolved). But the possibility was palpable: congressional resolution would certainly have loomed, much as Congress was the ultimate dispute resolver in the 1876

---

9. 24 Stat 373 (1887), codified at 3 USC §§ 5–7, 15–18 (1994).

10. For example, seven dissenting members of the House committee that reported the Act made this constitutional objection as one of the central grounds for their dissent:

> In accord with the principles I have mentioned, seven of the committee are of the opinion that, so far as casting the vote is concerned, the State has all the constitutional power conferred, and that Congress can not prescribe that a State shall make its determination within a limited time prior to the day of casting the vote.
>
> When the Constitution of the United States says that the day on which the electoral votes shall be cast shall be the same throughout the United States, the Constitution thereby imposes a limitation upon the appointing power of the States. The appointment must be made, all determinations concerning it must be made, all disputes concerning it must be settled, prior to that day; but Congress has no power, as is attempted here, to put a statute of limitations other than the limitation imposed by the Constitution on the appointing power of the State, by enacting that the determination of such question must be made six days, or at any other period, before the vote is cast. That is our point of difference [with the committee majority].

Electoral Count Act, 49th Cong, 2d Sess, in 18 Cong Rec H 47 (Dec 8, 1886) (Rep Dibble).

Hayes-Tilden election or in the internal civil war in Rhode Island that lay behind *Luther v Borden*.[11] Congress, self-consciously deliberating in as non-partisan a context as could be selected,[12] a decade after Hayes-Tilden with no disputed election on the horizon, chose exactly this political solution for disputed presidential elections in the Electoral Count Act, specifically re-jecting the alternative of United States Supreme Court resolution.[13]

When a justice stares at this kind of political resolution of a disputed pres-

11. 48 US (7 How) 1 (1849). Although the case is well known for its holding that "the guarantee of republican government" clause, US Const Art IV, § 4, is not justiciable, less well appreciated is that the context involved the state's declaration of martial law, com-peting governments claiming legitimate title to rule in Rhode Island, efforts at armed re-bellion, convictions for treason, and possible national military intervention. The Dorr Rebellion also became an issue in the 1844 presidential elections. With all these political modes of recourse open and Supreme Court intervention closed, the historical record suggests that the conflict was well resolved even absent Supreme Court intervention. For the leading histories of the Dorr Rebellion, see George M. Dennison, *The Dorr War: Re-publicanism on Trial, 1831–1861* (Kentucky 1976); Arthur May Mowry, *The Dorr War or The Constitutional Struggle in Rhode Island* (Preston & Rounds 1901). For the Supreme Court's role, see Carl B. Swisher, 5 *History of the Supreme Court of the United States: The Taney Period 1836–64* 515–27 (Macmillan 1974).

12. See, for example, Counting of Electoral Votes, 49th Cong, 1st Sess, in 17 Cong Rec S 815 (Jan 21, 1886) (Sen Sherman):

[The proposed Electoral Count Act] comes before us again at the beginning of an ad-ministration, when no party advantage can be derived from our decision, when the Senate is clearly on one side in party politics and the House clearly is on the other; and now, if ever, this matter ought to be settled upon some basis of principle.

13. 3 USC § 15 (1994) provides the mechanism for a congressional resolution, with ul-timate default rules, in the case of a state presenting competing slates of electors. In ex-plaining and justifying this political method of resolution, Senator Sherman, one of the primary speakers in support of the proposed statute, asserted that the method of resolv-ing a disputed presidential election was "a question that is more dangerous to the future of this country than probably any other." Counting of Electoral Votes, 17 Cong Rec at S 815 (cited in note 12). In justifying congressional, rather than Supreme Court, resolu-tion, he went on to argue:

Another plan which has been proposed in the debates at different times, and I think also in the constitutional convention, was to allow questions of this kind to be certi-fied at once to the Supreme Court for its decisions in case of a division between the two Houses. If the House should be one way and the Senate the other, then it was pro-posed to let the case be referred directly to the prompt and summary decision of the Supreme Court. But there is a feeling in this country that we ought not to mingle our great judicial tribunal with political questions, and therefore this proposition has not

idential election, does that justice see the specter of a "constitutional train-wreck?"[14] A dangerous mechanism to be avoided at nearly all costs, a mechanism that conjures up images of disorder, turbulence, political instability, indeed, "crisis?"[15] Does the very novelty of the Electoral Count Act process, one not invoked for over a hundred years, increase the judicial sense of a system racing to the brink, a race from which judicial rescue is desperately needed?[16] Or does a justice see other disputed presidential elections of 1800 and 1876—elections freighted with profound substantive conflicts genuinely tearing the country apart, unlike in 2000—and yet elections in which political institutions adequately resolved the dispute. Were these earlier moments "constitutional trainwrecks" or, more to the point, would the consti-

---

met with much favor. It would be a very grave fault indeed and a very serious objection to refer a political question in which the people of the country were aroused, about which their feelings were excited, to this great tribunal, which after all has to sit upon the life and property of all the people of the United States. It would tend to bring that court into public odium of one or the other of the two great parties. Therefore that plan may probably be rejected as an unwise provision. I believe, however, it is the provision made in other countries.

Id at S 817–18.

14. For the suggestion that the Supreme Court's decision "might well have averted chaos," see Cass R. Sunstein, *Order Without Law*, in this volume, page 216; for the view that the Court's decision avoided a "trainwreck," see Richard A. Posner, Bush v Gore: *Prolegomenon to an Assessment*, in this volume; for an effort to demonstrate that "[b]eyond that point of no return were the furies of civil commotion, chaos, and grave dangers—no longer imminent, but real," involving reports of the political actions that would have allegedly followed in Florida had the Supreme Court not acted, see Gary C. Leedes, *The Presidential Election Case: Remembering Safe Harbor Day*, 35 U Rich L Rev (forthcoming 2001).

15. For academic invocation of the language of "constitutional crisis" to describe the political rather than the judicial resolution of the disputed election, see Cass R. Sunstein, *Order Without Law*, in this volume, page 206; Richard A. Posner, *Florida 2000: A Legal and Statistical Analysis of the Election Deadlock and the Ensuing Litigation*, 2000 S Ct Rev 1, 45 ("I cannot see the case for precipitating a political and constitutional crisis merely in order to fuss with a statistical tie that can never be untied.").

16. In a post *Bush v Gore* speech, Chief Justice William Rehnquist remarked on the temptation of the Court to view itself this way: as he put it, the argument in favor of the Supreme Court's intervention in contexts like the 2000 presidential election is "that there is a national crisis, and only you can avert it. It may be hard to say 'no.'" See Charles Lane, *Rehnquist: Court Can Prevent a Crisis: Chief Justice Cites 1876 Election Role*, Wash Post A24 (Jan 19, 2001) (quoting the remarks of the Chief Justice to the John Carroll Society on January 7, 2001).

tutional order have been better off had they been resolved through Supreme Court decisions? A deep historical sensibility about the elections of 1800 or 1876 is not needed to ask such questions. For we can also ask whether the recent presidential impeachment process was a "constitutional trainwreck" or, again more to the point, whether the constitutional order would have been improved had the Supreme Court determined for the country what constituted "high Crimes and Misdemeanors"[17] within the meaning of the Constitution?

The Electoral Count Act sought to codify, modify, and regularize the limited past political practices for resolving disputed presidential elections. As an alternative to the images of instability, crisis, and disorder, would the justices see in this Act the genius of a democratic order, one that had filled a gap in its own original design by creating a rule-of-law process for resolving even one of the most incendiary issues any system can confront, the disputed choice of its chief executive? If the Electoral Count Act opts for congressional resolution of such disputes, does a justice see partisan politics as a politically representative and politically accountable means of resolution—a democratic system working out its own imperfections in a potentially self-correcting way?[18] If political resolution of election disputes appears unseemly, it is, warts and all, the conventional remedy for the other elective national offices. The Constitution makes both the United States House and Senate "the Judge"—note the intriguing choice of words—"of the Elections, Returns, and Qualifications of its own members."[19] The same is true for many state legislatures.[20] Moreover, according to the Supreme Court of a previous era, in a close Senate election states are free to conduct

17. US Const Art II, § 4.

18. For the contrasting picture of what congressional resolution would mean, see Posner, 2000 S Ct Rev at 46 (cited in note 15):

> Had the responsibility for determining who would be President fallen to Congress in January, there would have been a competition in indignation between the parties' supporters, with each side accusing the other of having stolen the election. Whatever Congress did would have been regarded as the product of raw politics, with no tincture of justice.

19. US Const Art I, § 5.

20. Florida among them. See Fla Stat Ann § 102.171 (West 2000):

> The jurisdiction to hear any contest of the election of a member to either house of the Legislature is vested in the applicable house, as each house, pursuant to s. 2, Art III of the State Constitution, is the sole judge of the qualifications, elections, and returns of its members.

manual recounts, with the Senate then free to use or reject those recounted figures in forming its own independent judgment.[21] (Interestingly, the Senate has at times exercised this power by engaging in its own manual recounts—including selective recounts of only that small subset of ballots actually in dispute, as well as recounts that override state law in order to ensure that the "intent of the voter" has been honored.[22]) But the Electoral College is not the kind of institution that could be made the judge of its own disputed elections, for the Electoral College has no continuous, institutional existence at all. Intentionally designed to be an evanescent body, which comes into being for a single and transitory function, immediately dissolves, and never meets collectively in a single place, the Electoral College simply could not play the same role the House and Senate do in resolving their own disputed elections. The longstanding[23] historical question has therefore been what alternative institution should play this role. In the Electoral Count Act, Congress chose the political process that might be thought of as the closest surrogate for disputed presidential elections to the constitutional structure for disputed House and Senate elections.

We must keep in mind—whether the justices did or not—that this political process, if not curtailed by the Court, would have taken place in a world in which the Court had already intervened to regulate the manner of the recount. That is, any recount totals presented to Congress would have resulted from a process overseen by the Supreme Court, one in which consistent, uniform, clearly specified vote-counting standards would have been required at the state level, including the revision of results from earlier recounts not completed under such constitutionally required rules. We should also keep in mind—as the justices surely did—that any such process very likely would not have been completed by December 18, the day con-

---

21. *Roudebush v Hartke*, 405 US 15, 26 (1972) (finding that Art I, § 5 of the Constitution does not prohibit a state recount in a Senate election). Note that this full process required nearly two years after election day before Hartke, the Senate's choice, was finally seated officially.

22. Anne M. Butler and Wendy Wolff, *United States Senate: Election, Expulsion and Censure Cases 1793–1990* 312–15, 421–25 (GPO 1995).

23. Congressional debate over the Electoral Count Act took note of the recurrent congressional efforts to create a mechanism for resolving disputed presidential elections. See, for example, Electoral Count Act, 18 Cong Rec at H 52 (cited in note 10) ("I will now remind the House that this question has been discussed since 1800. It has been discussed repeatedly. Repeatedly attempts have been made to legislate.").

gressionally assigned for the electors to vote.[24] In envisioning this kind of political, not judicial, process as the *dénouement*, what exactly did the Court, self-consciously or viscerally, imagine?

II. IMAGES OF DEMOCRACY BEFORE *BUSH V GORE*

A.

In 1996, by a margin of 60 to 40 percent, with nearly identical support among Republican and Democratic voters, over three million voters in California replaced the state's "closed" political primary with the "blanket primary."[25] In a blanket primary, voters can choose office by office in which party's primary they want to vote. Washington has used blanket primaries since 1935, as has Alaska since 1947.[26] Supporters of blanket primaries argue that they increase voter turnout and participation, partly by giving voters more choices, partly by enabling candidates closer to the median voter— more moderate candidates—to make it to the general election. The political parties, which believed this structure would weaken their control, chose not to attempt to make their case in the political process of the initiative contest,[27] but pursued ex post constitutional litigation. Seven federal

24. Michael McConnell suggests that it would have been *unconstitutional* for Congress to have accepted Florida's votes after this date, a suggestion I have not seen elsewhere. Michael W. McConnell, *Two-and-a-Half Cheers for* Bush v Gore, in this volume, page 120, note 93.

25. In a "closed" primary, eligibility is limited to voters who have registered as party members a specified period of time in advance of the primary. Fifteen states employ closed primaries. In an "open" primary, a registered voter may choose the party primary in which he or she prefers to vote on election day, whether or not the voter has registered previously as a member of that party; but the voter may vote only in that one party's primaries on election day. Twenty-one states use this structure. In addition, eight states permit independents to participate in party primaries along with party members; these are sometimes called "semi-open" or "semi-closed" primaries. California would have been the fourth state to use either a blanket or nonpartisan primary. *California Democratic Party v Jones*, 984 F Supp 1288, 1291–92 (E D Cal 1997) (discussing different types of primaries and noting the number of states with each type), affd 169 F3d 646 (9th Cir 1999), revd 120 S Ct 2402 (2000).

26. See Wash Rev Code Ann § 29-18.200 (West 1993) (authorizing blanket primary); Alaska Stat §§ 15.05.010, 15.25.090 (Michie 2000) (making general election rules apply to primaries). From 1960–66, Alaska temporarily shifted back to an open primary. See *O'Callaghan v Alaska*, 914 P2d 1250, 1256, 1263 (Alaska 1996) (noting the history of Alaska's blanket primary and upholding such primaries as constitutional). Louisiana also allowed a type of blanket primary, see La Rev Stat Ann § 18:401B (West 1979), but the Fifth Circuit found Louisiana's primary system unconstitutional, see *Love v Foster*, 147 F3d 383, 386 (5th Cir 1998).

27. Richard L. Hasen, *Parties Take the Initiative 'and Vice Versa,'* 100 Colum L Rev 731, 745–51 (2000) ("Republicans spent $48,899 opposing [a California blanket primary] measure; Democrats spent a mere $4,630.").

judges concluded blanket primaries were not constitutional, six federal judges concluded they were, and because all seven of the former were on the Supreme Court, the initiative was invalidated in *California Democratic Party v Jones.*[28] My concern here is not with which side is more convincing, as a matter of constitutional law or of policy, but with how different judges picture democracy when deciding such cases.

The district court put great weight on expert empirical evidence—the best expertise in political science testified at trial, but it was sharply divided—regarding the possible effects of blanket primaries on voter behavior and the strength of political parties. But at the same time, the imagery of the opinion celebrated "experiment[s] in democratic government"[29] and viewed the blanket primary against that narrative background. As the district court told the story, "Proposition 198 is the latest development in a history of political reform measures that began in the Progressive Era."[30] Reading the opinion, one is struck by how much the district judge emphasized the significance of longstanding and widespread popular support for blanket primaries in California. And because "[t]he history of election law is one of change and adaptation as the States have responded to the play of different political forces and circumstances," the district court expressed confidence in a future in which, whether the blanket primary turned out well or not, democratic politics would be self-correcting enough to respond.[31]

The seven justices on the Supreme Court who reversed—the *Bush v Gore* majority plus Justices Souter and Breyer—project a strikingly different image of the case. The Court consistently casts the active agent in the case as "the State," an abstract entity, which is pitted against the "rights" of political parties.[32] While the voters are present throughout the district court

28. 120 S Ct 2402, 2414 (2000).

29. *California Democratic Party,* 984 F Supp at 1303.

30. Id at 1301.

31. Id at 1303. The Court of Appeals panel unanimously adopted the district court's opinion. See *California Democratic Party,* 169 F3d at 647.

32. Contrast the opening lines, for example, of the Court's opinion with the concurrence of Justice Kennedy. Compare *California Democratic Party,* 120 S Ct at 2405 ("This case presents the question whether the State of California may [adopt a blanket primary].”), with id at 2414 (Kennedy concurring) ("Proposition 198, the product of a statewide popular initiative, is a strong and recent expression of the will of California's electorate."). Justice Kennedy's interesting concurrence, which cannot be explored here, is noteworthy because, in partial spirit with the dissenters and unlike the majority, he puts considerable stress (though not enough to change his vote) on an image of "a strong, participatory democratic process." Id.

opinion, the Supreme Court majority makes bare legal reference to popular adoption of the blanket primary and none to the level, breadth, or history of popular support. The most dramatic instance occurs when the Court rejects any appeal to the democratic interest in enhancing voter participation: "The voter's desire to participate does not become more weighty simply because the State supports it."[33] What is the separation between the state and the voters that is being imagined here in the context of a voter initiative? Moreover, the Court sees democratic politics and political organizations as fragile and potentially unstable entities that require judicial protection, for as the Court worries, a single election in a blanket primary "could be enough to destroy the party."[34] Without strong, well-ordered political organizations, enforced by constitutional law that denies popular majorities the power to shape the electoral process in the service, benighted or not, of enhanced participation, the Court sees a threat to the stability of the democratic order. A vision further from that of democratic experimentalism and a self-correcting, adaptive democratic system is hard to imagine.

Contrast, now, Justice Stevens's dissent, which Justice Ginsburg joined. This opinion, like the district court's, makes "the people" and "citizens" and "the electorate" the actors behind the blanket primary, not "the State."[35] At work in this case, for the dissent, are "competing visions of what makes democracy work," and for this very reason, "[t]hat choice belongs to the people."[36] The image of a resilient democratic system, not a fragile one, reappears; states "should be free to experiment with reforms designed to make the democratic process more robust."[37] Moreover, the value of voter participation is central in Justice Stevens's dissent; indeed, if that opinion gives one value priority in the justification of democracy over any other, it is the value of participation. Thus, Justice Stevens *structures* the case around the value of voter participation,[38] and his dissent would make the entire structure of constitutional analysis turn on whether regulations of politics expand or constrict voter participation: regulations that broaden participation should not face the same close judicial scrutiny, and their further consequences are for politics itself to work out.[39]

33. Id at 2413.
34. Id at 2410.
35. See, for example, id at 2421–22 (Stevens dissenting).
36. Id at 2421.
37. Id at 2422.
38. Id at 2416.
39. Id at 2419.

Though the various opinions confront each other with social-scientific facts and predictions, it seems unlikely that these facts—tentative and disputed as they were—in any way determined judicial judgment. Even if we somehow knew exactly how much blanket primaries would weaken political parties, change the governing behavior of public officials, and influence voter participation, how ought those effects be traded off against each other? Debates cast in empirical terms often masquerade for deeper, underlying disagreements about cultural assumptions and normative ideals.[40] The rhetoric, imagery, and narrative interpretations infusing these opinions, and others involving democratic politics, are a window into those conceptions. Is American democracy fragile, so that relatively novel political structures require aggressive constitutional evaluation? Or is American democracy experimental and self-revising, so that such structures are to be celebrated, or at least judicially tolerated, as contemporary, popular manifestations of a healthy democratic impulse? Should such popular, direct participation in addressing these questions itself be a preeminent value, to be weighed heavily in any judicial judgment? Or is such participation legally irrelevant, so that all regulation of politics, whether emerging from state legislatures—or from voter initiatives to which the party-dominated state legislature is affirmatively hostile—should be conceived as the action of a singular, undifferentiated entity, "the State?" The cultural attitudes judges bring toward these kind of questions surely influence, if they do not completely dominate, how judges respond to empirical claims and open-ended precedents—which is why, perhaps, most justices end up consistently on the same side of these cases, despite differences in facts, partisan consequences, and precedents among the various cases involving democracy that have recently been before the Court.

For that reason, the way the Court responds to open primaries,[41] a question it will find hard to avoid, will be particularly revealing. Blanket primaries may viscerally seem a bizarre novelty, in use in only a few places. But twenty-nine states use open primaries;[42] many have done so since primary elections themselves were mandated early in the twentieth century.

Unless the American democratic system has been suffering throughout this entire period as a result, the historical experience with open primaries— perhaps the most telling "empirical fact" of all—would not seem to support invalidating open primaries. On the one hand then, the open primary might

40. A theme masterfully developed in Dan M. Kahan, *The Secret Ambition of Deterrence,* 113 Harv L Rev 413, 497–500 (1999).

41. For the differences among types of primaries, see note 25.

42. See *Tashjian v Republican Party of Connecticut,* 479 US 208, 222–23 nn 11–12 (1986).

viscerally seem traditional, unthreatening, and consistent with the stability and strength of American democratic culture. For the Court to invalidate it would itself produce a massive and radical restructuring of a central feature of twentieth-century American democracy. On the other hand, there does not appear to be any meaningful distinction—for now, you will have to accept my word on that[43]—in legal principle or empirical fact for distinguishing the open from the blanket primary. The legal reasons the Court offers for invalidating blanket primaries appear equally applicable to open primaries. Thus, if the Court upholds open primaries, it will have to invoke largely formalistic distinctions;[44] doing so would therefore signal it is the novelty of the blanket primary, and cultural attitudes among the justices toward such popularly adopted innovations, not any deep-rooted matter of substantive legal principle or empirical fact, that divides the conventional open primary from the unconstitutional blanket primary. I will hazard only the following: faced with the choice between the principles of the blanket-primary case and the more familiar, longstanding conventional practice of the open primary, the seven-justice majority of *California Democratic Party v Jones* will splinter.

B.

"Fusion" politics flourished in the late nineteenth century.[45] Fusion candidacies entail joint nomination by two parties—typically a minor party and

43. Other scholars have reached similar views. See, for example, Richard L. Hasen, *Do the Parties or the People Own the Electoral Process?*, 149 U Pa L Rev 815, 830 n 60 (2001). In an open primary, the only act of party "affiliation" that is required is to ask for that party's ballot on election day; in a closed primary, the voter must be registered a defined period of time in advance as a party member. If the mere formality of asking for the party ballot is enough to distinguish open from blanket primaries, the distinction is hard to see as meaningful. See, for example, Samuel Issacharoff, *Private Parties with Public Purposes: Political Parties, Associational Freedoms, and Partisan Competition*, 101 Colum L Rev 274 (2001). In addition, open primaries permit a voter to vote only in one party's primary for all offices that particular election day; if there is a meaningful distinction here from blanket primaries, it would have to be that the power to pick and choose among party primaries for various offices leads, as an empirical matter, to greater rates of actual, undesirable (unconstitutional) cross over voting. No convincing empirical data support this conclusion, as far as I am aware.

44. See note 43.

45. The classic treatment is Peter H. Argersinger, *"A Place on the Ballot": Fusion Politics and the Antifusion Laws*, 85 Am Hist Rev 287, 288 (1980). For greater context on the legal questions discussed here, see Samuel Issacharoff and Richard H. Pildes, *Politics as Markets: Partisan Lockups of the Democratic Process*, 50 Stan L Rev 643, 683–88 (1998).

one of the two major parties—of the same candidate. The candidate appears on the ballot under both party lines; voters can choose either party line in voting for the candidate. The ability to form fusion candidacies was critical to the existence of active third-party politics in the late nineteenth century, which included the Populists, Greenbackers, and other third parties. Deep structural features of the American system make it unlikely that third parties will displace a major party—it has not happened nationally since the pre–Civil War era—but cross-endorsement enables third parties potentially to influence the positions that the two major parties adopt, as well as to afford organizational expression to dissenting voices within the major parties. Most importantly, stringent ballot-access rules in the United States require parties to achieve a fairly high level of support to be automatically included on the ballot in subsequent elections, rather than having to devote scarce resources to signature gathering. Yet if fusion is not permitted, voters who would otherwise support a third party decline to do so because such a vote seems wasted; with fusion, voters can support both the party of their choice and a major party candidate with a serious chance of winning.

Precisely because fusion challenged the conventional two-party structure, many state legislatures banned the practice at the turn of the twentieth century, even when voluntary between major and minor party.[46] In response to the nascent re-emergence of third parties today, these fusion bans were challenged in litigation that culminated in *Timmons v Twin Cities Area New Party*.[47] Again, a divided Supreme Court, six to three, reversed a unanimous court of appeals.[48] Again, there are no obvious partisan consequences to the issue between the two major parties; a ban on fusion does not clearly advantage either the Democratic or Republican party in their mutual competition. Here too, of greatest present interest is not the analytical structure of the formal First Amendment analysis, but the dramatically different cultural images of democracy that inform the views of different judges and that might provide a cultural prism through which *Bush v Gore* can be refracted.

46. Argersinger, 85 Am Hist Rev at 288–90, 303–4 (cited in note 45).

47. 520 US 351 (1997).

48. A different court of appeals in a 2–1 decision had upheld another state's fusion ban, see *Swamp v Kennedy*, 950 F2d 383 (7th Cir 1991), with Judges Easterbrook, Posner, and Ripple dissenting from the en banc court's refusal to review the case, see id at 388, 389 ("A state's interest in political stability does not give it the right to frustrate freely made political alliances simply to protect artificially the political status quo.").

To the Eighth Circuit, fusion candidacies invigorate the democratic process. While the state argued that protecting the integrity of elections justified its ban on fusion, the court of appeals conjured up just the opposite imagery: "consensual multiple party nomination may invigorate [democracy] by fostering more competition, participation, and representation in American politics. As James Madison observed, when the variety and number of political parties increases, the chance for oppression, factionalism, and nonskeptical acceptance of ideas decreases."[49] For empirical debates about the effects of fusion, the court of appeals turned to historical experience and interpreted that experience this way: "History shows that minor parties have played a significant role in the electoral system where multiple party nomination is legal, but have no meaningful influence where multiple party nomination is banned."[50] Like lower court judges in California, the Eighth Circuit also envisioned self-correcting internal mechanisms within democratic politics itself if fusion made for bad politics; major parties could simply refuse to consent to fusion.[51]

Now consider how democracy appeared to the decisive Supreme Court—this time, the *Bush v Gore* majority plus Justice Breyer. The central image in this opinion is not that of invigorated democracy through "political competition," but that of a system whose crucial "political stability" is easily threatened.[52] The word "stable" (and variations of it) appears a remarkable ten times in the brief majority opinion.[53] The central fact about fusion candidacies is the risk to political stability they are pictured to pose; thus, states must surely be able to "temper the destabilizing effects of party splintering and excessive factionalism."[54] Far from seeing Federalist 10 as supporting fusion candidacies, the Supreme Court sees such candidacies as the very embodiment of the factionalism Madison sought to avoid. Where the court of appeals saw the historically significant role of minor parties in American democracy, the Supreme Court worried about "campaign-related disorder."[55] Rather than looking at historical experience to assess

---

49. *Twin Cities Area New Party v McKenna*, 73 F3d 196, 199 (8th Cir 1996).

50. Id.

51. Id.

52. See, for example, *Timmons*, 520 US at 366 ("States also have a strong interest in the stability of their political systems.").

53. Id at 351, 353, 355, 364, 366, 367, 368, 370.

54. Id at 367.

55. Id at 358.

whether fusion candidacies had actually generated these concerns, or at contemporary empirical facts from states that permit fusion, like New York, the Court majority did not require "empirical verification of the weightiness of the State's asserted justifications" for banning fusion candidacies.[56] Indeed, because the risk of political instability was so high, the Court expressly concluded, for the first time in its history, that the states' interest in political stability justified electoral regulations that "favor the traditional two-party system."[57]

Once again, Justice Stevens led the dissent, joined by Justice Ginsburg. In contrast, his unifying metaphor is "robust competition," not political stability. Indeed, he calls this concern the "central theme" of the Court's democracy jurisprudence: "the entire electorate, which necessarily includes the members of the major parties, will benefit from robust competition in ideas and governmental policies," and this principle, Justice Stevens asserts, is "the core of our electoral process."[58] To the extent that the dispute between the Court and Justice Stevens was over the "empirical facts" about the effects of fusion, Justice Stevens viewed historical experience as showing that the majority's fears for stability were "fantastical."[59] Fusion, in fact, is "the best marriage"[60] of the virtues of minor parties with the level of political stability democracy requires; fusion offers a means by which major parties will be responsive to the view of minor party adherents, without actually threatening to divide a legislature. Interestingly, Justice Souter—who, with Justice Breyer, moves across the voting line in the quadrology of cases I consider in this essay—also dissented, but in a far more equivocal way. Writing in the double negative, he thought "it may not be unreasonable to infer that the two-party system is in some jeopardy" today.[61] If it were, he

56. Id at 364.

57. Id at 367. For the demonstration that the Court has never previously invoked such a justification, see Richard L. Hasen, *Entrenching the Duopoly: Why the Supreme Court Should Not Allow the States to Protect the Democrats and Republicans from Political Competition*, 1997 S Ct Rev 331.

58. *Timmons*, 520 US at 382 (Stevens dissenting).

59. Id at 375 n 3.

60. Id at 380.

61. Id at 384 (Souter dissenting). Ironically, Justice Souter cites a 1992 *New York Times* essay by Professor Theodore J. Lowi, which asserts that 1992 will historically be viewed "as the beginning of the end of America's two-party system," although Lowi celebrates this purported fact precisely because he believes demise of the two-party system will enhance,

would not be prepared to reject the majority's constitutional enshrinement of that system as a necessary means toward political stability. But for Justice Souter, the state had simply not yet argued this point adequately enough to permit judgment.[62]

Is the debate over fusion an empirical debate, in any meaningful sense? If we look back to historical moments at which fusion flourished, how do we interpret that past? Was it a time of political instability, excessive factionalism, campaign disorder, and party splintering? Or was it a time of vibrant democracy, robust competition, more responsive government (to those eligible to vote), and more engaged democracy? If the choice about fusion cannot be determined by empirical inquiry, can it be determined by the internal logic of doctrinal analysis? Does the First Amendment protect the right of voters and parties to the seemingly expanded choice fusion facilitates? But surely political stability is a value against which constitutional doctrines must be assessed? If neither facts nor doctrine compel a particular constitutional judgment, and if partisan political stakes point in no particular direction, yet federal judges divide so evenly over questions like this, what explains those differences? Perhaps, the suggestion is here, it is different cultural assumptions about how important order and stability, as opposed to competition and fluidity, are to democracy.

C.

How specific must the legal norms be that regulate aspects of democracy? Procedural judgments of this sort depend upon evaluations of the particular aspect of democracy at stake; how the values justifying that aspect will be affected; and whether potentially countervailing values will be compromised (and by how much), should greater or lesser degrees of specificity be required. In addition, the specificity of a legal norm can be generated through two alternative sources. The most obvious is the relevant legal text itself; in theory, a norm can always be made more specific if the enact-

---

not threaten, American democracy. See Theodore J. Lowi, *Toward a Responsible Three-Party System*, in Daniel M. Shea and John C. Green, eds, *The State of the Parties: The Changing Role of Contemporary American Parties* 45 (Rowman & Littlefield 1994) ("One of the best kept secrets in American politics is that the two-party system has long been brain-dead—kept alive by support systems like state electoral laws that protect the established parties from rivals and by public subsidies and so-called campaign reform.").

62. *Timmons,* 520 US at 384 (Souter dissenting).

ing body is willing or required to provide greater determinate content ex ante as to how that norm is to be applied in a range of contexts, at least to the extent those contexts are foreseeable. A second source through which legal norms can potentially gain sufficient precision and specificity is through institutional structures and processes that give post-enactment content to a more general norm in the process of applying it. "Intent of the voter" is a statutory norm, for example, that could be assessed against questions of this sort, questions which, with respect to the vote, are now grounded on the Equal Protection Clause in the wake of *Bush v Gore*.[63]

In another recent, signal case for the law of democracy, the Supreme Court confronted the process by which public television stations are constitutionally permitted to make judgments about which ballot-qualified candidates to include in publicly sponsored candidate debates. In Arkansas, the state-owned public television broadcaster sponsored congressional debates; in one of the state's four congressional districts, an independent candidate had qualified for the ballot. But the station refused to permit him to join the Democratic and Republican candidates in the debate. Lacking a previously established policy, the station excluded him based, it argued, on its conclusion that he was not "a serious candidate." A jury found that he had not been excluded because of his political views. But the central question was not whether this particular judgment was substantively appropriate; the question was whether government actors had to make such judgments in advance, through more clearly specified norms, that would protect against potentially inconsistent or biased judgments if the norms were left ex ante at a high level of generality and specified only at the moment that specific decisions were being made. "Not a serious candidate," in other words, is a legal norm that can be assessed against constitutionally mandated procedural standards, such as whether the criteria for access to public debates must be specified in advance rather than developed ad hoc on a case-by-case basis.

By now you can no doubt nearly complete the story yourself: in *Arkansas Educational Television Commission v Forbes*,[64] a divided Supreme Court, the *Bush v Gore* majority plus Justice Breyer, reversed a unanimous court of appeals. Justice Stevens penned the dissent, joined again by Justice Ginsburg,

63. Along with the question whether equal protection requires statewide uniformity in the substantive issue of what counts as a legal vote.

64. 523 US 666 (1998).

and, less equivocally this time, by Justice Souter.[65] As in the previous two cases, no distinctly mainstream partisan stakes seem apparent in the issue; neither the Republicans nor the Democrats appear likely to benefit systematically from broad or narrow rules of candidate inclusion and exclusion.

What images of democracy form the backdrop for judges in such procedural disputes about how specific legal norms must be? Do multiple-candidate debates raise the prospect of robust, competitive exchange or the threat of disorder, tumult, and confusion? Here is how the Court majority pictured the choice: public broadcasters would be faced with "the prospect of cacophony, on the one hand" if Forbes's First Amendment claim were accepted; or, on the other hand, when confronted with such a senseless and chaotic prospect, public broadcasters might well withdraw from the role of sponsoring debates at all.[66] The striking image is that of "cacophony," about which we can first ask some preliminary questions. Is cacophony itself a factual or normative matter? We can all agree that, at some point, too many speakers can frustrate the point of a debate. But is a six-candidate debate "cacophonous?" In the 1992 Democratic presidential primary, six candidates debated in early debates; so too in the 1988 Republican primary.[67] Yet at stake in *Forbes* was whether a third candidate, qualified to be on the ballot, would be permitted into the public debate.

But more interesting than when exactly a debate becomes mere noise is the way the *image* of cacophony seems to have obscured from the Court other legal possibilities, as well as other competing cultural images. Those other procedural possibilities, rather than any profound difference of principle, are what the dissenters emphasized. Thus, the dissents did not require public debate sponsors to open debates to all candidates, nor even to all ballot-qualified candidates. Instead, the dissent would have required greater procedural regularity in advance, through specific, pre-established criteria, of the bases for candidate inclusion—rather than what the dissent called the "ad hoc" and "standardless character of the decision to exclude" that was actually made.[68] Indeed, several debate-sponsoring entities, such as the Commission on Presidential Debates, filed briefs arguing that they had

65. Id at 683.

66. Id at 681.

67. Jamin B. Raskin, *The Debate Gerrymander,* 77 Tex L Rev 1943, 1973 (1999). Of course, early primaries might be viewed differently than general election debates, but the Court's opinion relies not at all on these kinds of distinctions.

68. *Arkansas Educational Television,* 523 US at 684.

developed precisely such pre-established, transparent, objective allocative criteria and thereby managed to avoid cacophony, or withdrawal from debate sponsorship, while ensuring consistent and uniform treatment.[69] Particularly in light of this experience, it seems that a fear of this image of disordered, chaotic debates, rather than meaningful factual evidence, led the Court to worry that requiring procedural protections for access would cause public stations to flee the debate-sponsoring role.

How much pre-established specificity judges demand, of course, depends in part on how valued the particular activity is. Here, too, what divided federal judges so evenly might well have been whether multicandidate debate itself was viewed as a benefit or as a cost to "democracy." Thus, Justice Stevens emphasized that a third-party candidate who was not likely to win might nonetheless change electoral outcomes by taking votes from a dominant-party candidate; even if Forbes himself were properly characterized as "not a serious candidate," excluding him from the debate "may have determined the outcome of the election."[70] For Justice Stevens, the power to affect electoral outcomes self-evidently makes a candidate's participation a benefit to democracy. But while the Court's opinion says nothing about that issue, one wonders whether a group of justices who, in *Timmons*, expressed fear of the "destabilizing effects of party splintering and excessive factionalism,"[71] would consider an independent candidate's outcome-determinative effects on elections a *cost* to democracy rather than a self-evident benefit.

Because many aspects of elections implicate constitutional values—the vote, access to the ballot, participation in public debates, access to other public fora—legal issues inevitably will arise concerning the levels of specificity required of regulation. Whether that specificity must be provided in advance through a formal legal text, whether it can be generated through

69. See Brief of Amicus Curiae Commission on Presidential Debates in Support of Petitioner, *Arkansas Educational Television Commission v Forbes*, No 96-779 (filed May 30, 1997) (available on Lexis at 1996 US Briefs 779). See also 11 CFR § 110.13(c) (2000); New York City Admin Code § 3-709.5 (1999); Commission on Presidential Debates, Nonpartisan Candidate Selection Criteria for 2000 General Election Debate Participation, available online at <http://www.debates.org/pages/candsel.html> (visited Apr 10, 2001). Even once pre-established, objective criteria are specified, those criteria might of course be challenged substantively.

70. *Arkansas Educational Television*, 523 US at 685.

71. *Timmons*, 520 US at 367.

institutional processes, or whether it is required at all are questions that judges will confront repeatedly. That empirical facts could in themselves resolve these issues seems unlikely; does Jesse Ventura's victory in Minnesota, made possible partly by his third-party participation in debates, enhance or threaten appropriate democratic politics?[72] That narrow partisan concerns could explain or motivate results in cases like *Forbes* seems equally implausible. That constitutional doctrine is itself specific enough to determine the level of specificity required of state actors in *Forbes* is also challenged by the divisions, again, among a large group of federal judges. That cultural assumptions and images of ideal democracy play a significant role in explaining differences in cases like *Forbes*—assumptions and images not falsifiable as facts, or provable through internal legal analysis—is the alternative I mean to raise here for understanding the emerging constitutional law of democracy.

III. *BUSH V GORE* REVISITED

The cases selected in this essay are defining moments in the recent law of democracy. In more conventional legal-analytic terms, much could be said to argue for the coherence of the majority opinions, or of the dissents, or perhaps of certain decisions but not others. After all, they arise in different contexts; they place the Court in different postures. In some, the Court upholds state laws, in others, it finds them unconstitutional. I have said nothing here about those possible distinctions. Yet it is striking that across these defining cases, the five-justice majority in *Bush v Gore* is also consistently together, though also noteworthy that it is joined consistently by Justice Breyer; that the two strongest dissenters in *Bush v Gore*, Justices Stevens and Ginsburg, are always in dissent; and that Justice Souter, between these two poles in *Bush v Gore*, also moves back and forth, majority to dissent, in this overall map of cases. Four cases do not a social-scientific sample make, but they nonetheless suggest an intriguing cultural pattern.

Whether democracy requires order, stability, and channeled, constrained forms of engagement, or whether it requires and even celebrates relatively wide-open competition that may appear tumultuous, partisan, or worse, has long been a struggle in democratic thought and practice (in-

72. For discussion of the crucial role that less restrictive electoral laws and debate practices played in enabling Ventura's success, see Richard H. Pildes, *The Theory of Political Competition*, 85 U Va L Rev 1605, 1617–18 (1999).

deed, historically it was one of the defining set of oppositions in arguments about the desirability of democracy itself). Of course, the answer is that democracy requires a mix of both order (law, structure, and constraint) and openness (politics, fluidity, and receptivity to novel forms). But people, including judges and political actors, regularly seem to group themselves into characteristic and recurring patterns of response to new challenges that arise. These patterned responses suggest that it is something beyond law, or facts, or narrow partisan politics in particular cases, that determine outcomes; it is, perhaps, cultural assumptions and historical interpretations, conscious or not, that inform or even determine these judgments. Whatever the analytical truth about the necessity of both order and openness to democracy, the cultural question is, from which direction do particular actors, such as judges, tend to perceive the greatest threat. Is the democratic order fragile and potentially destabilized easily? Or is the democratic order threatened by undue rigidity, in need of more robust competition and challenge? Does democratic politics contain within itself sufficient resources to be self-correcting? Or must legal institutions carefully oversee political processes to ensure their continued vitality?

Bush v Gore can be assessed legally, politically, or as I prefer to here, culturally. I cannot purport to separate the contributing role each of these dimensions might have played in the decision, particularly when *Bush v Gore* is analyzed as an isolated single event. But when we examine the decision in the full tapestry of the Supreme Court's emerging and increasingly active role in the constitutionalization of democratic politics—a role initiated forty years ago in *Baker v Carr*—we can see images, metaphors, and assumptions about democracy that consistently recur. These images of the relationship of law and order—constitutional law and judicially structured order—to democracy are aspects of a broader jurisprudential culture. They emerge most revealingly in cases in which the partisan political consequences are nonexistent, or certainly not obvious.[73] Nor do the divisions in these cases map onto conventional, political characterizations of the justices, in the narrow sense of partisan political orientation; Justice Breyer, for example, consistently joins the five-member *Bush v Gore* majority. Yet nonetheless, they do divide in these nonpartisan cases in much the same way they did in *Bush v Gore*.

73. Again, as throughout, I mean the partisan consequences to the Republican and Democratic Parties, as third parties and independent candidates *are* consistently disadvantaged by these decisions.

The suggestion here is that, whatever role law and conventional politics might be debated to have played in *Bush v Gore,* a cultural dimension must be considered as well. Because this cultural orientation toward democracy transcends law and narrow partisan politics, and because it itself is not determined by "facts," but leads facts to be understood in particular ways, this cultural dimension plays a powerful role in judicial responses to cases involving democratic politics. When the Court envisioned a political resolution of Bush v Gore, the election, how much was it moved by a cultural view, not a narrowly partisan preference, that "democracy" required judicially ensured order, stability, and certainty, rather than judicial acceptance of the "crisis" that partisan political resolution might be feared by some to have entailed?[74] If the Court were so moved—by the country's perceived need for what Frank Michelman calls "judicial salvation"—*Bush v Gore* would be of a piece with the current Court's general vision of democratic politics and the role of constitutional law.[75] That general vision transcends the election, and it transcends narrow partisan interpretations, for it is a vision that Justice Breyer seems generally to embrace, if not in the specific context of *Bush v Gore.* I cannot offer any sophisticated account here for why Justice Breyer seems to share this disposition, or for why Justice Stevens resists it so strenuously. But perhaps for one who believes in the authoritative role of expertise in policymaking, as Justice Breyer does,[76] it is not such a far leap to believe that democracy also requires the expertise of judges, through constitutional law, to ensure order and stability.[77] And perhaps for Justice Stevens, it is familiarity with the hurlyburly of Chicago politics that reassures him that out of the chaos of democracy itself, sufficient order, stability, and resolution will be generated.[78]

The fear that democratic institutions would be unable to secure their own stability, and the perceived need for constitutionally imposed order, would be

74. John Yoo, for example, praises the Court's decision precisely because it "restored stability to the political system." John C. Yoo, *In Defense of the Court's Legitimacy,* in this volume, page 225.

75. For the view that *Bush v Gore* does reflect "a larger distrust of politics," see Elizabeth Garrett, *Leaving the Decision to Congress,* in this volume.

76. See, for example, Stephen Breyer, *Breaking the Vicious Circle: Toward Effective Risk Regulation* (Harvard 1993).

77. Frank I. Michelman, *Suspicion, or the New Prince,* in this volume, pages 137–39.

78. For a fascinating analysis of Justice Stevens's distinct approach to cases of democratic politics, see Pamela S. Karlan, *Cousins' Kin: Justice Stevens and Voting Rights,* 27 Rutgers L J 521 (1996).

consistent with each of the Court's interventions into the election. The Court acted with surprising alacrity to assert control over the dispute, an alacrity suggested by its choice to hear *Bush v Palm Beach County Canvassing Board*,[79] followed by its conclusion that no substantive issue of law was yet ready to be decided at that point (a decision that was minimalist only in the most technical, formal sense, for all actors subsequently behaved as if the Court had actually decided that Article II of the Constitution or the Electoral Count Act would be violated were state courts to rely on the state constitution or make "new law").[80] The stay order, too, was an assertion of the power to establish order and control even before the moment of final decision. Whatever the various possible reasons for these actions, individually and as a whole, they are consistent with the manifestation of considerable anxiety about the capacity of other institutions, including political ones such as Congress, to avoid unleashing "the furies of civil commotion, chaos, and grave dangers"—precisely the terms in which the defense of the Court is now being cast.[81] To the extent that what might be called this "cultural conservatism" toward democracy underlies *Bush v Gore*, and the current Court's jurisprudence of politics more generally, it is a cultural disposition more pervasive than one confined to the current Court. In closing, I want to suggest a way of understanding these powerful, competing visions of democracy in a broader historical context.

Two great foundational crises confronted American democracy in the twentieth century. The first was the challenge to the economic order posed by the worldwide Depression of the 1920s and 1930s. If capitalism were to endure, how should the economic system be structured so as to avoid the recurrence of a similar catastrophe? The second was the challenge to the democratic order posed by the rise of fascism and totalitarianism in formerly democratic Europe. If democracy were to endure, how should the political order be structured so as to avoid similar moral nightmares here? In both contexts, the initial diagnosis and remedy were strikingly similar. The Great Depression had been caused, in the classic phrase, by "ruinous competition," by a disordered, tumultuous economic system that lacked structure, order, and stability.[82] Thus, the early New Deal sought to constrain competition through

79. 121 S Ct 510 (2000).

80. For endorsement of this decision as an act of judicial minimalism, see Cass R. Sunstein, *Order Without Law*, in this volume.

81. Leedes, 35 U Rich L Rev (cited in note 14).

82. For a summary of early New Deal beliefs that the economic order required state "rationalization," see Alan Brinkley, *The End of Reform* 34–39 (Knopf 1995).

cartel-like legislation, such as the National Industrial Recovery Act, that would bring the necessary regularity, order, and stability to the economic system. Post–World War II democratic thought, in a way that might be seen as analogous, similarly located the causes of totalitarianism in an overly competitive, overly chaotic, and fragmented political system.[83] To ensure "political stability" and avoid "ruinous competition," American democracy required regular organizations, a highly ordered two-party system, a style of politics that was channeled and contained, lest too much politics undermine democracy itself. Perhaps it also required, or came to be seen as requiring, an active judicial role to ensure that too much democratically adopted restructuring did not undermine the stability of democracy itself.

In the economic realm, we came to abandon the post-Depression view that aggressive state "rationalization" was necessary to ensure stability and order; competition, seeming disorder, and tumult came to be seen as signs of vigor and robustness, not paths to ruination. Yet in the political realm, we cling much more tenaciously to the fear that too much politics, or too competitive a political system, will bring instability, fragmentation, and disorder. By we, I mean the institutional structures of democracy with which we live, the legal framework of national democratic practices, and the dispositions of judges and many others toward novel or revived forms of democratic practice—blanket primaries, fusion candidacies, multiparty and multicandidate competition, and, perhaps, political resolution of disputed presidential elections. Given the strength and endurance of American democracy, including its capacity for self-revision and correction, is that fear the appropriate stance to take?

83. This is the theme in the book still considered "the political masterpiece of the postwar era," Richard H. Pells, *The Liberal Mind in a Conservative Age: American Intellectuals in the 1940s and 1950s* 83–84 (Harper & Row 1985), which is Hannah Arendt's *The Origins of Totalitarianism* (Harcourt 1951). For variations on this fixation with the need for order and constrained political competition, see Daniel Bell, *The End of Ideology: On the Exhaustion of Political Ideas in the Fifties* 94–95 (Free Press 1960); Seymour Martin Lipset, *Political Man: The Social Bases of Politics* 74–75 (Doubleday 1960) ("Inherent in all democratic systems is the constant threat that the group conflicts which are democracy's lifeblood may solidify to the point where they threaten to disintegrate the society. Hence conditions which serve to moderate the intensity of partisan battle are among the key requisites of democratic government."). The sociologist David Riesman diagnosed this 1950s intellectual sensibility: "[intellectual elites of this era] are frightened by the ideal of a pluralistic, somewhat disorderly, and highly competitive society. . . ." David Riesman, *Individualism Reconsidered and Other Essays* 423–24 (Free Press 1954).

Bush v Gore

Prolegomenon to an Assessment

RICHARD A. POSNER

The Supreme Court's decision terminating the Florida recount and, in consequence, effectively confirming George W. Bush as President has been fiercely criticized by liberal critics. One theme of the critics, though directed less at the decision itself than at its effect, is that, had the recount continued, Al Gore would have been shown to be the "real winner" of the Florida presidential vote. That is incorrect. The recount ordered by the Florida Supreme Court might have given Gore a popular-vote majority. But the recount should never have been ordered. There was no basis for it in Florida law and no reason to believe that Gore had "really" won the election. The basis of that belief was a misunderstanding of statistics and of Florida law.

A separate question, one I examine elsewhere,[1] is whether the U.S. Supreme Court should have intervened. Separate, but not unrelated; that the Florida court was acting arbitrarily was the premise of the equal protection argument that the Supreme Court eventually accepted, and that it was acting in violation of Florida law was the premise of the Article II argument that three Justices found persuasive and that I consider the stronger of the two arguments.[2]

Bush v Gore: *Prolegomenon to an Assessment* © 2001 by Richard A. Posner. I thank Bryan Dayton for his very helpful research assistance, and Christopher DeMuth, John Donohue, Frank Easterbrook, Eldon Eisenach, Einer Elhauge, Elizabeth Garrett, Dennis Hutchinson, Lawrence Lessig, Michael McConnell, Edward Morrison, Eric Posner, Stephen Stigler, David Strauss, and Cass Sunstein for their very helpful comments on earlier versions of this essay.

1. See Richard A. Posner, *Florida 2000: A Legal and Statistical Analysis of the Election Deadlock and the Ensuing Litigation,* 2000 S Ct Rev 1, where I also discuss at greater length the issues discussed in this essay.

2. See id at 2.

I. WOULD A PROPERLY CONDUCTED RECOUNT HAVE PRODUCED VICTORY FOR GORE?

After the machine recount of the Florida votes and the addition to the tally of the late-arriving absentee ballots, Bush was ahead by only 930 votes out of almost six million cast in Florida. It was natural to suppose that the voting machines might have made enough mistakes (even after the machine recount) to have given Bush his victory, so that a hand recount might show that Gore had really won. A hand recount might indeed have shown this, but it would not follow that Gore had really won. The hand recount might be as unreliable as the machine count that it was intended to correct. While machines can be poorly designed, defectively manufactured, and inadequately maintained, and as a result make many errors, human counters can be fatigued, biased, or simply unable to infer, with any approach to certainty, what the voter's intent was from a ballot that the machine refused to count; so they can make many errors too. The Democrats asked for hand recounts in only four counties (Broward, Palm Beach, Miami-Dade, and Volusia), in all of which Gore had prevailed in the machine count and the canvassing boards were dominated by Democrats. A recount in these circumstances was highly likely to produce more votes for Gore than for Bush; indeed, all Gore had to do was to pick up the same percentage of recovered votes as he had won in the machine count to increase his lead in these counties.[3] By the same token, a recount in counties won by Bush would have been likely to increase Bush's lead in those counties, though not necessarily by enough to offset Gore's gain in the four counties.

Even without regard to the possible effects of recounts in other counties, Gore would have been likely to overcome Bush's statewide lead only if the votes in the four counties that Gore sought recounts in had been recounted in accordance with the criteria used in Broward County. Gore's net gain of 582 votes in the Broward County recount represented 0.15 percent of his total votes there; that is, the recount gave him a net addition of 15 votes for every 10,000 votes that he had obtained from the original tabulation. If his votes in Palm Beach and Miami-Dade counties are multiplied by the same

---

3. To illustrate, suppose that in some precinct Gore had 7,000 votes counted by the machine and Bush 3,000, and 300 had not been counted, so that Gore led Bush by 4,000 votes. If now the 300 were counted and they split in the same proportion as the votes that had been counted previously, Gore would get 210 more votes and Bush 90 more, increasing Gore's lead by 120 votes.

percentage and the product added to his net gain in Broward, his aggregate net gain is 1,480 votes and overcomes Bush's 930-vote lead.[4] But the 1,480 figure is suspect, and not only because Gore's margin in the other two counties was smaller than his margin in Broward, and so he could not have expected to pick up as large a share of the recovered votes; and also not only because of the domination of the canvassing boards by Democrats, who would be likely to give the edge to Gore in close cases. Democratic domination of the boards also made them likely to use criteria designed to maximize the number of recovered votes, since, as I have explained, the more votes recovered in counties Gore had carried, the more Bush's lead would erode. But when the criteria designed to maximize the number of recovered votes, which is to say the criteria used by Broward County's canvassing boards, are projected to the other counties to give Gore an estimated net gain of 1,480 votes, these projections are bound to be unreliable.

This point is essential, and must be explained. The counties in question used the punchcard voting method. A card is placed on a tray, and the voter votes by punching a hole next to the candidate's name. The piece of the card thus dislodged, the "chad," falls to the bottom of the tray. The card is then removed and placed in a machine that counts votes by beaming light through the holes. If the chad is not punched through, the light will be blocked and the vote not registered. A chad that though punched remains dangling from the ballot by one or two corners, with the result that the vote was not counted by the tabulating machine, may be pretty good evidence of an intent to vote for the candidate whose chad was punched, provided the voter did not also punch the chad of another candidate for the same office (a significant qualification, however, as we will see). But inferring a voter's intentions from a merely dimpled chad, or a chad only one of whose corners has been separated from the ballot, is chancy. Nevertheless, Broward County's canvassing board apparently counted all such chads in undervotes (ballots that the machines had recorded as containing no vote for a presidential candidate) as valid votes. It did this even though a faint dimple might be created by the handling of the ballot or by its being repeatedly passed through the vote-counting machines; even though the voter may have started to vote for the candidate but then changed his mind, perhaps

4. Volusia County completed its hand recount before the November 14 statutory deadline and therefore the 98-vote net gain that it produced for Gore was included in calculating Bush's 930-vote official margin. As we will see, the Volusia recount probably produced an excessive net gain for Gore.

realizing he had made a mistake; even though there were many undecided voters in the 2000 presidential election, some of whom may have gone into the voting booth still undecided and, in the end, "decided" they could not make up their minds which presidential candidate to vote for; and even though some voters (probably more than the undecideds) undoubtedly misunderstood the ballot instructions. Those instructions were clear, but only if one could read. Voters voting on the basis of their recollection of oral instructions received from party activists would be bound often to make a mistake and spoil their ballot. In addition, the punchcard method of voting used in these counties requires a minimum of manual dexterity, and some voters lack even that.

Because the undercounted votes were only a small fraction of the total number of votes cast, it would not be surprising if a large fraction of them had been cast by undecided, confused, clumsy, inexperienced, or illiterate voters. This inference is especially compelling in the case of ballots in which the voter punched through the chads of all but the presidential candidates, indicating that the voting machine was not defective. This was the ground on which the Palm Beach County Canvassing Board decided eventually to exclude such ballots while counting those that had several, though apparently as few as three, dimpled chads. It was also why the Miami-Dade County Board could not, had it decided to count dimpled ballots, reasonably have confined the recount to the 10,750 undervotes in that county. Some of the ballots counted for the presidential candidate whose chad had been punched through may have contained a hanging chad in the other presidential candidate's hole. A hand recount would suggest that the voter had voted for two presidential candidates, voiding the ballot. Yet a ballot in which the voter punched through both presidential chads but left one dangling is as good evidence that the voter tried to vote for both candidates as a dangling chad in an undervote is evidence that the voter tried to vote for that candidate. It would not take a large percentage of such ballots, out of the more than 600,000 ballots cast in Miami-Dade County, to offset irregular ballots among the 10,750 undervoted ballots.

The hand-recount criterion most favorable to the Democrats yet at least minimally objective was Palm Beach's three-dimples rule. A more conservative method would have counted dimples only in ballots in which no chads had been punched through, a pattern particularly suggestive of the voter's having tried unsuccessfully to punch through and perhaps been thwarted by a defect in the voting machine (for example, chad buildup). Palm

Beach's method produced either 176 or 215 extra votes for Gore; the Florida Supreme Court declined to decide which number was correct, leaving the matter to further proceedings that were interrupted before the correct number could be determined. Assume, favorably to Gore, that the higher one was correct. It was still only 0.08 percent of the votes (8 in 10,000) that the machine had counted for Gore in Palm Beach County. Had the Broward and Miami-Dade Canvassing Boards used the Palm Beach method and produced the same percentage of additional votes for Gore, he would not have overtaken Bush's lead. His total gain in all three counties would have been only 788 votes (215 in Palm Beach as mentioned, 263 in Miami-Dade, and 310 in Broward).[5] The 168 additional votes that Gore netted in Miami-Dade from the first 20 percent or so of the recounted precincts before the recount was interrupted are a meaningless figure, because these precincts are far more heavily Democratic than the county as a whole.

Of the disputed votes awarded to either Gore or Bush that yielded Gore's net gain of (at most) 215 votes in Palm Beach County, 61 percent went to Gore and 39 percent to Bush, compared to a 62 percent/38 percent split of the total machine-counted Palm Beach vote. This suggests that Gore would probably not have received more than 50 percent of the undervotes in a statewide hand count, since that was his percentage of the statewide machine count. It also underscores the meaninglessness of the 168-vote gain for him from the partial recount in heavily Democratic precincts in Miami-Dade County. He received 70 percent of the additional votes recorded by the recount, though his margin in the county as a whole was only 53 percent.

An alternative method of estimating how the undervotes might have split between the two candidates is to compare Gore's vote gain in Palm Beach County with the number of disputed ballots in that county, 14,500. His net vote gain of 215 from that batch of ballots was only 1.5 percent of the votes that he got from that batch in the machine count. The same percentage of the 10,750 undervotes in Miami-Dade County would have meant a net gain of only 161 votes, compared to 263 by my earlier method. And even the 161-vote estimate is inflated. Gore received a lower percentage of the total Gore-Bush vote in Miami-Dade County—53 percent, compared with 62 percent in Palm Beach County. If a 24 percent margin (62–38) would have yielded Gore 161 extra votes over Bush, a 6 percent margin (53–47)

5. In addition, he would have had a net gain of only 78, not 98, votes in Volusia County, reducing his overall net gain from 788 to 768.

would have yielded him only 40. Finally, it might make sense to average the machine-count and hand-recount results, since if their errors are independent averaging the two results will cause many of the errors to cancel out. But averaging Bush's 930-vote machine lead with a smaller but still positive lead obviously would not produce a victory for Gore.

Some voters in Palm Beach County who cast ballots that the machine counted were misled by the "butterfly" ballot (in which the candidates are listed on both sides of the ballot rather than all on one side) used in that county and voted for Buchanan when they meant to vote for Gore.[6] This ballot, the brainchild of the Democratic supervisor of elections for the county, was intended both to enable the candidates' names to be printed in large type, in consideration of the number of elderly voters in the county, and to place before the voter all the candidates for each office without need to turn the page. Another ballot design, while less confusing, would have disenfranchised an unknown number of voters who had poor eyesight or cast their vote before realizing that there were additional candidates on the next page of the ballot. Even if, as widely and I think correctly believed, the butterfly design was on balance a mistake, it was an irremediable one for purposes of the 2000 election—not only because there was no reliable method of determining within any reasonable deadline for selecting Florida's electors the true intent of these voters, but also because altering an election outcome on the basis of the confusing design of the ballot would open a Pandora's box of election challenges.

Gore's best chance for overcoming Bush's lead, it turns out, as we will see in the next Part, would have been to recount overvotes as well as undervotes; for there is evidence of recoverable overvotes, in particular ballots in which the voter had both punched a candidate's chad and written in the name of the same candidate in the place for write-in votes. But Gore did not want overvotes recounted. In all likelihood, therefore, a fairly designed and

6. Bush was listed first on the left-hand side of the ballot and Gore second. Buchanan was listed first on the right-hand side, between Bush and Gore rather than opposite to Bush. The candidates' chads were in the middle of the ballot, which meant that Buchanan's chad was between Bush's and Gore's. A voter who wanted to vote for Gore had to punch the third chad down; if he punched the second, which was almost level with the word "Democratic" above Gore's and Lieberman's names, he was voting for Buchanan. It would be an easy mistake to make, especially for an inexperienced voter or one with poor eyesight, though, as mentioned in the text below, the butterfly format enables larger type and in that respect helps people with poor eyesight.

administered hand recount would not have enabled Gore to overcome Bush's 930-vote lead.

Let us now see what the Florida Supreme Court did to unsettle that lead.

II. WHAT THE FLORIDA SUPREME COURT DID TO FLORIDA'S ELECTION STATUTE

A. THE STATUTE

Florida's election statute requires counties to certify their vote totals within seven days of the election, which in 2000 meant by November 14,[7] except that overseas ballots are as a consequence of federal law to be counted up to the tenth day after the election and added to the seventh-day totals.[8] Up to that seventh day a candidate may "protest" the result of the election in a county as "being erroneous" and "may . . . request . . . a manual recount" and the county canvassing board "may authorize" it.[9] This hand recount is of just a sample of precincts, but if it "indicates an error in the vote tabulation which could affect the outcome of the election,"[10] the board must take corrective action, which can include a hand recount of all the ballots cast in the county.[11] Should that recount not be completed by the seventh day, its results "may be ignored" by the Florida Secretary of State.[12] Once the Secretary of State has received the certified county totals and certified the election winner, the loser can "contest" the result by filing a lawsuit.[13] If he can prove that enough "legal votes" were rejected to have "change[d] or place[d] in doubt the result of the election," the court can "provide any relief appropriate under such circumstances."[14] A "damaged or defective" ballot is not to be declared invalid if it contains "a clear indication of the intent of the voter."[15]

---

7. Fla Stat Ann § 102.111(1) (West 2000).

8. See *Palm Beach County Canvassing Board v Harris,* 772 S2d 1273, 1288 (Fla Dec 11, 2000).

9. Fla Stat Ann §§ 102.112(1), 102.166(1), (4)(a), (c) (West 2000).

10. Id § 102.166(5).

11. Id § 102.166(5)(c).

12. Id § 102.112(1). The preceding Section (§ 102.111(1)) says "shall be ignored," creating the only real inconsistency in the statute. I have no quarrel with the Florida Supreme Court's preferring "may," which was also the interpretation of the Secretary of State.

13. Id § 102.168(1).

14. Id §§ 102.168(3)(c), (e)(8).

15. Id § 101.5614(5).

None of the hand recounts sought by Gore, except the one in Volusia County,[16] was complete by November 14, and the Secretary of State said she would refuse to consider them. She interpreted the statute to mean that unless there was evidence of fraud or statutory violations, or some disaster (a hurricane, for example) that had interrupted the recount, the seven-day deadline was firm.[17] The Director of the Division of Elections in the Secretary of State's office interpreted, presumably with her concurrence, the statutory term "error in the vote tabulation" to mean a failure of the tabulating machine to count properly marked ballots, rather than the machine's failing to record a vote because the voter had failed to follow the instructions for casting a valid, machine-readable vote or to complain to a precinct worker if the voter could not follow the instructions because the voting machine was defective.[18] The instructions were clear. The many dimpled and dangling chads were the result of voters' either failing to follow the instructions or, if the voting machine itself was defective, so that the instructions could not be followed, failing to seek the assistance of an election official—a failure that was also a form of voter error. If voter error was not a valid basis for a hand recount, there was no possible justification for extending the statutory deadline for submission of a county's votes in order to permit an effort to recover votes from ballots rejected because of voter error. The only reason the county canvassing boards needed extra time was to complete the laborious hand recounts necessary to recover votes from ballots that the voters spoiled, a process of interpretation rather than of mere inspection.

When on November 21 the Florida Supreme Court reversed the Secretary of State and extended the November 14 deadline for protest recounts to November 26,[19] the consequence was to postpone till then the certification of the election results and hence the commencement of the contest proceeding, thus squeezing the time for completing such a proceeding so

16. See note 4.

17. Her written statement is quoted in *Palm Beach County Canvassing Board v Harris,* 772 S2d 1220, 1226–27 n 5 (Fla Nov 21, 2000), vacd and remd as *Bush v Palm Beach County Canvassing Board,* 121 S Ct 471 (2000) (per curiam).

18. Roberts's interpretation can be found in the Joint Appendix to the Respondent's Supplemental Brief, *Bush v Palm Beach County Canvassing Board,* No 00-836, *52–58 (filed Nov 30, 2000) (available on Westlaw at 2000 WL 1793147) (including letters from Roberts regarding the meaning of error in tabulation).

19. *Palm Beach County Canvassing Board v Harris,* 772 S2d at 1240.

tightly as to make completion by any realistic deadline chancy. This implication of the court's ruling suggests that the Secretary of State's statutory interpretation was the correct one after all. As does the statutory text: "error
in vote *tabulation*" does not sound like an error by the voter; it sounds like
an error by the mechanical or human tabulator. The machinery for counting punchcard ballots, which are the form of ballot used in 40 percent of
Florida's counties, containing 63 percent of the state's population, was not
designed to tabulate dimpled or otherwise unpunched-through ballots; so
how could its failure to count such ballots be thought an error in tabulation? And because that "failure" was built into the design of the machine,
to deem it the result of an error in vote tabulation would make hand recounts mandatory in all close elections in the many counties that use
punchcard voting machines. The legislature was unlikely to have intended
this when it passed the statute, especially given the vagaries of hand recounting of spoiled ballots.[20]

The statute does not specify the circumstances if any in which the Secretary of State is required or even permitted to include in her certification of
the election results the results of a recount not completed by the statutory
deadline. But the statute authorizes the Secretary of State to interpret the
statute,[21] implying that her interpretation if reasonable is conclusive. The
interpretation by the director of her division of elections, the interpretation that voter error is not a ground for extending the deadline, *was* reasonable and should therefore have been conclusive on the Florida
Supreme Court. Indeed, it was the natural and sensible interpretation of

20. In contrast, the absence of a postmark on some absentee ballots of military personnel, a defect the Secretary of State did not think invalidated those ballots, was akin to
a tabulating error. The voter does not affix the postmark. The overseas voters had followed instructions to the letter and had thus done all they could do to cast a legal vote;
the mistake was in the transmission machinery.

The Democrats, after being accused of being anti-military, decided not to make an
issue of the absence of postmarks on military ballots. Another irregularity in the pro-
cessing of absentee ballots, however, was challenged. Republican campaign workers had
been permitted to enter the election offices in two counties to affix voter identification
numbers to absentee ballots that were missing them. The Florida courts rebuffed the
challenge on the ground that the voters' intentions were clear. See *Jacobs v Seminole
County Canvassing Board*, 773 S2d 519, 2000 Fla LEXIS 2404, *5–9 (Dec 23) (per curiam).
The numbers were affixed before the votes were counted, and so there was no question
of an error in the tabulation of the votes.

21. Fla Stat Ann § 97.012(1) (West 2000).

"error in the vote tabulation," which, to repeat, is the only basis in the statute for a complete hand recount of a county's votes.[22]

Against this conclusion, Michael McConnell, without addressing the question of the Secretary of State's interpretive authority, argues that the election statute does not limit the reasons for conducting a manual recount.[23] But this is incorrect. A full countywide manual recount (as distinct from the initial sample recount) is permitted only "if the [sample] manual recount indicates an error in the vote tabulation which could affect the outcome of the election."[24] McConnell also cites a provision of the election law which states that if during the manual recount the counters are "unable to determine a voter's intent in casting a ballot, the ballot shall be presented to the county canvassing board for it to determine the voter's intent."[25] But as McConnell himself notes, the Florida Supreme Court never cited this provision; and I cannot see its bearing on the meaning of "error in the vote tabulation." If because of such an error all the ballots have to be inspected by hand, some of them are bound to be spoiled ballots; and if it is unclear whether or not a ballot is spoiled, the question is properly referred to the canvassing board. That is all the provision in question means.

The statute also provides that the Secretary of State may ignore recount results received after the seventh day following the election.[26] This implies that she has discretion to ignore results from recounts not barred by the statute (for example, a hand recount conducted because of an error in the vote tabulation that might have affected the outcome of the election) as well as being compelled to ignore those that are barred.[27] So even if she erred in thinking her hands tied by the statute, and therefore failed to exercise her discretion to ignore or not to ignore late recount results designed to correct

22. Id § 102.166(5).

23. Michael W. McConnell, *Two-and-a-Half Cheers for* Bush v Gore, in this volume, pages 106–7.

24. See Fla Stat Ann §§ 102.166(5), (5)(c).

25. Id § 102.166(7)(b); McConnell, page 106 in this volume (cited in note 23).

26. Fla Stat Ann § 102.112(1).

27. As Judge Lewis explained in upholding her refusal to include late recount results, "Florida law grants to the Secretary [of State], as the Chief Elections Officer, broad discretionary authority to accept or reject late filed returns." *McDermott v Harris*, 2000 WL 1714590, *1 (Fla Cir Ct Nov 17), revd as *Palm Beach County Canvassing Board v Harris*, 772 S2d 1220 (Fla Nov 21, 2000), vacd and remd as *Bush v Palm Beach County Canvassing Board*, 121 S Ct 471.

voter error, the court should have directed her to exercise her discretion; that is the remedy for a failure to exercise discretion.[28] It would have been well within her discretion to ignore the late recount results—as the expense, delays, near riots, litigation avalanche, and general turmoil that attended the Florida Supreme Court's refusal to uphold her decision demonstrate.

B. WHAT THE FLORIDA SUPREME COURT DID TO THE STATUTE

The Florida Supreme Court reversed Judge Lewis and extended the statutory deadline to November 26, at the same time holding that the recount should include spoiled ballots in which the voter's intent was discernible. The justices thought it okay to strong-arm the statute because they thought it internally inconsistent inasmuch as it allowed a recount to be sought right up to the seventh day after the election even though a recount requested on the last day could not be completed by the end of that day, the deadline for submission by the counties of their vote totals.[29] There is no inconsistency. If the recount is not requested promptly after the election and so cannot be completed by the seventh day, the losing candidate has mainly himself to blame for not having acted faster; and the only consequence is that he must fall back on his remedy of filing a contest proceeding. The Florida Supreme Court in its second opinion, that of December 8, reversing the dismissal of the contest proceeding, ruled in effect (though erroneously, as I shall argue) that the certification has no presumptive validity in such a proceeding.[30] This implies that the disap-

---

28. See, for example, *Chathas v Local 134 IBEW,* 233 F3d 508, 514 (7th Cir 2000) (remanding the case to enable lower court judge to make the required discretionary judgment); *Campanella v Commerce Exchange Bank,* 137 F3d 885, 892–93 (6th Cir 1998) (remanding because the "district court appears not to have recognized that it had supplemental jurisdiction, and thus failed to actually undertake an exercise of discretion"); *Channell v Citicorp National Services, Inc,* 89 F3d 379, 387 (7th Cir 1996). As the court said in *Channell,* "Because he held that [28 USC] § 1367(a) did not authorize the exercise of supplemental jurisdiction, [the district judge] did not exercise the discretion § 1367(c) confers. It belongs to him rather than to us, so we remand for its exercise." *Channell,* 89 F3d at 387.

29. *Palm Beach County Canvassing Board v Harris,* 772 S2d 1220, 1235 (Fla Nov 21, 2000), vacd and remd as *Bush v Palm Beach County Canvassing Board,* 121 S Ct 471 (2000) (per curiam).

30. *Gore v Harris,* 772 S2d 1243, 1260 (Fla Dec 8, 2000) (holding that votes hand

pointed candidate loses very little by being remitted to his contest remedy. The more important point is that seven days is plenty of time to correct an error in vote tabulation, even when a hand recount is necessary, since the voter's intention in a ballot that has been filled out in accordance with the instructions can be determined by a simple inspection of the ballot; debatable interpretation is not required. The Secretary of State was entitled in the exercise of her discretion in the interpretation and application of the statute to conclude that wanting to recover votes from ballots spoiled by the voter was not a proper reason for an extension of the statutory deadline—especially in a presidential election, where delay in certifying the results of the election could well cause chaos.[31] It is precisely in adapting the statute to the exigencies of a presidential election that the Secretary of State might have been expected to be given a freer rein in statutory interpretation and application. Her decision not to delay the certification of the winner of the presidential election deserved considerable deference; it received none.

The Florida Supreme Court made no effort to conceal the fact that in interpreting the statute differently from the Secretary of State it was appealing to a higher law than the statute. It derided "sacred, unyielding adherence to statutory scripture"[32] and "hyper-technical reliance upon statutory

---

counted in the contest proceeding "must be included in the certified vote totals"), revd and remd as *Bush v Gore,* 121 S Ct 525 (2000) (per curiam).

31. See Posner, 2000 S Ct Rev at 27 (cited in note 1).

32. *Palm Beach County Canvassing Board v Harris,* 772 S2d at 1228, quoting *Boardman v Esteva,* 323 S2d 259, 263 (Fla 1975). The court did not, however, quote the following passage from *Boardman:* "the results of elections are to be efficiently, honestly and promptly ascertained by election officials to whom some latitude of judgment is accorded, and . . . courts are to overturn such determinations only for compelling reasons when there are clear, substantial departures from essential requirements of law." 323 S2d at 268–69 n 5 (quoting the trial court with approval). The question in *Boardman*—and in another decision from which the Florida Supreme Court in *Palm Beach County Canvassing Board v Harris* quoted sonorous right-to-vote language, *Beckstrom v Volusia County Canvassing Board,* 707 S2d 720, 725 (Fla 1998)—was whether substantial compliance with the rules governing absentee ballots was sufficient to allow a vote to be counted. The court held that it was, thus presaging its decision regarding irregularities in the absentee ballots challenged in Seminole and Martin Counties in the 2000 election. See note 20. Compare *Chappell v Martinez,* 536 S2d 1007, 1008–9 (Fla 1988), and *Carpenter v Barber,* 198 S 49 (Fla 1940).

provisions"[33] and said that "the abiding principle governing all election law in Florida" was to be found in the statement in Florida's constitution that "all political power is inherent in the people."[34] The court was using the Florida constitution, or perhaps some principle of natural law, to trim the statute. "[T]he will of the people is the paramount consideration. . . . This fundamental principle, *and* our traditional rules of statutory construction, guide our decision today."[35] Armed with a principle as vague and all-encompassing as "people power," a court can do anything with an election law in the name of interpretation. The court's later explanation that it had been using the ordinary principles of statutory interpretation after all, and specifically that the "plain meaning" of the statutory term "error in the vote tabulation" included an error resulting from a voter's mistake that made his ballot unreadable by the machine,[36] was lame. The Secretary of State's interpretation *was* the plain meaning of that term.[37]

After the Secretary of State on November 26 (the court-imposed extended deadline for certification following protest) certified Bush as the winner, albeit with a diminished lead (Broward having completed its recount by then), Gore brought suit against the *Democratic* canvassing boards of Palm Beach and Miami-Dade,[38] contesting the election results in those two counties. On December 4, after a two-day trial, Florida Circuit Judge

33. *Palm Beach County Canvassing Board v Harris,* 772 S2d at 1227.

34. Id at 1230, quoting Fla Const Art I, § 1.

35. *Palm Beach County Canvassing Board v Harris,* 772 S2d at 1228 (emphasis added).

36. *Palm Beach County Canvassing Board v Harris,* 772 S2d 1273, 1283–84 (Fla Dec 11, 2000) (per curiam).

37. David A. Strauss, in his contribution to this volume, *Bush v Gore: What Were They Thinking?,* pages 200–201, argues that the Florida Supreme Court's interpretations of other provisions of the election statute, such as "legal vote," were "consistent with the plain language of the contest statute" and therefore that "there is a plain language defense for the Florida Supreme Court's action." This suggests a misunderstanding of the "plain meaning" interpretive principle. The principle is that if statutory language is plain, that is, clear as a linguistic matter (regardless of the real world context of application, which might expose an ambiguity), the court should follow it, unless the result is totally absurd. All Strauss means is that some of the statutory language is not plain. But "error in the vote tabulation" is plain, and it is merely bizarre for the Florida Supreme Court to have claimed that its interpretation, which violated the plain meaning of the term, *was* the plain meaning.

38. Also Nassau County, but that part of Gore's case went nowhere, and I will ignore it.

Sauls dismissed Gore's suit.[39] Gore appealed and four days later the Florida Supreme Court reversed in another indefensible opinion.[40]

Judge Sauls had interpreted Florida's election statute as establishing the contest as a judicial proceeding to review administrative action.[41] The purpose of the contest trial was thus to determine whether the canvassing boards, the organs charged with tabulating election results, had abused their discretion in failing to conduct a hand recount in a certain way (that is, the Broward way, sought by Gore), or at all (the Miami-Dade County Canvassing Board had begun a hand recount, then changed its mind and stopped).[42] As there was no reason to believe that the result of the statewide election would change in favor of Gore if reasonable recounting procedures were followed,[43] of which the most favorable method to Gore that could be considered reasonable was Palm Beach's three-dimples method, Judge Sauls found no abuse of discretion and so refused to order a further recount. By reversing him and holding that the decision of a canvassing board is entitled to no deference in a contest proceeding, the Florida Supreme Court made the protest a meaningless preliminary to the contest and expanded, without any basis in the statute, the power of the courts relative to that of the officials (the members of the canvassing boards and the Secretary of State) to whom the legislature had actually confided the conduct and supervision of elections, including election recounts. And while the statute as we have seen limits the canvassing boards to correcting errors in the vote tabulation,[44] the December 8 opinion authorizes (even requires) judges in contest cases to conduct recounts intended to rectify voter errors as well.[45] The court, even though it lacks staff and experience for counting and interpreting ballots (especially thousands or tens of thousands or millions of ballots), becomes the primary tabulator, rather than the election officials. That is upside down.[46]

39. *Gore v Harris*, 2000 WL 1790621, *5 (Fla Cir Ct Dec 3), revd and remd as *Gore v Harris*, 772 S2d 1243, revd as *Bush v Gore*, 121 S Ct 525.

40. *Gore v Harris*, 772 S2d 1243. The vote this time was 4–3 (the November 21 decision had been unanimous), with powerful dissents.

41. *Gore v Harris*, 2000 WL 1790621 at *4.

42. Id.

43. Id at *3.

44. Fla Stat Ann § 102.166(5).

45. *Gore v Harris*, 772 S2d at 1260–62.

46. The Chief Justice forcefully argued this point in his dissenting opinion. Id at 1262–65 (Wells dissenting).

It is true that the election statute does not confine contests to situations in which there has been an error in the vote tabulation. The grounds include fraud or other misconduct by an election official, bribery, the counting of illegal votes, and the ineligibility of a candidate.[47] The only ground available to Gore, however, was the failure to count "legal votes." And in context that was merely a complaint about the canvassing boards' handling of spoiled ballots. The principles of administrative law required the contest court, as Judge Sauls ruled, to defer to the canvassing boards as the experts in counting votes, and thus to uphold their decisions unless unreasonable. Given the problems of interpreting spoiled ballots, the decisions of the Palm Beach and Miami-Dade boards were not unreasonable, as Judge Sauls correctly concluded.

As well as upsetting the balance between court and agency, the Florida Supreme Court set the threshold for relief in a contest proceeding at an implausibly low level. No human or machine fault in the conduct of the election, and no external circumstances (such as a natural disaster) that might interfere with the conduct of the election, had to be shown. It was enough that the election had been close and that a hand recount using unspecified criteria might recover enough undervotes to change the outcome.[48] Successful contests, in the sense of contests eventuating in judicial orders for selective or comprehensive hand recounts, would become the norm in close elections.

On November 21, the Florida Supreme Court had extinguished the Secretary of State's discretion. On December 8, it extinguished the canvassing boards' discretion. The justices said in effect: if the election is close and we think there were a lot of voter errors, we have carte blanche to order any mode of recount that strikes us as likely to recover a substantial number of the rejected votes. The Florida election statute could provide that electors are to be picked by the state's supreme court after it knows (and maybe does not like) the result of the election, using a standard of the voter's unclear intent and the principles of natural law, even when there is no reason to suppose that an infallible hand recount would reverse the result of the election. But the legislature did not say anything like that.

The court ordered that Gore's 215-vote net gain in the Palm Beach recount (or 176—the court left it to the trial court to decide which number was correct), plus his 168-vote net gain from the partial recount in Miami-Dade

---

47. See Fla Stat Ann § 102.168(3).

48. *Gore v Harris,* 772 S2d at 1254–55.

County, be added to Gore's certified total.[49] The court thus was changing that total after the deadline (November 26) that it itself had set for determining the certified vote totals after the completion of the protest recounts. The court ordered a hand recount of all the remaining undervotes not only in Miami-Dade but throughout the state,[50] which have been estimated at sixty thousand.

The trial before Judge Sauls had made crystal clear, if it was not already, that the hand recounts were neither uniform[51] nor reliable. There were Broward rules, which favored Gore unduly, as we have seen, and a medley of different Palm Beach rules, the three-dimples rule having emerged after the recount had begun (earlier iterations had been a "sunshine rule"—light must be visible through the chad hole—and a "no dimple" rule, the rule followed in Palm Beach county in previous recounts[52]). No one knew what standard the Miami-Dade counters had used before they abandoned the recount. Yet while acknowledging that "practical difficulties may well end up controlling the outcome of the election"[53] (that is, may terminate the contest proceeding before its completion), the Florida Supreme Court gave Gore the votes he had gained in Miami-Dade County before the recount was interrupted, even though the precincts counted were unrepresentative and time might be called on the complete recount. The court refused to prescribe a uniform standard, and thus was ordering a recount that could not be expected to be accurate, or even concluded. Yet if Gore was ahead in the recount when time was called, the court's opinion implied (probably inadvertently) that he would be declared the winner even if the disputed ballots in precincts likely to favor Bush had yet to be recounted. For the court had given Gore the votes he had received in Miami-Dade's partial recount even though the full recount might never be completed.

Critics of the U.S. Supreme Court's intervention in the election litigation blame that Court for the Florida Supreme Court's failure to set a uniform standard. The argument is that by doing so the Florida court would have stoked the fires of Bush's argument based on Article II of the U.S.

49. Id at 1248, 1262.

50. Id at 1261–62.

51. See, for example, Trial Transcript, *Gore v Harris,* No 00-2808, *91–104 (Fla Cir Ct Dec 2, 2000) (available on Westlaw at 2000 WL 1802941) (testimony of Judge Charles Burton, chairman of the Palm Beach canvassing board).

52. See id.

53. *Gore v Harris,* 772 S2d at 1261–62 n 21.

Constitution that the court was revising rather than interpreting the election statute. But what is more likely to have stopped the court (since filling a gap in a statute is not rewriting the statute) is that a uniform standard based on Broward procedures would have been completely untenable, yet a uniform standard that was inconsistent with those procedures would have made the inclusion of the Broward recount result in Gore's certified vote total nonsensical—it would amount to crediting Gore with votes recovered by a procedure that the court itself was rejecting as unreliable.

There is more wrong with the December 8 opinion. In ordering that only undervotes be recounted, the court was ignoring the fact that Gore's gains in Broward, Palm Beach, Miami-Dade, and Volusia counties may have included overvotes. An overvote is less likely to be recovered by a hand recount than an undervote is. But if the chad for one candidate is cleanly punched through and the chad for his rival slightly dislodged because the voter started to vote for the rival and then realized he was making a mistake, the machine might read the second dislodgement as a vote and void the ballot. And if the voter both punched a candidate's chad and wrote the candidate's name in the space provided for write-in votes, the machine would automatically reject the ballot, even though the voter's intention was plain.[54] There were 110,000 overvotes statewide, so given the closeness of the election the refusal to order them recounted could not easily be justified, except for the shortness of time. More to the point, if Gore was given votes recovered from overvotes in the four counties' recounts, those ballots had to be recounted, because some of them may well have been true overvotes, where, as I explained earlier, the voter had punched through the chads for two presidential candidates but one of the chads had been left hanging and so the machine, which cannot be relied on to count hanging chads as votes, had failed to reject the ballot.

Despite the shortness of time, the Florida Supreme Court assumed on December 8 that a responsible recount might be completed and the state's electoral votes certified by December 12; electoral votes certified after that date could be challenged in Congress when the votes were counted in January.[55] There was no way in which sixty thousand votes could be recounted by the

---

54. Gore's own people thought that the second type of error had been made in Duval County and had cost Gore a significant number of votes. Richard T. Cooper, *A Different Florida Vote*, LA Times A1 (Dec 24, 2000). According to Cooper, the Gore team did not discover the overvote problem in Duval County in time to request a recount there.

55. 3 USC § 5 (1994).

twelfth yet allow time for the contestants' lawyers to challenge, and a judge to review, the decisions made by the counters on particular ballots, especially when the counters would be using different criteria for what constituted a "legal vote." Either the court meant to condone a bobtailed procedure or it was expecting the recount to fizzle and did not want to be blamed.

Granted, the Florida statute is vague when it comes to relief. Remember that the court in a contest proceeding that finds that enough "legal votes" were rejected to "change or place in doubt the result of the election" can "provide any relief appropriate under such circumstances."[56] "Appropriate" is not defined; it has been left to the courts to work out on a case-by-case basis. But even a term as vague as "appropriate" does not give a court carte blanche. No reasonable person could consider the relief ordered by the Florida Supreme Court on December 8 appropriate. Once again the court had misinterpreted it.

CONCLUSION

It is natural to conclude that if the critics are right and the U.S. Supreme Court lacked adequate grounds for intervening in the election litigation and therefore should not have halted the recount ordered by the Florida Supreme Court on December 8, an injustice was done. But if my analysis is correct, the conclusion is erroneous, if by "injustice" one means that Gore would have been the legal winner had the recount continued. Even with Bush's lead carved down to as few as 150 votes by the Florida Supreme Court's decision of December 8, it is unclear whether Gore would have prevailed in the recount ordered by that court. It is true that he needed to pick up only a few more than that number of votes from the nine thousand undervotes not yet recounted in Miami-Dade County to pull ahead, assuming the other fifty thousand or so undervotes statewide that had not yet been recounted would have split evenly. We do not know what rule the Miami-Dade canvassing board would have used had it resumed recounting. But if it would have used Palm Beach rules on all 10,750 disputed ballots in Miami-Dade County, then by my earlier analysis it probably would have given Gore only 263 additional votes—fewer than 100 more than the 168 vote gain that the Florida Supreme Court had already given Gore in Miami-Dade. Had Gore gained only 100 more net votes, Bush would still have won the state, albeit by as few as 50 votes.

56. Fla Stat Ann §§ 102.168(3)(c), (e)(8).

Gore *might* have prevailed in the recount—Miami-Dade's canvassing board might have used Broward rules, with results similar to what they produced in Broward County—but only by virtue of the Florida Supreme Court's having violated state law. The decisions of November 21 and December 8 made a hash of that law. Abstention by the federal courts would not have erased the fact that the Florida Supreme Court had erred grievously in interpreting the Florida election law. It should not have extended the deadline for hand recounting that had been fixed by the Secretary of State, or interpreted "error in the vote tabulation" to include a voter's error in voting, or reversed Judge Sauls's dismissal of the contest proceeding, or extinguished the discretionary authority of the state and local election officials, or authorized relief in a contest proceeding on the basis merely that the election was close and there were a number of undervotes, or credited Gore with the Broward and the partial Miami-Dade recount results, or ordered a statewide recount of undervotes but not overvotes.[57] In all these respects it was deforming Florida's election law. There was no legal basis for compelling the Secretary of State to accept late hand recounts; Bush really did win by 930 votes. Had Gore been declared the winner on the basis of the recount ordered by the Florida court on December 8, he would have owed his victory to legal error, whether or not it was a legal error that the U.S. Supreme Court should have corrected. The result of the Supreme Court's intervention was, therefore, at the least, rough justice; whether it was legal justice is the question I have left for another occasion.

57. Gore might well have benefited from a hand recount of overvotes statewide, see note 54, but he did not seek such a recount. More to the point, voter error is not a basis under Florida law for recounting.

9

Bush v Gore

What Were They Thinking?

DAVID A. STRAUSS

There is an old question: does a judge decide how a case will come out, and then find a justification in the law? Or does the judge approach the case with no strong prior inclination and follow the legal materials where they lead? If we confine the question to judges who are reasonably able and conscientious, the answer is surely that cases lie on a continuum between these poles. In some cases judges may have no strong intuitions, and they more or less try to figure out the right answer from the legal materials, perhaps approaching them with a weak and rebuttable prior view that one position is correct. One would expect that to be true in cases involving relatively technical bodies of law that engage no strong moral sentiments, or perhaps in areas that are so infrequently litigated that the law is unfamiliar.

In other cases one would expect a judge to have strong intuitions, from the start, about how the case should come out. There is nothing necessarily wrong with this, at least as long as the judge is willing to change her mind if the legal materials, upon investigation, make it clear that the intuition is unsustainable. It is sensible, as well as inevitable, for people immersed in the legal culture to trust their intuitions about what the law must be before they have specifically investigated an issue.

The extraordinary litigation that led to the Supreme Court's decision in *Bush v Gore*[1] allows us to speculate, with more confidence than usual, about how the justices approached the issues

I am grateful to Michael Klarman and Richard Pildes for comments on an earlier draft, and to Crista Leahy for com ments and expert research assistance.

1. 121 S Ct 525 (2000) (per curiam).

presented by that case. The fast pace of the proceedings, and the relative novelty of the legal issues, made the justices' thought processes unusually visible. They could not, as they ordinarily would, wait for the lower court proceedings to be fully completed and take as much time as they needed before committing themselves publicly to a position. They had to respond to two separate decisions of the Florida Supreme Court very quickly and very publicly.

The conclusion that emerges, in my view, is that several members of the Court—perhaps a majority—were determined to overturn any ruling of the Florida Supreme Court that was favorable to Vice President Gore, at least if that ruling significantly enhanced the Vice President's chances of winning the election. They acted on the basis of strong intuitions—which, as I said, is by no means necessarily inappropriate in itself—but the intuitions were intuitions about the outcome, not about the law. The specific legal questions presented in the litigation were shifting, complex, and esoteric. It is hard to see how the justices could have strong legal intuitions about any of those specific questions. To the extent those questions raised familiar broad issues—like federalism and the relationship between the courts and the political process—the majority's reaction in this litigation contradicted their normal inclinations. During the litigation, the justices in the majority appear to have accepted, at one time or another, four different arguments offered by Governor Bush's lawyers, all of which were questionable—one of which, based on 3 USC § 5,[2] even the majority subsequently abandoned—but which had one common element: they required that the Florida Supreme Court be reversed. On the crucial remedial question that ensured Governor Bush's election, the majority's decision appears to be simply indefensible. And the majority opinion insisted that its rationale was to be applied, essentially, only in this case—basically conceding that the result, not the legal principle, dictated the outcome.

What explains this extraordinary behavior by the Supreme Court? The most plausible hypothesis, I believe, is that several members of the United States Supreme Court were convinced that the Florida Supreme Court would try to give the election to Vice President Gore and would act improperly if necessary to accomplish that objective. The governing intuition was that the Florida Supreme Court had to be stopped from doing this. The majority's actions in the litigation show a relentless search for some reason

---

2. 3 USC § 5 (1994). See text accompanying notes 9–10.

that could be put forward to justify a decision reversing the Florida Supreme Court. The outcome was a foregone conclusion.

If this is correct, then the United States Supreme Court's decision was not even on the continuum I described above. It was not comparable, for example, to judges' having an intuition that school segregation is unconstitutional, then groping for a theory that would justify that conclusion. School segregation was a familiar thing, as were the basic principles of the Equal Protection Clause. It is hard to believe that anyone on the Supreme Court really had strong intuitions about (or even more than a bare familiarity with) the provisions of Article II of the Constitution, or Title 3 of the United States Code, that played such a large role in the *Bush v Gore* litigation. The Equal Protection Clause was the ultimate basis for the decision, but the majority essentially admitted (what was obvious in any event) that it was not basing its conclusion on any general view of what equal protection requires. The decision in *Bush v Gore* was not dictated by the law in any sense—either the law found through research, or the law as reflected in the kind of intuitive sense that comes from immersion in the legal culture.

In the rest of this essay, I will try to support this speculation. Perhaps the most obvious way to support it would be to demonstrate that the Court's decision was wrong on the merits. But that case has been made, not least by the dissenting opinions.[3] Besides, it is no sin for a court to get a case wrong, especially if the issues are complex and the time is brutally short. Other aspects of the litigation are, I believe, more revealing about how the justices approached this case, and I will examine them in Part I below.

Then in Part II, I will consider whether the majority, irrespective of whether it was following the law, was actually right about the Florida Supreme Court—and if so, whether the United States Supreme Court's decision might be, in some sense, justifiable. The argument in defense of the United States Supreme Court would have to be that it engaged in a kind of morally justified civil disobedience. It deliberately acted in a way that could not be legally justified in order to prevent some greater harm. I do not think that argument can be sustained. But it would be enough of a breakthrough if it were generally accepted that the United States Supreme Court's decision has to be justified, if at all, in those terms.

---

3. *Bush v Gore*, 121 S Ct at 539 (Stevens dissenting); id at 542 (Souter dissenting); id at 546 (Ginsburg dissenting); id at 550 (Breyer dissenting).

I. FIVE REVEALING ACTS

A. THE REMEDY

Seven justices concluded that the recount ordered by the Florida Supreme Court in the contest proceedings violated the Equal Protection Clause. A majority of the Court reasoned that the procedures under which the Florida Supreme Court proposed to conduct the recount "do not satisfy the minimum requirement for non-arbitrary treatment of voters necessary to secure the fundamental right" to vote.[4] Among other things, the majority said, the "intent of the voter" standard that the Florida court used, while "unobjectionable as an abstract proposition and a starting principle," requires "specific standards to ensure its equal application."[5] "The formulation of uniform rules to determine intent based on these recurring circumstances is practicable and, we conclude, necessary."[6]

On the merits, this holding is very adventuresome—it goes well beyond anything the Court had previously said—but it is not wholly implausible. It would not have been shocking if the Warren Court had interpreted the Equal Protection Clause in this way (although there would no doubt have been much criticism of it for doing so). In fact, this interpretation can be seen both as an extension of the Warren Court's vision of democracy and as a logical implication of the view, seriously proposed a generation ago, that the Constitution limits the degree to which discretion can be vested in executive officials of both the state and federal governments.[7] For the majority of this Court, the equal protection holding was wildly out of character. And it seems very questionable for the Court to announce and apply a novel principle like this for the first time in a case that effectively decides a presidential election. But on the underlying merits, the Court's interpretation of the Equal Protection Clause was not indefensible.

What does seem indefensible is the Court's remedy. Of the seven justices who concluded that the recount procedures ordered by the Florida Supreme

4. Id at 530.

5. Id.

6. Id.

7. See Kenneth Culp Davis, *Discretionary Justice: A Preliminary Inquiry* (LSU 1969); James Vorenberg, *Decent Restraint of Prosecutorial Power,* 94 Harv L Rev 1521, 1521–22 (1981). A few court of appeals cases seemed to adopt this approach, but they were generally not followed. See, for example, *Holmes v New York City Housing Authority,* 398 F2d 262 (2d Cir 1968); *Hornsby v Allen,* 326 F2d 605 (5th Cir 1964).

Court violated the Equal Protection Clause, two would have followed what seems like the normal course: a remand to allow the Florida Supreme Court to dispose of the case in a way that was consistent with both the United States Supreme Court's ruling and Florida law. But by a vote of five to four, the Court refused to allow the Florida Supreme Court to try to implement its ruling on remand. The majority stated that complying with the Court's ruling would require "substantial additional work."[8] It then reasoned as follows:

> The Supreme Court of Florida has said that the legislature intended the State's electors to "participat[e] fully in the federal electoral process," as provided in 3 U.S.C. § 5[, which] requires that any controversy or contest that is designed to lead to a conclusive selection of electors be completed by December 12. That date is upon us, and there is no recount procedure in place under the State Supreme Court's order that comports with minimal constitutional standards. . . . Because the Florida Supreme Court has said that the Florida Legislature intended to obtain the safe-harbor benefits of 3 U.S.C. § 5, Justice Breyer's proposed remedy—remanding to the Florida Supreme Court for its ordering of a constitutionally proper contest until December 18—contemplates action in violation of the Florida election code, and hence could not be part of an "appropriate" order authorized by [Florida law].[9]

The federal statute to which the Court referred—3 USC § 5, the so-called safe harbor provision—provides that when a state has made a "final determination of any controversy" concerning the appointment of electors "at least six days before" the date the electors meet in the state capital to vote, "such determination . . . shall be conclusive" on Congress.[10] By law the electors met on December 18, 2000, so December 12 was the cutoff for taking advantage of the safe harbor.

What the majority did in this passage was to attribute to the Florida legislature not just an intention to adhere to Section 5, but an intention to adhere to Section 5 at any cost. The majority said, in effect, that the Florida state legislature would want to take advantage of Section 5 even if that meant awarding the state's electoral votes to the candidate who lost the election—"lost" according to the state's election laws, as interpreted by the state's high-

8. *Bush v Gore,* 121 S Ct at 532.
9. Id at 532–33.
10. 3 USC § 5.

est court and modified by any federal constitutional requirements. That is an unlikely intention for any legislature to have. Certainly one would expect that the legislature would rather send forward challengeable electoral votes for the winner of the state's popular vote, rather than unchallengeable votes for the loser. To attribute a contrary intention to Florida on the basis of a general statement in the Florida Supreme Court's opinion[11] is very strained. In fact, the Florida Supreme Court's opinion suggests, if anything, that it would *not* have wanted to abandon the effort to count votes; the majority of that court explicitly rejected the argument, advanced in a dissenting opinion, that "because of looming deadlines and practical difficulties we should give up any attempt to have the election of the presidential electors rest upon the vote of Florida citizens as mandated by the Legislature."[12]

At the very least, it was uncertain what the Florida Supreme Court would have said if forced to choose between the safe harbor and continued counting. In the face of any uncertainty about the Florida legislature's intentions, for the United States Supreme Court to attribute such an unlikely intention to the Florida legislature without even remanding, to see what the Florida Supreme Court would say, is inexplicable—unless, of course, the United States Supreme Court simply did not trust the Florida Supreme Court to play it straight.

B. THE STAY

On December 9, the Court, by the same vote of 5 to 4 that would ultimately decide the case, issued a stay of the Florida Supreme Court's second decision.[13] The effect of the stay was to stop the counting of the ballots ordered by the Florida Supreme Court. The Supreme Court's standard rule for granting a stay of a lower court's order is that the party seeking the stay must demonstrate a substantial probability of success on the merits, and the "balance of equities"—the harm faced by the petitioner if the stay is denied, compared to the harm to the respondent if the stay is granted—must favor the petitioner.[14]

11. See *Gore v Harris,* 772 S2d 1243, 1261 (Fla Dec 8, 2000), revd and remd as *Bush v Gore,* 121 S Ct 525.

12. *Palm Beach County Canvassing Board v Harris,* 772 S2d 1220, 1261–62 n 21 (Fla Nov 21, 2000), vacd and remd as *Bush v Palm Beach County Canvassing Board,* 121 S Ct 471 (2000) (per curiam).

13. *Bush v Gore,* 121 S Ct 512 (2000) (application for stay).

14. See, for example, *Rubin v United States,* 524 US 1301, 1301 (1998) (discussing the conditions under which stays should be granted).

By that measure, the stay seems impossible to justify. To begin with, it is not clear that the harm to Governor Bush should have carried any weight at all. Justice Scalia, in an opinion defending the stay, explained that "[t]he counting of votes that are of questionable legality . . . threaten[s] irreparable harm to [Governor Bush], and to the country, by casting a cloud upon what he claims to be the legitimacy of his election."[15] The premise of this argument is that there is a legitimate interest in suppressing truthful information—information about what the recount ordered by the Florida Supreme Court would have disclosed—in order to protect the President of the United States from political harm. Ordinarily it is a fundamental principle of our system of freedom of expression that the government cannot limit what people hear about politics because it mistrusts their ability to evaluate that information rationally. The majority's apparent conclusion that then-Governor Bush had a legitimate interest in suppressing certain information may not be wholly unsupportable, but it is at least problematic.

But if one accepts the possible political damage to Governor Bush as a legitimate harm, the potential harm to Vice President Gore was vastly greater. Had Vice President Gore prevailed on the merits in the Supreme Court, the stay might easily have deprived him of his victory, by preventing the counting of the ballots before the electors were to cast their votes on December 18. It is true that the failure to grant a stay might have inflicted political damage on a Bush presidency; but granting a stay might have wholly deprived Vice President Gore of the presidency.

There is only one circumstance in which the balance of equities might have favored Governor Bush: if a majority of the Supreme Court had already decided how it was going to rule. If there had been any chance that the Vice President would win in the Supreme Court, the stay was indefensible. But if it were a foregone conclusion that the Florida Supreme Court's decision would be reversed, even the administrative expense of counting might justify a stay. In addition, if five justices had already made up their minds that they were going to rule in favor of Governor Bush, the stay, however controversial, ensured that they would not be in the awkward position of reversing an apparent Gore victory. The hypothesis that best explains the majority's decision to grant a stay despite the imbalance in the equities and

15. *Bush v Gore,* 121 S Ct at 512 (Scalia concurring).

the questionable nature of Governor Bush's interest is that the majority knew, when it granted the stay, how the case would come out.

That, too, is not necessarily a reason to criticize the justices. It is probably pretty common for justices to know, from reading the certiorari petition, how they will vote in a case. But this was not a run-of-the-mill case presenting a slight variant on a subject that the justices have thought about dozens of times. The Florida Supreme Court's decision in *Bush v Gore* concerned a state election law statute with which the justices surely had no prior familiarity—even from *Bush v Palm Beach County Canvassing Board*,[16] which concerned an entirely different state statute. Governor Bush's arguments also drew on broader aspects of Florida election law and Florida administrative law; he argued, for example, that the Florida Supreme Court should have required deference to the decisions of the county canvassing boards even though the contest statute did not say that explicitly. The equal protection argument that was the basis of the majority's opinion depended on a detailed familiarity with the facts about the various recounts that had been underway, as well as an assessment of what was "practicable."[17]

The Florida Supreme Court issued the opinion at 4:00 P.M. on December 8.[18] The United States Supreme Court granted the stay at 2:45 P.M. on December 9.[19] In less than twenty-three hours, five justices evidently had decided that Governor Bush was sure to prevail, because in view of the harm to the Vice President, the stay could not possibly be justified if there had been any doubt. The justices reached this decision even though they had little or no prior familiarity with the state law involved, and even though they were acting on the basis of a very hastily prepared stay application and opposition. It is hard to resist the conclusion that they knew all along what they were going to do.

C. THE GRANT OF CERTIORARI IN *BUSH V PALM BEACH COUNTY CANVASSING BOARD*

Governor Bush's certiorari petition in *Bush v Palm Beach County Canvassing Board* relied primarily, and very heavily, on 3 USC § 5. Section 5 was the basis of the first question presented in the petition, and the twenty-seven page petition did not begin to discuss any other arguments until page eight-

16. 121 S Ct 471 (2000) (per curiam).

17. *Bush v Gore*, 121 S Ct at 530.

18. *Gore v Harris*, 772 S2d 1243 (Fla Dec 8, 2000), revd and remd as *Bush v Gore*, 121 S Ct 525.

19. *Bush v Gore*, 121 S Ct 512.

een.[20] This is a pretty clear indication that Governor Bush's lawyers thought Section 5 provided their best argument by far. That argument—repeatedly asserted in the petition—was that Section 5 forbade Florida from altering its election laws after the date of the election.[21] This passage—the emphasis is in the original—is representative:

> The application of 3 U.S.C. § 5 in these circumstances is straightforward. . . . [T]his Court has not previously been called upon to decide whether or not the States must adhere to preexisting law in resolving election disputes. But the plain language of the federal statute indicates that they *must* do so. [22]

This interpretation of Section 5 is wrong. No one, now, believes otherwise. Section 5 does not prohibit states from "changing the rules"; it just provides that the consequence of doing so is that their choice of electors may be challenged before Congress. This is in fact clear from the language of the statute, once one untangles its syntax, and by the time *Bush v Gore* was decided even the three justices who concluded that the Florida Supreme Court had changed the law did not assert that that court's action was forbidden by Section 5.

Governor Bush's lawyers really cannot be faulted for writing the petition as they did. They were scrambling, under enormous time pressure, to find some basis to get the Supreme Court involved in what was really a dispute over the meaning of state law, and like almost everyone else they did not have prior familiarity with the esoteric provisions of Title 3. In fact, Vice President Gore's brief in opposition to the petition did not recognize the plain error in the interpretation of Section 5.[23] In his brief on the merits,

20. Petition for Writ of Certiorari, *Bush v Palm Beach County Canvassing Board,* No 00-836, *27 (filed Nov 22, 2000) (available on Lexis at 2000 US Briefs 836).

21. Id at *12.

22. Id at *18. For similar statements, see, for example, id at *17–22; id at *12 (stating that "[t]he evident purpose of this federal law is to ensure that the applicable rules cannot be changed once the voters have gone to the polls"); id at *13 (noting "the express federal statutory prohibition against the *post hoc* creation of new legal rules"); id at *15–16 ("Congress's federally imposed requirement that controversy over the appointment of electors be resolved solely under legal standards 'enacted prior to' the date of the election.").

23. See Brief in Opposition to Petitions for Writs of Certiorari, *Bush v Palm Beach County Canvassing Board,* No 00-836, *6 (filed Nov 24, 2000) (available on Lexis at 2000 US Briefs 836).

Vice President Gore did demonstrate that Section 5 was only a safe harbor;[24] in fact, by the time Governor Bush's lawyers wrote their brief on the merits, they had realized, too, that they had gone too far, and their Section 5 arguments in the merits brief were much more hedged.[25]

But if one cannot fault the lawyers, one can certainly raise concerns about the actions of the Supreme Court, which made a very questionable decision to intervene in the litigation on the basis of a misunderstanding of the law—and an even more questionable decision not to back out when its misunderstanding became clear. The Court granted certiorari on the question presenting the Section 5 issue. (It also agreed to review a question raising an Article II issue, but it did not grant certiorari on the question in the Bush petitions that raised the Equal Protection Clause issue.[26]) The Court then instructed the parties to address the question: "What would be the consequences of this Court's finding that the decision of the Supreme Court of Florida does not comply with 3 U.S.C. Section 5?"[27] This question reflects a misunderstanding of Section 5; if the Court had understood that Section 5 was most plausibly understood only to create a safe harbor, it would have asked the parties to address directly the question whether Section 5 did more than that. The Court's actions also suggested that the Court believed the Section 5 issue would be the central issue in the case.

The Court's decision to grant certiorari was very surprising to most observers, and it was a highly significant event. Among other things, it gave credibility to the extremely harsh attacks that Governor Bush's representatives made on the Florida Supreme Court. There was no obvious legal reason for the Court to intervene; that is why its decision to do so surprised most observers. The central issues were ones of state law and, as their treatment of Section 5 shows, even Governor Bush's lawyers, with every incentive to find a federal question in the case, struggled to do so.

In these circumstances—a highly charged political context raising difficult

---

24. See Brief of Respondents Al Gore, Jr., and Florida Democratic Party, *Bush v Palm Beach County Canvassing Board,* No 00-836, *1 (filed Nov 28, 2000) (available on Lexis at 2000 US Briefs 836).

25. See Brief for Petitioner, *Bush v Palm Beach County Canvassing Board,* No 00-836, *12–13 (filed Nov 28, 2000) (available on Lexis at 2000 US Briefs 836).

26. See Petition for Writ of Certiorari, *Bush v Palm Beach County Canvassing Board* at *i (cited in note 20) (available on Lexis at 2000 US Briefs 836); *Bush v Palm Beach County Canvassing Board,* 121 S Ct 510 (2000) (granting writ of certiorari).

27. *Bush v Palm Beach Canvassing Board,* 121 S Ct at 510.

issues of state law and no obvious issues of federal law—the Supreme Court would ordinarily operate with a strong presumption against granting certiorari. That is what it should have done in this case. Its attitude should have been that unless it found a compelling argument that the Florida Supreme Court violated federal law, it would stay out of the case. It did not find such an argument; if it had, it would not have focused the parties' attention on an argument that turned out to be plainly wrong. To put the point another way, before it made a grant of certiorari that was momentous in itself, the Supreme Court should have examined the Section 5 argument carefully enough to discover the error that soon became clear to everyone. The fact that it didn't is another indication that the Court was reacting viscerally on the basis of an inchoate sense, not grounded in any legal principle, that something had to be done.

D. THE RULING IN *BUSH V PALM BEACH COUNTY CANVASSING BOARD*

The Court's decision in *Bush v Palm Beach County Canvassing Board* bears out the impression that a majority of the justices, having made up their minds that the Florida Supreme Court's decision should not be allowed to stand, was seeking only a suitable means of overturning it. By the time of the oral argument, no justice was receptive to the interpretation of Section 5 that had been put forward in the petition. Chief Justice Rehnquist and Justice Scalia, however, raised, at argument, the question whether the Florida Supreme Court had violated Article II, Section 1 by relying on the state constitution in interpreting state voting laws.[28] The Court subsequently issued a unanimous opinion vacating the decision of the Florida Supreme Court and remanding the case to that court, principally to determine if the Florida Supreme Court had relied on the Florida Constitution. The Supreme Court explained its remand by saying that "[t]here are expressions in the opinion of the Supreme Court of Florida that may be read to indicate that it construed the Florida Election Code without regard to the extent to which the Florida Constitution could, consistent with Art. II, § 1, cl. 2, 'circumscribe the legislative power.'"[29]

This decision was praised as statesmanlike by some, and it did tem-

---

28. Transcript of Oral Argument, *Bush v Palm Beach County Canvassing Board,* No 00-836, *50–51 (Dec 1, 2000) (available on Lexis at 2000 US Trans Lexis 70).

29. *Bush v Palm Beach County Canvassing Board,* 121 S Ct at 474, quoting *McPherson v Blacker,* 146 US 1, 25 (1892).

porarily paper over the sharp disagreements among the justices that surfaced at the argument. But in other respects the decision was anything but a careful and prudent use of the Supreme Court's power.

It is, for example, entirely clear that the Court did not grant certiorari in order to address the issue on which it remanded. Not only was the Court focused on 3 USC § 5 when it granted certiorari, but—more significantly—the petition did not at any point argue that the Florida Supreme Court violated Article II by relying on the provisions of the Florida Constitution.[30] That argument, which later persuaded the Court, did not merit as much as a single sentence in the certiorari petition. If the Court had granted the petition in order to consider this question, it would have directed the parties to address it specifically, as it directed the parties to address a question that it mistakenly thought was raised by 3 USC § 5.

When the Court realized that it had agreed to review the case on the basis of a misunderstanding of the law (that is, of 3 USC § 5), it might have done one of several things. It might have dismissed the writ as improvidently granted. If that were too embarrassing, the Court might have found some other ground to dismiss the writ; for example, by the time of the Court's decision, the case was at least close enough to being moot to justify dismissing the petition. Conceivably, once it decided that the important issue was one that both it and the parties had all but ignored, it could have asked for briefing on that issue. But the Court did none of those things. Instead, it appears to have issued as severe a rebuke to the Florida Supreme Court as it could, while still maintaining unanimity.

There were several things wrong with this course of action. First, the constitutional question is in fact a complex one. It is far from clear what the relationship is between a state's constitution and the power that a state "legislature" may exercise under Article II, Section 1 to "direct" the "manner" in which electors are appointed. Presumably a state constitution may not itself direct how electors are chosen, at least if the constitution is not the work of the legislature.[31] But the other polar position—that a legislature

---

30. The issue was comprised within one of the questions presented in the petition and therefore was technically before the Court, but it was not argued in the petition in any form.

31. Vice President Gore's lawyers argued that the Florida Constitution is in fact the work of the legislature, thus making the issue even more complex and the Court's conclusion even more questionable. See Brief For Respondents Al Gore, Jr., and Florida Democratic Party, *Bush v Palm Beach County Canvassing Board,* No 00-836, *42–43 (filed Nov 28, 2000) (available on Lexis at 2000 US Briefs 836).

may wholly disregard the state constitution when it directs how electors are appointed—cannot possibly be correct. A state legislature is a creature of the state constitution: you cannot tell the difference between a state's real legislature and a group of usurpers without looking at the state constitution. Beyond that, state constitutions often specify such things as when the legislature meets, how it is convened and adjourned, what constitutes a quorum, and so on.[32] It would be very surprising if a state legislature could simply ignore such state constitutional provisions when it was directing the manner in which presidential electors are appointed. Determining the ways in which a state constitution may and may not limit the legislature's decisions about presidential electors will, therefore, be a difficult and complex task.

Second, as the Court must have been aware, its decision was generally viewed as resolving—not just raising—the question whether Article II, Section 1 precludes state constitutional limits on legislative action. The Court did not even acknowledge that some state constitutional limits on legislative power would be unproblematic, much less explain where the line might be drawn between acceptable and unacceptable limits. The Court's formulation of the reason for vacating the Florida Supreme Court's decision—"we are unclear as to the extent to which the Florida Supreme Court saw the Florida Constitution as circumscribing the legislature's authority under Art. II, § 1, cl. 2"[33]—was quite naturally taken to mean that any such "circumscription" might be unconstitutional. Thus the effect of the Supreme Court's remand was not only to suggest that the Florida Supreme Court had acted unconstitutionally but to affect the further proceedings in that court.

Finally, the decision of the Florida Supreme Court by no means forced the United States Supreme Court to confront this question. The Florida Supreme Court did not declare that something the legislature had done was unconstitutional under the state constitution. At worst, the Florida Supreme Court relied on the state constitution for general principles of a kind that could easily be seen as part of the background against which the legislature knowingly enacted the Florida election laws—which is how the Florida Supreme Court explained its opinion on remand. Significantly,

32. See, for example, Fla Const Art III, § 3, cl a–c (specifying when the legislature meets); id cl c, e (specifying how the legislature is convened and adjourned); id § 4, cl a (specifying what constitutes a quorum).

33. *Bush v Palm Beach County Canvassing Board,* 121 S Ct at 475.

Governor Bush did not press this argument at any point in the litigation until it was raised by members of the Court. The argument was, as I said, not mentioned at all in the petition; it was made perfunctorily in Governor Bush's merits brief (in only three paragraphs, on page forty-seven of a fifty-page brief); and it was not mentioned at oral argument until members of the Court brought it up.

In other words, the Court—having evidently granted certiorari under a misapprehension about 3 USC § 5—issued a politically sensitive decision that was bound to be misinterpreted on a complex question that was not squarely raised, not adequately briefed, and not aggressively pushed by the petitioner. Why did the Court do this? In theory, because it was possible (although very unlikely) that the Florida Supreme Court would acknowledge that its decision relied on the state constitution to reject a legislative directive, and because it was possible (although again unlikely) that such a decision, on the basis of the kind of general principles discussed in the Florida Supreme Court's opinion, might transgress constitutional limits that the United States Supreme Court did not seriously try to define. As an exercise of the Supreme Court's certiorari jurisdiction, this is irregular to the point of being inexplicable. As an effort to thwart, by any means necessary, a perceived illegitimate act by the Florida Supreme Court, it begins to make sense.

E. THE EQUAL PROTECTION HOLDING, LIMITED "TO THIS CASE"

The Court's own statements provide the final piece of evidence that the Court was responding not to any legal principle but to a perception that something needed to be done in this particular case. *Bush v Gore* held that the recount procedures mandated by the Florida Supreme Court "do not satisfy the minimum requirement for non-arbitrary treatment of voters."[34] The Court identified a number of aspects of the ruling that seemed arbitrary to it—for example, that the lower court included in the vote totals partial recounts from some counties, and manually recounted overvotes from some jurisdictions but not others.[35] But those problems could have been cured by directing the Florida Supreme Court to modify the vote totals; they did not justify the United States Supreme Court in holding that the recount could not go forward.

34. *Bush v Gore,* 121 S Ct at 530.
35. Id at 531–32.

That aspect of the Court's holding, which may have determined the outcome of the presidential election, was justified on the basis of a plausible but potentially far-reaching principle: that at least where the right to vote is concerned, the states may not use discretionary standards if it is practicable to formulate rules that will limit discretion. In particular, the Court concluded that the standard that the Florida Supreme Court specified to govern the counting of votes—that the intention of the voter be honored—is "unobjectionable as an abstract proposition" but requires "specific standards to ensure its equal application."[36] The Court acknowledged, of course, that discretionary inquiries into intent are common in many areas of the law. But it said that here, "[t]he search for intent can be confined by specific rules designed to ensure equal treatment."[37]

This is a recognizable principle: a state must make decisions according to rules, rather than according to discretionary standards, at least when the costs of doing so are not too great. The Court's decision to limit this principle to voting—rather than to allow it to be extended to, for example, the criminal justice system, where it might have dramatic effects—is at least supported by precedent, which can be read to treat voting rights differently from most other individual interests.[38] Even as applied to voting rights, this principle would have far-reaching implications given the ubiquity of the "intent of the voter" standard[39] and the wide local variations in voting and tabulation mechanisms and the like. But the effects would probably not be more dramatic than, say, those of the Court's reapportionment decisions of the 1960s.[40]

The problem is that the Court was not interested in the principle. It went out of its way to try to limit its ruling to the facts of *Bush v Gore*. The Court said that it was ruling only on "the special instance of a statewide recount under the authority of a single state judicial officer"[41]—without explaining

36. Id at 530.

37. Id.

38. See, for example, *Kramer v Union Free School District No 15*, 395 US 621, 626 (1969) (holding that the right to vote lies at "the foundation of our representative society" and classifications with regard to that right to vote are subject to strict scrutiny); *Harper v Virginia Board of Elections*, 383 US 663, 665 (1966) ("[T]he right to suffrage is subject to the imposition of state standards which are not discriminatory.").

39. See *Bush v Gore*, 121 S Ct at 541 (Stevens dissenting); Brief of Respondent Albert Gore, Jr, *Bush v Gore*, No 00-949, *36 (filed Dec 10, 2000) (available on Westlaw at 2000 WL 1809151).

40. See *Reynolds v Sims*, 377 US 533, 555 (1964); *Wesberry v Sanders*, 376 US 1 (1964).

41. *Bush v Gore*, 121 S Ct at 532.

why this was a special instance, different from all other aspects of the electoral process. The Court then tried even harder to limit its holding:

> Our consideration is limited to the present circumstances, for the problem of equal protection in election processes generally presents many complexities. The question before the Court is not whether local entities, in the exercise of their expertise, may develop different systems for implementing elections. Instead, we are presented with a situation where a state court with the power to assure uniformity has ordered a statewide recount.[42]

There is no obvious reason—and the Court gave none—for using a different rule when a state legislature "with the power to assure uniformity" is acting, or for why the recount itself does not present as many "complexities" as other aspects of voting, or why "local entities, in the exercise of their expertise" could not "develop different systems for implementing" the voter intent standard.

The Court's attempt to limit its holding, with barely a fig leaf of principle, gives the game away. The majority was not concerned with principle. It smelled a rat in this case. It thought the Florida Supreme Court was up to no good. It could not explain what the Florida Supreme Court was up to in terms that engaged general principles that it was willing to embrace, but it was determined to intervene and stop that court. If the actions of the United States Supreme Court are to be defended, they must be defended in those terms.

II. WAS IT JUSTIFIED?

The most straightforward way to determine whether the Florida Supreme Court was acting in such an illegitimate way as to warrant the United States Supreme Court's intervention is, of course, to consider the merits of the issues. The United States Supreme Court's ruling on the equal protection issue, although potentially defensible in principle, was certainly novel, and surely the Florida Supreme Court did not act illegitimately when it failed to anticipate that ruling. Most of the attacks on the Florida Supreme Court's decision instead seem to assert—as the three-justice concurring opinion did in *Bush v Gore*—that that court's interpretation of Florida election law was so indefensible that it violated Article II, Section 1. The merits of this position have been extensively discussed, beginning in the opinions themselves, and there seems little to add.

42. Id.

One point should be emphasized, however. The Florida Supreme Court decision that was overturned in *Bush v Gore* was consistent with the plain language of the principal statute involved—the Florida statute governing contests of election certifications[43]—and neither the concurring opinion nor, as far as I am aware, anyone else, has seriously contended otherwise. Richard A. Posner specifically addresses this argument in his contribution to this symposium, but his remarks betray the weakness of his position.[44] Judge Posner does not contend that the Florida Supreme Court's interpretation of the contest statute is inconsistent with its plain meaning. Judge Posner says that the term "error in vote tabulation" has a plain meaning. That seems implausible to me, but in any event that term occurs in the protest statute, not the contest statute, and was not at issue in *Bush v Gore*.

In fact, Judge Posner's suggestion that I misunderstand the "'plain meaning' interpretive principle" neatly reveals where the argument in his essay goes wrong. That principle bears on the question whether the Florida Supreme Court correctly interpreted Florida law. But that question was not before the United States Supreme Court. The position of the three concurring Justices was a usurpation precisely because they—like Judge Posner—acted as if that were the question. The question before the United States Supreme Court was whether what the Florida court did was so far wrong that it violated Article II, Section 1—and for purposes of *that* question, the fact (implicitly conceded by Posner) that the Florida court's action was consistent with the plain meaning of the contest statute is a strong point in the Florida court's defense. That statute provides that "rejection of a number of legal votes sufficient to change or place in doubt the result of the election" is a "ground[ ] for contesting [the] election."[45] The statute does not define what a "legal vote[ ]" is. The statute also includes an exceptionally broad grant of power to the trial court: "The circuit judge to whom the contest is presented may fashion such orders as he or she deems necessary to ensure that each allegation in the complaint is investigated, examined, or checked, to prevent or correct any alleged wrong, and to provide any relief appropriate under such circumstances."[46] It is not eccentric, as a matter of English usage, to say that a "legal vote" has been "reject[ed]"

---

43. Fla Stat Ann § 102.168 (West 2000).

44. Richard A. Posner, Bush v Gore: *Prolegomenon to an Assessment,* in this volume, page 177, note 37.

45. Fla Stat Ann § 102.168(3), (3)(c).

46. Id § 102.168(8).

when a ballot is not counted in accordance with the intentions that the voter indicates on it. The election in Florida was close enough that those rejected votes "place[d] in doubt the result of the election."[47] And the procedures that the Florida Supreme Court ordered were well within the broad remedial power granted by the statute.[48]

The fact that there is a plain language defense for the Florida Supreme Court's action does not establish that the Florida Supreme Court's decision was correct—although the concurring opinion asserted that under Article I, Section 2, "the text of the election law itself . . . takes on independent significance."[49] But unless there is at least a clearly settled line of precedent to the contrary—which there was not in Florida; among other things, the contest statute had been extensively revised in 1999—the fact that the Florida Supreme Court's decision was consistent with the plain language of the contest statute should be enough to show that that court was not acting in a fundamentally illegitimate way that warranted the United States Supreme Court's determined effort to derail it.

The concurring opinion's attack on the Florida Supreme Court was that the Florida court interpreted the contest statute in a way that fit badly with the provisions of Florida law that allow for a "protest" before votes are certified.[50] The relationship of the "protest" and the "contest" statutes is an obvious concern; indeed, from the face of the contest statute it looks as if a judge could intervene in almost any close election. The Florida Supreme

47. Id § 102.168(3)(c).

48. Those powers are granted to the trial judge, but in exigent circumstances, it is not extraordinary for an appellate court to direct a lower court to exercise its discretion in a certain way. The Florida Supreme Court did leave the trial court supervising the recount with substantial discretion; that discretion was part of what led the majority to find an equal protection violation. Neither the concurring opinion nor, so far as I am aware, anyone else, has shown that the Florida legislature meant to prevent the Florida Supreme Court from exercising the normal range of appellate powers over the lower courts in this case.

49. *Bush v Gore,* 121 S Ct at 534. The full quotation is: "the text of the election law itself, and not just its interpretation by the courts of the States, takes on independent significance." It is not clear why the concurring opinion said this. If a legislature acted with the understanding that courts would interpret statutes in a way that did not follow "the text . . . itself," then attaching significance to the text, rather than judicial interpretations, would defeat the legislature's intentions, presumably in contravention of Article I, Section 2.

50. See Fla Stat Ann § 102.166 (West 2000); *Bush v Gore,* 121 S Ct at 536–37.

Court tried to come to grips with this problem, holding, for example, that the decisions of the canvassing boards at the protest stage would be evidence admissible in the contest proceedings.[51] This is not the only plausible reading of the Florida statutory scheme—the dissenters in the Florida Supreme Court, and the concurring opinion, thought the canvassing boards should get more deference—but so far as I am aware no one has identified either a statute or a precedent that precludes the Florida Supreme Court's view.

Beyond the substantive merits of the case, there are other indications that the Florida Supreme Court was not simply trying to ensure that Vice President Gore would win the election. On several occasions, the Florida Supreme Court ruled against Vice President Gore on important issues. For example, before the election results were certified, the Florida Supreme Court rejected Vice President Gore's effort to require Miami-Dade County to resume the recount it had started, then stopped. The Vice President believed that the remaining votes in that county would give him the statewide lead. It is not out of the question—and at the time it seemed entirely possible, indeed perhaps probable—that the Florida Supreme Court's decision on this issue cost the Vice President the election.

Later, the Florida Supreme Court summarily affirmed lower court decisions from Seminole and Martin Counties. In those cases, Republican Party officials were shown to have engaged in clearly improper conduct in the handling of absentee ballots. The trial courts nonetheless denied relief, holding that the election results were not tainted.[52] The clear impropriety might well have provided an opening for the Florida Supreme Court to rule in favor of the Vice President, had it been seeking opportunities to do so. The Florida Supreme Court also upheld a lower court decision that refused to declare the Palm Beach County "butterfly ballot" unlawful and to order a revote.[53]

Finally, in the contest case that led to the United States Supreme Court's decision in *Bush v Gore*, the Florida Supreme Court rejected several claims by the Vice President that were at least colorable. The Supreme Court refused to intervene when Vice President Gore complained that the trial

---

51. *Gore v Harris,* 772 S2d 1243, 1252 (Fla Dec 8, 2000), revd and remd as *Bush v Gore,* 121 S Ct 525.

52. *Taylor v Martin County Canvassing Board,* 773 S2d 517 (Fla Dec 12, 2000).

53. *Fladell v Palm Beach County Canvassing Board,* 772 S2d 1240 (Fla Dec 1, 2000).

judge—whom the Supreme Court ultimately reversed—was proceeding too slowly, even though it was clear that the passage of time could be fatal to the Vice President's chances.[54] This was a self-defeating thing for the Florida Supreme Court to do, if it simply wanted to ensure the Vice President's election. When it heard the case on the merits, the Florida Supreme Court rejected the Vice President's argument that 3,300 votes from Palm Beach County that had been manually counted should be recounted.[55] The Florida Supreme Court also rejected the Vice President's argument that Nassau County authorities acted improperly by refusing to certify the vote totals disclosed by a mandatory machine recount, reverting instead to the initial machine count that was more favorable to Governor Bush:[56] David Boies, the Vice President's lead counsel, regarded this as such a strong claim that he said beforehand, "If I can't win that argument, I'm going to give up the practice of law."[57]

Of course, these rulings may simply have been in accordance with the law. Certainly the fact that the Florida Supreme Court ruled against Vice President Gore on some occasions does not establish that its rulings in his favor were correct. But the United States Supreme Court, I have argued, was not prompted by a reasoned judgment that the Florida Supreme Court made specific legal errors. The United States Supreme Court's actions seem to be the product of a general sense that the Florida Supreme Court was illegitimately manipulating the law to ensure that Vice President Gore won. Even if the Florida Supreme Court was doing so, that would not by itself justify the actions of the United States Supreme Court: one of the consequences of a federal system of government is that sometimes state authorities will abuse their power in ways that the federal government is powerless to correct. But the fact that the Florida Supreme Court passed up opportunities to rule in favor of Vice President Gore, even when it was plausible to do so and when such a ruling would have greatly helped him, is evidence that the United States Supreme Court's perception was wrong.

54. *Palm Beach County Canvassing Board v Harris,* 772 S2d 1220, 1240 (Fla Nov 21, 2000), vacd and remd as *Bush v Palm Beach County Canvassing Board,* 121 S Ct 471.

55. *Gore v Harris,* 772 S2d 1243, 1259–60 (Fla Dec 8, 2000), revd and remd as *Bush v Gore,* 121 S Ct 525.

56. *Gore v Harris,* 772 S2d at 1260.

57. David Firestone and David Barstow, *Counting the Vote: The Overview: Florida Legislature Plans to Enter Legal Fray, Backing Bush's Suit,* NY Times A1 (Nov 25, 2000).

CONCLUSION

No one, not even the most enthusiastic supporter of Governor Bush's campaign, should feel entirely comfortable with the result in *Bush v Gore*. If I am right about what the Supreme Court did, then the best that can be said is that the Court trumped the supposed lawlessness of the Florida Supreme Court with lawlessness of its own. As I have suggested, I do not believe the United States Supreme Court had adequate reason to suspect the Florida Supreme Court of a nakedly partisan effort to "steal" the election. But the more troubling question is whether, even if the justices' view of the Florida Supreme Court was correct, they were justified in acting without really being concerned about whether they had a sound legal basis for doing so.

Judges, like everyone else, sometimes act on instinct. That is inevitable and, as I said at the outset, often unobjectionable, within limits. But a close election is sure to inflame partisan passions and to skew judgment in a partisan direction. That makes it all the more important for judges to hesitate, to question their own motives, and to make sure that their judgments have a solid basis in the law before they act. That may be a lot to expect. But if there is any court of which we should expect it, it is the United States Supreme Court. In *Bush v Gore*, a majority of the Court, prompted by a general and unjustified sense that something needed to be done, plunged in, splintered along ideological lines, and played a prominent role in deciding the election. This was not a triumph for the rule of law.

10

Order Without Law

CASS R. SUNSTEIN

Under the leadership of Chief Justice William Rehnquist, the Supreme Court of the United States has generally been minimalist, in the sense that it has attempted to say no more than is necessary to decide the case at hand, without venturing anything large or ambitious.[1] To some extent, the Court's minimalism appears to have been a product of some of the justices' conception of the appropriately limited role of the judiciary in American political life. To some extent, the tendency toward minimalism has been a product of the simple need to assemble a majority vote. If five or more votes are sought, the opinion might well tend in the direction of minimalism, reflecting judgments and commitments that can command agreement from diverse people.

To be sure, the Court has been willing, on occasion, to be extremely aggressive. In a number of cases, the Court has asserted its own, highly contestable vision of the Constitution against the democratic process. This aggressive strand has been most evident in a set of decisions involving federalism;[2] it can be found

---

I am grateful to Richard Posner and Mary Anne Case for helpful comments on an earlier draft. Apologies for the title choice to Professor Robert C. Ellickson. See his superb (and unrelated) *Order Without Law: How Neighbors Settle Disputes* (Harvard 1991).

1. For a general discussion of judicial minimalism, see Cass R. Sunstein, *One Case at a Time: Judicial Minimalism on the Supreme Court* (Harvard 1999).

2. *United States v Morrison*, 120 S Ct 1740, 1759 (2000) (striking down the Violence Against Women Act as beyond the power of Congress under the Commerce Clause); *City of Boerne v Flores*, 521 US 507, 536 (1997) (holding that the Religious Freedom Restoration Act exceeded Congress's remedial powers under the Fourteenth Amendment); *United States v Lopez*, 514 US 549, 567–68 (1995) (holding that the prohibition of firearm possession near schools was outside the power of Congress).

elsewhere as well.[3] But generally these decisions have been minimalist too. Notwithstanding their aggressiveness, they tend to decide the case at hand, without making many commitments for the future. Sometimes those decisions have even been "subminimalist," in the sense that they have said less than is required to justify the particular outcome.[4]

In the Court's two decisions involving the 2000 presidential election, minimalism was on full display. The Court's unanimous decision in *Bush v Palm Beach County Canvassing Board*[5] was firmly in the minimalist camp. Here the Court refused to resolve the most fundamental issues and merely remanded to the Florida Supreme Court for clarification. The Court's 5–4 decision in *Bush v Gore*[6] was also minimalist in its own way, for it purported to resolve the case without doing anything for the future. But here the Court effectively ended the presidential election. It did so with rulings, on the merits and (especially) on the question of remedy, that combined hubris with minimalism.

The Court's decision in *Bush v Gore* did have two fundamental virtues. First, it produced a prompt and decisive conclusion to the chaotic post-election period of 2000. Indeed, it probably did so in a way that carried more simplicity and authority than anything that might have been expected from the United States Congress. The Court might even have avoided a genuine constitutional crisis. Second, the Court's equal protection holding carries considerable appeal. On its face, that holding has the potential to create the most expansive, and perhaps sensible, protection for voting rights since the Court's one-person, one-vote decisions of mid-century.[7] In the fullness of time, that promise might conceivably be realized within the federal courts, policing various inequalities with respect to vot-

3. Justices Antonin Scalia and Clarence Thomas are fairly consistent maximalists, on the ground that they favor rule-bound decisions. See Antonin Scalia, *The Rule of Law as a Law of Rules*, 56 U Chi L Rev 1175, 1178–86 (1989) (discussing reasons to prefer rules over judicial discretion).

4. See *Romer v Evans*, 517 US 620, 635 (1996) (holding law forbidding special government protections for homosexuals to be invalid under the Equal Protection Clause, without fully explaining its consistency with earlier decisions).

5. 121 S Ct 471 (2000) (per curiam).

6. 121 S Ct 525 (2000) (per curiam).

7. See *Reynolds v Sims*, 377 US 533, 568 (1964) (holding an apportionment decision violative of the Equal Protection Clause because of the different weight given to different votes); *Baker v Carr*, 369 US 186, 208–37 (1962) (holding state apportionment decision not to present nonjusticiable political questions).

ing and voting technology. But it is far more likely that the Court's decision, alongside the evident problems in the Florida presidential vote, will help to spur corrective action from Congress and state legislatures.

The Court's decision also had two large vices. First, the Court effectively resolved the presidential election not unanimously, but by a 5–4 vote, with the majority consisting entirely of the Court's most conservative justices. Second, the Court's rationale was not only exceedingly ambitious but also embarrassingly weak. However appealing, its equal protection holding had no basis in precedent or in history. It also raises a host of puzzles for the future, which the Court appeared to try to resolve with its minimalist cry of "here, but nowhere else." Far more problematic, as a matter of law, was the majority's subminimalist decision on the issue of remedy. By terminating the manual recount in Florida, the Court resolved what it acknowledged to be a question of Florida law, without giving the Florida courts the chance to offer an interpretation of their own state's law.

In a case of this degree of political salience, the Court should assure the nation, through its actions and its words, that it is speaking for the law, and not for anything resembling partisan or parochial interests. A unanimous or near-unanimous decision can go a long way toward providing that assurance, because agreement between diverse people suggests that the Court is really speaking for the law. So too for an opinion that is based on reasoning that, whether or not unassailable, is so logical and clear as to dispel any doubt about the legitimacy of the outcome. The Court offered no such opinion.

From the standpoint of constitutional order, the Court might well have done the nation a service. From the standpoint of legal reasoning, the Court's decision was very bad. In short, the Court's decision produced order without law.

I. PRELIMINARIES

Bush v Gore was actually the fourth intervention, by the United States Supreme Court, in the litigation over the outcome of the presidential election in Florida. In sequence, the Court's interventions consisted of the surprising grant of certiorari on November 24, 2000;[8] the unanimous, minimalist remand on December 4, 2000;[9] the grant of a stay, and certio-

---

8. *Bush v Palm Beach County Canvassing Board*, 121 S Ct 510 (2000) (granting first writ of certiorari).

9. *Bush v Palm Beach County Canvassing Board*, 121 S Ct 471.

rari, on December 9, 2000;[10] and the decisive opinion in *Bush v Gore* on December 12, 2000.[11]

A. THE UNANIMOUS, MINIMALIST REMAND

On November 13, Florida Secretary of State Katherine Harris announced that the statutory deadline of November 14, 2000, was final, and that she would not exercise her discretion so as to allow extensions.[12] On November 21, the Florida Supreme Court interpreted state law to require the Secretary of State to extend the statutory deadline for a manual recount.[13] This was a highly controversial interpretation of Florida law, and it might well have been wrong.[14] At the time, however, any errors seemed to raise issues of state rather than federal law.

In seeking certiorari, Bush raised three federal challenges to the decision of the Florida Supreme Court.[15] First, he argued that by changing state law, the Florida Court had violated Article II of the United States Constitution, which provides that states shall appoint electors "in such Manner as the Legislature," and not any court, may direct.[16] Second, Bush invoked a federal law saying that a state's appointment of electors is "conclusive" if a state provides for the appointment of electors "by laws enacted prior to the day fixed" for the election.[17] According to Bush, the Florida court did not follow, but instead changed, the law "enacted prior" to Election Day, and in his view this change amounted to a violation of federal law.[18] Third, Bush argued that the manual recount would violate the Due Process and Equal Protection Clauses, because no clear standards had been established to ensure that similarly situated people would be treated similarly.[19]

10. *Bush v Gore,* 121 S Ct 512 (2000).

11. *Bush v Gore,* 121 S Ct 525.

12. See *Palm Beach County Canvassing Board v Harris,* 772 S2d 1220, 1225–26 (Fla Nov 21, 2000), vacd and remd as *Bush v Palm Beach County Canvassing Board,* 121 S Ct 471.

13. *Palm Beach County Canvassing Board v Harris,* 772 S2d at 1240.

14. See, for example, Michael W. McConnell, *Two-and-a-Half Cheers for* Bush v Gore, in this volume (discussing how the state supreme court's decision that the law mandates an extension is wrong); Richard A. Posner, Bush v Gore: *Prolegomenon to an Assessment,* in this volume (same).

15. Petition for Writ of Certiorari, *Bush v Palm Beach County Canvassing Board,* No 00-836 (filed Nov 22, 2000) (available on Lexis at 2000 US Briefs 836).

16. Id at *18–20, citing US Const Art II § 1, cl 2.

17. Petition for Writ of Certiorari at *12–18 (cited in note 15), citing 3 USC § 5 (1994).

18. Petition for Writ of Certiorari at *12–18 (cited in note 15).

19. Id at *20–26.

At the time, most observers thought it exceedingly unlikely that the Court would agree to hear the case. Even if the Florida Supreme Court had effectively "changed" state law, it appeared improbable that the United States Supreme Court could be convinced to say so. Whatever the merits, the Court seemed unlikely to intervene into a continuing controversy over the presidential vote in Florida. This was not technically a "political question,"[20] but it did not seem to be the kind of question that would warrant Supreme Court involvement, certainly not at this preliminary stage. To the general surprise of most observers, the Court agreed to grant certiorari, limited to the first two questions raised by Bush.[21]

Bush asked the United States Supreme Court to hold that because the Florida Supreme Court had violated the federal Constitution and federal law, Florida's Secretary of State had the authority to certify the vote as of November 14. For his part, Gore wanted the Court to affirm the Florida Supreme Court on the ground that that court had merely interpreted the law.[22] The United States Supreme Court refused these invitations and took an exceptionally small step, asking the state supreme court to clarify the basis for its decision.[23] Did the state court use the Florida Constitution to override the will of the Florida legislature? In the Court's view, that would be a serious problem, because the United States Constitution requires state legislatures, not state constitutions, to determine the manner of appointing electors.[24] The Supreme Court also asked the state court to address the federal law requiring electors to be appointed under state law enacted "prior to" Election Day.[25] In its own opinion, the Florida Supreme Court had said nothing about that law.

This was judicial minimalism in action. Why did the Court proceed in this way? It seems possible that some of the justices refused to settle the merits on principle, thinking that the federal judiciary should insert itself as lit-

20. For a discussion of what constitutes a nonjusticiable political question, see *Baker v Carr*, 369 US 186, 208–37 (1962).

21. *Bush v Palm Beach County Canvassing Board*, 121 S Ct 510 (2000) (granting certiorari).

22. See Brief of Respondents Al Gore, Jr., and Florida Democratic Party, *Bush v Palm Beach County Canvassing Board*, No 00-836, *13–21, 50 (filed Nov 28, 2000) (available on Lexis at 2000 US Briefs 836).

23. See *Bush v Palm Beach County Canvassing Board*, 121 S Ct at 475 (remanding for further proceedings).

24. Id at 474.

25. Id.

tle as possible into the continuing electoral struggle. But the most likely explanation is that the Court sought unanimity and found, as groups often do, that unanimity is possible only if as little as possible is decided.

B. THE ASTONISHING STAY

On December 8, the Florida Supreme Court ruled, by a vote of 4 to 3, that a manual recount was required by state law, and it thus accepted Gore's contest.[26] This decision threw the presidential election into apparent disarray. With the manual recount beginning, it became quite unclear whether Bush or Gore would emerge as the winner.

On December 9, the Supreme Court issued a stay of the decision of the Florida Supreme Court.[27] This was the first genuinely extraordinary action taken by the United States Supreme Court. It was not only extraordinary but also a departure from conventional practice, and one that is difficult to defend on conventional legal grounds—not because Bush lacked a substantial probability of success, but because he had shown no irreparable harm.

To be sure, some harm would have come to Bush from the continuation of the manual recount. It is entirely possible that the recount would have narrowed the gap between Bush and Gore. This would have been an unquestionable harm to Bush, in the nontrivial sense that it would have raised some questions about the legitimacy of his ensuing presidency, if it had subsequently been determined that the manual recount was unlawful.[28] But the question remains: How serious and irreparable would this "harm" have been? If the manual recount was soon to be deemed unlawful, would the Bush presidency really have been "irreparably" harmed? This is extremely doubtful.

At the same time, the stay of the manual recount would seem to have worked an irreparable harm to Gore. For Gore, time was very much of the essence, and if the counting was stopped, the difficulty of completing it in the requisite period would become all the more serious. By itself, the Supreme Court's stay of the manual recount did not hand the election to Bush. But it came very close to doing precisely that.

26. *Gore v Harris*, 772 S2d 1243, 1260–62 (Fla Dec 8, 2000), revd and remd as *Bush v Gore*, 121 S Ct 525.

27. *Bush v Gore*, 121 S Ct 512 (2000) (granting certiorari and staying the implementation of the Florida Supreme Court's decision).

28. As emphasized by Justice Scalia, see id at 512 (Scalia concurring).

In these circumstances, can anything be said on behalf of the stay? A reasonable argument is available, at least in retrospect. Suppose that a majority of the Court was entirely convinced that the manual recount was unlawful, perhaps because in the absence of uniform standards, similarly situated voters would not be treated similarly. If the judgment on the merits was clear, why should the voting be allowed to continue, in light of the fact that it would undoubtedly have to be stopped soon in any case, and its continuation in the interim would work some harm to the legitimacy of the next president? The question suggests that if the ultimate judgment on the merits was clear, the stay would not be so hard to defend. If the likelihood of success is overwhelming, the plaintiff should not be required to make the ordinary showing of irreparable harm.[29] The problem, then, was less the stay than the Court's ambitious, poorly reasoned judgment on the merits.

II. ORDER AND LAW

A. MERITS: WHAT THE COURT SAID

On the merits, there are two especially striking features to the Court's decision. The first is that six justices were unwilling to accept Bush's major submission, to the effect that the Florida Supreme Court had produced an unacceptable change in Florida law.[30] The second is that five members of the Court accepted the adventurous equal protection argument.

The equal protection claim does have considerable appeal, at least as a matter of common sense. If a vote is not counted in one area when it would be counted in another, something certainly seems to be amiss. Suppose, for example, that in one county, a vote will not count unless the stylus goes all the way through, whereas in another country, a vote counts merely because it contains a highly visible "dimple." If this is the situation, some voters can legitimately object that they are being treated unequally for no good reason.

In its per curiam opinion, the Court spelled out the equal protection rationale in some detail. "In some cases a piece of the card—a chad—is hang-

---

29. *Cuomo v United States Nuclear Regulatory Commission,* 772 F2d 972, 974 (DC Cir 1985).

30. I will not discuss that issue here. In brief, I think that the argument becomes less convincing the more one reflects on it. To be sure, a decision by a state court to disregard state law would raise serious questions under Article II. And I do not believe that the Florida Supreme Court correctly interpreted state law. But the majority's view was not so implausible as to amount to a change, rather than an interpretation. See *Bush v Gore,* 121 S Ct at 543–45 (Souter dissenting); id at 554 (Breyer dissenting).

ing, say by two corners. In other cases there is no separation at all, just an indentation."[31] The disparate treatment of these markings in different counties was unnecessary, because the "search for intent can be confined by specific rules designed to ensure uniform treatment."[32] In Florida, that search was not so confined, for the record suggested that in Miami-Dade County, different standards had been applied in defining legal votes; and Palm Beach County appeared to go so far as to change its standards during the process of counting. To this, the Court added "further concerns."[33] These included an absence of specification of "who would recount the ballots," leading to a situation in which untrained members of "ad hoc teams" would be involved in the process.[34] And "while others were permitted to observe, they were prohibited from objecting during the recount."[35] Thus the Court concluded that the recount process "is inconsistent with the minimum procedures necessary to protect the fundamental right of each voter in the special instance of a statewide recount under the authority of a single state judicial officer."[36]

The Court was well aware that its equal protection holding could have explosive implications for the future, throwing much of state election law into constitutional doubt. Thus the Court emphasized the limited nature of its ruling: "The question before the Court is not whether local entities, in the exercise of their expertise, may develop different systems for implementing elections. Instead, we are presented with a situation where a state court with the power to assure uniformity has ordered a statewide recount with minimal procedural safeguards."[37]

B. MERITS: THREE PROBLEMS

There are three problems with this reasoning. First, the Court's decision lacked any basis in precedent. Second, the Court's effort to cabin the reach of its decision seemed ad hoc and unprincipled—a common risk with minimalism. And third, the system that the Court let stand seemed at least as problematic, from the standpoint of equal protection, as the system that the Court held invalid.

31. Id at 530.
32. Id.
33. Id at 532.
34. Id.
35. Id.
36. Id.
37. Id.

1. Precedent. Nothing in the Court's previous decisions suggested that constitutional questions would be raised by this kind of inequality. The cases that the Court invoked on behalf of the equal protection holding—mostly involving one-person, one-vote and the poll tax[38]—were entirely far afield. To be sure, the absence of precedential support is not decisive; perhaps the problem had simply never arisen. But manual recounts are far from uncommon, and no one had ever thought that the Constitution requires that they be administered under clear and specific standards.

To make the problem more vivid, suppose that in 1998, a candidate for statewide office—say, the position of attorney general—lost after a manual recount, and brought a constitutional challenge on equal protection grounds, claiming that county standards for counting votes were unjustifiably variable. Is there any chance that the disappointed candidate would succeed in federal court? In all likelihood the constitutional objection would fail; in most courts, it would not even be taken seriously. The rationale would be predictable, going roughly like this: "No previous decision of any court supports the view that the Constitution requires uniformity in methods for ascertaining the will of the voter. There is no violation here of the principle of one-person, one-vote. Nor is there any sign of discrimination against poor people or members of any identifiable group. There is no demonstration of fraud or favoritism or self-dealing. In the absence of such evidence, varying local standards, chosen reasonably and in good faith by local officials, do not give rise to a violation of the federal Constitution. In addition, a finding of an equal protection violation would entangle federal courts in what has, for many decades, been seen as a matter for state and local government."

Of course it is possible to think that this equal protection holding would be wrong. Whether the federal Constitution should be read to cabin local discretion in this way is a difficult question. The problem is that in a case of such great public visibility, the Court embraced the principle with no support in precedent, with little consideration of implications, and as a kind of bolt from the blue.[39]

---

38. *Harper v Virginia Board of Elections*, 383 US 663, 666 (1966); *Reynolds v Sims*, 377 US 533, 568 (1964).

39. One of the real oddities of the majority opinion is that it was joined by two Justices—Scalia and Thomas—who have insisted in their commitment to "originalism" as a method of constitutional interpretation. There is no reason to think that by adopting the Equal Protection Clause, the nation thought that it was requiring clear and specific

2. Reach. It is not at all clear how the rationale of *Bush v Gore* can be cabined in the way that the Court sought to do. What is missing from the opinion is an explanation of why the situation in the case is distinctive, and hence to be treated differently from countless apparently similar situations involving equal protection problems. The effort to cabin the outcome, without a sense of the principle to justify the cabining, gives the opinion an unprincipled cast.

Suppose, for example, that a particular area in a state has an old technology, one that misses an unusually high percentage of intended votes. Suppose that many areas in that state have new technology, capable of detecting a far higher percentage of votes. Suppose that voters in that area urge that the Equal Protection Clause is violated by the absence of uniformity in technology. Why doesn't *Bush v Gore* make that claim quite plausible? Perhaps it can be urged that budgetary considerations, combined with unobjectionable and longstanding rules of local autonomy, make such disparities legitimate. In the context of a statewide recount administered by a single judge—the situation in *Bush v Gore*—these considerations appear less relevant. But it is easy to imagine cases in which those considerations do not seem weighty. I will return to these questions below.

3. Arbitrariness on all sides. The system that the recount was designed to correct might well have been as arbitrary as the manual recount that the Court struck down—and hence the Court's decision might well have created an even more severe problem of inequality. Consider the multiple inequalities in the certified vote. Under that vote, some machines counted votes that were left uncounted by other machines, simply because of different technology. Where optical scan ballots were used, for example, voters were far more likely to have their votes counted than where punchcard ballots were used. In Florida, fifteen of every one thousand punchcard ballots showed no presidential vote, whereas only three of every optically scanned ballot showed no such vote.[40] These disparities might have been reduced with a manual recount. If the broad principle of *Bush v Gore* is correct, manual re-

---

standards in the context of manual recounts in statewide elections. In fact it is controversial to say that the Fourteenth Amendment applies to voting at all. The failure of Justices Scalia and Thomas to suggest the relevance of originalism, their preferred method, raises many puzzles.

40. *Bush v Gore,* 121 S Ct at 552.

counts might even seem constitutionally compelled. But the Court's decision, forbidding manual recounts, ensured that the relevant inequalities would not be corrected.

Nor were the machine recounts free from inequality. Some counties merely checked the arithmetic; others put ballots through a tabulating machine. The result is a significant difference in the effect of the machine recount. If the constitutional problem consists of the different treatment of the similarly situated, then it seems entirely possible that the manual recount, under the admittedly vague "intent of the voter" standard, would have made things better rather than worse—and that the decision of the United States Supreme Court aggravated the problem of unjustified inequality.

4. Overall evaluation. On the merits, then, the most reasonable conclusion is not that the Court's decision was senseless—it was not—but that it lacked support in precedent or history, that it raised many unaddressed issues with respect to scope, and that it might well have authorized equality problems as serious as those that it prevented. In these ways, the majority's opinion has some of the most severe vices of judicial minimalism. In fact this was a subminimalist opinion, giving the appearance of having been built for the specific occasion.

C. REMEDY

Now turn to the Court's decision on the issue of remedy. If the manual recount would be unconstitutional without clear standards, what is the appropriate federal response? Should the manual recount be terminated, or should it be continued with clear standards? At first glance, that would appear to be a question of Florida law. If the Florida legislature would want manual recounts to continue, at the expense of losing the federal safe harbor, then manual recounts should continue. If the Florida legislature would want manual recounts to stop, in order to preserve the safe harbor, then manual recounts should stop.

Why did the Supreme Court nonetheless halt the manual recount? The simple answer is that the Court thought it clear that the Florida Supreme Court would interpret Florida law so as to halt the process. As the Court wrote,

> The Supreme Court of Florida has said that the legislature intended the State's electors to "participat[e] fully in the federal electoral process" . . . .

Because it is evident that any recount seeking to meet the December 12 date will be unconstitutional for the reasons we have discussed, we reverse the judgment of the Supreme Court of Florida ordering a recount to proceed.[41]

Thus the Court concluded that as a matter of Florida law, a continuation of the manual recount "could not be part of an 'appropriate' order authorized by" Florida law.[42]

This was a blunder. It is true that the Florida Supreme Court had emphasized the importance, for the Florida legislature, of the safe harbor provision.[43] But the Florida courts had never been asked to say whether they would interpret Florida law to require a cessation in the counting of votes, if the consequence of the counting would be to extend the choice of electors past December 12. In fact the Florida Court's pervasive emphasis on the need to ensure the inclusion of lawful votes[44] would seem to indicate that if a choice must be made between the safe harbor and the inclusion of votes, the latter might have priority. It is not easy to explain the United States Supreme Court's failure to allow the Florida Supreme Court to consider this issue of Florida law.

Here, then, is the part of the United States Supreme Court's opinion that is most difficult to defend on conventional legal grounds.

III. ALTERNATE HISTORY: WHAT MIGHT HAVE HAPPENED

Might anything unconventional help to defend the Court's conclusion? I have suggested that the Court's decision produced order. In fact it might well have averted chaos. It is worthwhile to spend some time on this question, because it provides the best explanation of the Court's otherwise inexplicable approach.

Let us briefly imagine what would have happened if the Court had affirmed the Florida Supreme Court, or remanded for continued counting under a constitutionally adequate standard. In the event of an affirmance, manual counting would of course have continued. In the event of a remand, the Florida Supreme Court would have had to sort out the relation-

41. Id at 533.

42. Id.

43. *Gore v Harris,* 772 S2d 1243, 1248 (Fla Dec 8, 2000), revd and remd as *Bush v Gore,* 121 S Ct 525.

44. *Gore v Harris,* 772 S2d at 1256–57.

ship between the legislature's desire to preserve the safe harbor and its desire to ensure an accurate count. That Court had been divided 4–3 on the question whether a manual recount should be required at all. It is reasonable to speculate that the three dissenters would continue to object to the manual recount. The question is whether any of the four members of the majority would conclude that the December 12 deadline took precedence over the continuation of the contest. There is certainly a chance that the Florida Supreme Court would have terminated the election at that point. But if it failed to do so, things would have gotten extremely messy.

Almost certainly, the Republican-dominated Florida legislature would have promptly sent a slate of electors, thus producing two (identical) slates for Bush—the November 26 certification and the legislatively specified choice. The legislative slate would in turn have been certified by the Secretary of State and the Governor of Florida. In the meantime the counting would, by hypothesis, have continued, well after the expiration of the December 12 safe harbor date. If Bush had won the manual recount, things would be very simple. But suppose Gore had won; what then? Would the Secretary of State have voluntarily certified the new count? Would the Governor of Florida have signed off on the certification? It is not at all clear that Florida's executive officials would do what the Florida courts wanted them to do. And if the Secretary of State and the Governor refused, how would the Florida courts have responded? Would they have threatened executive officials with contempt? How would they have responded to the threat? At the very least, there is a risk here of a minor constitutional crisis within Florida itself.

Suppose that this problem had been solved—and that three certified votes from Florida had come before Congress. At that point, both houses of Congress, acting separately, would have to vote on which certification to accept.[45] Almost certainly the Republican-dominated House of Representatives would have accepted a Bush slate. The Senate, split 50–50, would be much harder to call; perhaps some Democrats, in conservative states won by Bush, would have agreed to accept the Bush slate from Florida. But perhaps there would have been an even division within the Senate. If so, Vice President Gore would have been in a position to cast the deciding vote. Suppose that he did—and that he voted for the third Florida slate, and thus for himself, so as to ensure that the House and the Senate would come to different

45. See 3 USC § 15 (1994).

conclusions. At that point, the outcome is supposed to turn on the executive's certification.[46] But which was that? Here the law provides no clear answers. At this point, a genuine constitutional crisis might have arisen. It is not clear how it would have been settled. No doubt the nation would have survived, but things would have gotten very messy.

The Court's decision made all of these issues academic. It averted what would have been, at the very least, an intense partisan struggle, lacking a solution that is likely to have been minimally acceptable to all sides. I do not mean to suggest that the Supreme Court majority was correct. The Court owes a duty of fidelity to the law. Pragmatic concerns are certainly relevant in the face of ambiguous law, but there is a reasonable argument that the Court abandoned the law simply because of pragmatic concerns. What I hope to have shown is why the Court might have done the nation a big favor.

IV. A LARGE NEW RIGHT?

For the future, the most important question involves the scope of the right recognized in *Bush v Gore*. Notwithstanding the Court's efforts, that right is not at all easy to cabin, at least as a matter of basic principle. On its face, the Court appears to have created the most expansive voting right in many decades.

A. A MINIMALIST READING

At its narrowest, the Court has held that in the context of a statewide recount proceeding overseen by a single judge, the standard for counting votes must be (a) uniform and (b) concrete enough to ensure that similarly situated people will be treated similarly. This holding extends well beyond the context of presidential elections; it applies to statewide offices, not just federal offices.

By itself this is a substantial renovation of current law, since over thirty states fail to specify concrete standards for manual recounts.[47] This does not mean that state legislatures must set down clear standards in advance; a decision by state judges should suffice. But the inevitable effect of the opinion will be to increase the pressure for legislative reform at the state and possibly even the national level. Any state legislature would be well advised to specify the standard by which votes will be counted in the con-

46. Id.

47. See *Bush v Gore*, 121 S Ct at 540 n 2 (Stevens dissenting).

text of a manual recount. All this should count, by itself, as a gain for sense and rationality in the recount process.

B. EQUALITY IN VOTING

It is hard to understand why the principle of *Bush v Gore* does not extend much further than the case itself, at least in the context of voting. Consider the following easily imaginable cases:

1. Poor counties have old machinery that successfully counts 97 percent of votes; wealthy counties have newer machinery that successfully counts 99 percent of votes. Those in poor counties mount a constitutional challenge, claiming that the difference in rejection rates is a violation of the Equal Protection Clause.

2. Same as the immediately preceding case, except the division does not involve poor and rich counties. It is simply the case that some areas use machines that have a near-perfect counting rate, and others do not. The distribution of machines seems quite random.

3. Ballots differ from county to county. Some counties use a version of the controversial "butterfly ballot"; most do not. It is clear that where the butterfly ballot is used, an unusual number of voters are confused, and do not successfully vote for the candidate of their choice. Does this violate the Equal Protection Clause?

4. It is a national election. Citizens in Alabama use different machinery from that used by citizens in New York. The consequence is that citizens in Alabama are far more likely to have their votes uncounted than citizens in New York. Do they have a valid equal protection claim? What if the statistical disparity is very large?

The *Bush* Court's suggestion that ordinary voting raises "many complexities" is correct;[48] but how do those complexities justify unequal treatment in the cases just given? The best answer would point to two practical points: budgetary considerations and the tradition of local control. In light of these points, it might be difficult for some areas to have the same technology as others. Wealthy counties might prefer to purchase more expensive machinery, whereas poorer communities might devote their limited resources to other problems. Perhaps judicial caution in the cases just given can be justified in this way. But even if this is so, *Bush v Gore* plainly suggests the legitimacy of both state and national action designed to combat dispar-

---

48. *Bush v Gore,* 121 S Ct at 532.

ities of this kind. It is for this reason that the Court's decision, however narrowly intended, set out a rationale that might well create an extremely important (and appealing) innovation in the law of voting rights. Perhaps legislatures will respond to the invitation if courts refuse to do so.

C. A GENERAL REQUIREMENT OF RULES?

In fact the Court's rationale might extend more broadly still. Outside of the context of voting, governments do not impose the most severe imaginable constraints on official discretion. Because discretion exists, the similarly situated are treated differently.[49] Perhaps the most obvious example is the "beyond a reasonable doubt" standard for criminal conviction, a standard that different juries will inevitably interpret in different ways. Is this unacceptable?[50]

In the abstract, the question might seem fanciful; but analogous constitutional challenges are hardly unfamiliar. In the 1960s and 1970s, there was an effort to use the Due Process and Equal Protection Clauses to try to ensure more rule-bound decisions, in such contexts as licensing and admission to public housing.[51] Plaintiffs argued that without clear criteria to discipline the exercise of discretion, there was a risk that the similarly situated would not be treated similarly, and that this risk was constitutionally unacceptable. But outside of the most egregious settings, these efforts failed,[52] apparently on the theory that rule-bound decisions produce arbitrariness of their own, and courts are in a poor position to know whether rules are better than discretionary judgments. Does *Bush v Gore* require courts to extend the limited precedents here?

Perhaps it could be responded that because the choice between rule-

49. This is the basic theme of Kenneth Culp Davis, *Discretionary Justice: A Preliminary Inquiry* (LSU 1969).

50. A possible answer is that no more rule-bound approach would be better, all things considered. This is a difference from *Bush v Gore*, where it was easy to imagine a rule-bound approach that would add constraints on discretion without sacrificing any important value.

51. *Hornsby v Allen*, 326 F2d 605, 610 (5th Cir 1964); *Holmes v New York City Housing Authority*, 398 F2d 262, 264–65 (2d Cir 1968).

52. For examples of unsuccessful attempts to challenge unconditioned discretion violative of equal protection in these contexts, see *Phelps v Housing Authority of Woodruff*, 742 F2d 816, 822–23 (4th Cir 1984); *Atlanta Bowling Center, Inc v Allen*, 389 F2d 713, 715–17 (5th Cir 1968).

bound and more discretionary judgments is difficult in many cases, judicial deference is generally appropriate—but not when fundamental rights, such as the right to vote, are at risk. If so, *Bush v Gore* has a limited scope. But does this mean that methods must be in place to ensure against differential treatment of those subject to capital punishment? To life imprisonment? I cannot explore these questions here. But for better or for worse, the rationale in *Bush v Gore* appears to make it necessary to consider these issues anew.

CONCLUSION

If the Supreme Court is asked to intervene in an electoral controversy, especially a presidential election, it should try to avoid even the slightest appearance that the justices are speaking for something other than the law. Unanimity, or near-unanimity, can go a long way toward providing the necessary assurance. Whether or not this is possible, the Court's opinion should be well-reasoned and rooted firmly in the existing legal materials.

In *Bush v Gore,* the Court did not succeed on these counts. The 5–4 division was unfortunate enough; it was still worse that the five-member majority consisted of the most conservative justices. Regrettably, the Court's opinion had no basis in precedent or history. To be sure, the equal protection argument had a certain appeal in common sense. But even if it were correct, the natural remedy would have been to remand to the Florida Supreme Court, to ask that court to say whether Florida law would favor the manual recount over the safe harbor provision, or vice-versa. This remedy seems especially sensible in light of the fact that the inequalities that the Court condemned might well have been less serious than the inequalities that the recount would have corrected.

Nonetheless, there are two things to be said on behalf of the Court's ruling. First, the Court brought a chaotic situation to an abrupt end. From the standpoint of constitutional order, it is reasonable to speculate that any other conclusion would have been far worse. In all likelihood, the outcome would have been resolved in Congress, and here political partisanship might well have spiraled out of control. Second, the principle behind the equal protection ruling has considerable appeal. In a statewide recount, it is not easy to explain why votes should count in one area when they would not count elsewhere. In fact the principle has even more appeal if understood broadly, so as to forbid similarly situated voters from being treated differently because their votes are being counted through different technologies. Understood in that broader way, the principle of *Bush v Gore* should bring a range of questionable practices under fresh constitutional scrutiny.

Bush v Gore is likely to intensify public concern about unjustifiably aggressive decisions from the Supreme Court, and perhaps that concern will give the Court an incentive to be more cautious about unsupportable intrusions into the democratic arena. Far more important, *Bush v Gore* might come to stand for a principle, in legislatures if not courts, that greatly outruns the Court's subminimalist holding—a principle that calls for an end to the many unjustified disparities in treatment in voting and perhaps beyond. It would be a nice irony if the Court's weak and unprecedented opinion, properly condemned on democratic grounds, led to significant social improvements from the democratic point of view.

11

In Defense of the Court's Legitimacy

JOHN C. YOO

Even as it brought the 2000 presidential election to conclusion, *Bush v Gore*[1] gave rise to a flurry of attacks on the legitimacy of the Supreme Court. Many scholars criticized the Court for its creation of a new Equal Protection Clause claim never before seen, for its sudden imposition of a deadline that foreclosed any remedy, for its apparent hypocrisy in intervening into a local election dispute, and for its intervention into an utterly partisan dispute. Criticism usually would come as no surprise—it is merely the standard discussion about the actions of the institution that is the focus of much of our work in academia.

While early opinion polls show that most Americans have decided to move on,[2] it seems that many academic critics of *Bush v Gore* have decided to go beyond the usual mulling over of Supreme Court opinions. In the weeks following the Court's decision, prominent legal academics have voiced a number of objections that question the Court's very legitimacy, and in some cases have urged the political system to attack the Court. Many have characterized the decision as partisan and ungrounded in

During the Florida election crisis, the author testified before a special committee of the Florida legislature concerning the state's options for choosing its presidential electors. I thank Jesse Choper and Phil Frickey for their comments.

1. *Bush v Gore,* 121 S Ct 525 (2000) (per curiam).

2. Even though a bare majority of Americans initially agreed with the Court's ruling in *Bush v Gore,* 80 percent of respondents to a CNN/USA Today/Gallup poll conducted on December 13, 2000, accepted Bush as the legitimate winner of the 2000 presidential election. David W. Moore, *Eight in Ten Americans to Accept Bush as "Legitimate" President,* Gallup News Service (Dec 14, 2000), available online at <http://www.gallup.com/poll/releases/pr001214.asp> (visited Feb 22, 2001).

law.[3] Some have even compared the justices to partisan lobbyists.[4] As a result, these critics have called upon the Senate to refuse to confirm any Supreme Court justices during President Bush's term,[5] while others have hit upon the idea of reducing the number of justices on the Court.[6] Some have even gone so far as to compare the Court's alleged loss of legitimacy today to the Court's decision in *Dred Scott,* with all of the dire consequences that it portended.[7]

Much of this inflamed rhetoric, while good for grabbing headlines, no doubt resulted from the heat of the moment rather than from careful reflection and thought. But even if this criticism is shallow, it is broad. At least 585 law professors took the unusual step of signing an ad published in the New York Times on January 13, 2001, decrying *Bush v Gore* as an illegitimate, political decision.[8] The ad flatly declared: "when a bare majority of the U.S. Supreme Court halted the recount of ballots under Florida law, the five justices were acting as political proponents for candidate Bush, not as judges."[9]

Heady words. Such extraordinary criticism raises some questions worth pursuing. Did the Supreme Court somehow render an "illegitimate" decision in *Bush v Gore*? Has the Court undermined the institutional legitimacy that allows it to play a central role in American politics and society? What is the real threat to the Court's legitimacy in the aftermath of *Bush v Gore*?

This essay will argue that concerns about the Court's legitimacy are overblown. While it is certainly too early to be sure, the Court's actions, and their impact on the political system, come nowhere close to approaching the circumstances that surrounded earlier, real threats to the Court's standing. The Court did not decide any substantive issues—on a par with abortion or privacy rights, for example—that call upon the Court to remain con-

---

3. See, for example, Akhil Amar, *The Supreme Court: Should We Trust Judges?,* LA Times M1 (Dec 17, 2000) ("[T]his is not the rule of law: It is the rule of subjective sensibility.").

4. See, for example, Bruce Ackerman, *The Court Packs Itself,* Am Prospect 48 (Feb 12, 2001), available online at <http://www.prospect.org/print/V12/3/ackerman-b.html> (visited March 29, 2001).

5. See id.

6. Neal Katyal, *Politics Over Principle,* Wash Post A35 (Dec 14, 2000).

7. Id, discussing *Scott v Sanford,* 60 US 393 (1857).

8. On the problems with academics participating in such group letters or ads, see Neal Devins, *Bearing False Witness: The Clinton Impeachment and the Future of Academic Freedom,* 148 U Pa L Rev 165, 185–90 (1999) (warning of irrelevancy, loss of academic freedom, and reduced funding resulting from politically motivated letter writing).

9. Dave Zweifel, *Court Decision Still Rankles Law Profs,* Capital Times 6A (Jan 24, 2001) (reprinting text of ad).

tinually at the center of political controversy for years. Instead, the Court issued a fairly narrow decision in a one-of-a-kind case—the procedures to govern presidential election counts—that is not likely to reappear in our lifetimes. Rather than acting hypocritically and lawlessly, the Court's decision to bring the Florida election dispute to a timely, and final, end not only restored stability to the political system but was also consistent with the institutional role the Court has shaped for itself over the last decade.

I. LEGITIMACY AS PUBLIC OPINION

Legitimacy is a word often used in our political debate, but seldom defined precisely. We can think of institutional "legitimacy" as the belief in the binding nature of an institution's decisions, even when one disagrees with them.[10] This sociological or even psychological definition of the term is concerned with whether people will think the Court's decision in *Bush v Gore* was legitimate, and as a result will obey it.[11] It is different from philosophical legitimacy, in which one is concerned with moral obligations to follow the law.[12] Our Weberian definition of legitimacy is also different from the manner in which Critical Legal Studies scholars use the phrase to argue that because the legal system is radically indeterminate, and produces unjust results, it is illegitimate.[13]

One way, then, to judge whether *Bush v Gore* has undermined the Court's institutional legitimacy in American society would be to examine public attitudes toward the Court. Studies have shown that public support for the Court and its role in society run high, even though many have little knowledge about the Court's day-to-day activities.[14] While this is not the place to

10. Legitimacy in this sense is composed of both a belief that an institution's command is obligatory, and an action in compliance. See Max Weber, 1 *Economy and Society* 31–33 (Bedminster 1968). See also Alan Hyde, *The Concept of Legitimation in the Sociology of Law*, 1983 Wisc L Rev 379, 381–82 (discussing Weber's analysis of "legitimacy").

11. See Tom R. Tyler and Gregory Mitchell, *Legitimacy and the Empowerment of Discretionary Legal Authority: The United States Supreme Court and Abortion Rights*, 43 Duke L J 703, 711 n 25 (1994) (comparing sociological and philosophical notions of legitimacy).

12. See, for example, Ronald Dworkin, *Law's Empire* 190–215 (Belknap 1986); Joseph Raz, *The Authority of Law: Essays on Law and Morality* 1–27 (Clarendon 1979).

13. See Ken Kress, *Legal Indeterminacy*, 77 Cal L Rev 283, 285 (1989).

14. See, for example, Walter F. Murphy and Joseph Tanenhaus, *Publicity, Public Opinion, and the Court*, 84 Nw U L Rev 985, 1019 (1990) ("[A]nalyses show there is no necessary connection between knowledge and support for the Court.").

226 John C. Yoo

conduct a detailed study,[15] we may perhaps draw some initial conclusions from recent Gallup polling data. Over the last decade, poll respondents have usually held more confidence in the Supreme Court than in the other two branches of government.[16] In June 2000, 47 percent of those polled said that they held either a "great deal" or "quite a lot" of confidence in the Supreme Court, versus 42 percent for the presidency and 24 percent for Congress.[17] Even in light of the usual caveats surrounding the use of polling data, the resiliency in the Court's public support has been relatively deep and wide,[18] even as it has rendered a series of controversial decisions ranging from affirmative action to abortion to civil rights to religion.

Bush v Gore has not changed those overall numbers significantly. According to the Gallup poll, 59 percent of adults in January 2001 approved of the way the Supreme Court was handling its job, down only slightly from 62 percent in late August 2000.[19] While the Court's overall approval ratings have barely changed, however, the partisan composition of those numbers may be cause for concern. Approval of the Supreme Court among Republicans jumped from 60 percent in August 2000 to 80 percent by January 2001; among Democrats, that number fell from 70 percent in August to 42 percent in January.[20] But what may be most important is independents; there the Court's approval ratings dropped marginally from 57 to 54 percent.[21] While it is too early to tell whether this partisan split in attitudes to-

15. Political scientists have conducted several excellent studies about the relationship between public opinion and the Supreme Court. See, for example, Thomas R. Marshall, *Public Opinion and the Supreme Court* (Unwin Hyman 1989); Gregory A. Caldeira, *Public Opinion and the U.S. Supreme Court: FDR's Court-Packing Plan,* 81 Am Pol Sci Rev 1139 (1987).

16. *Confidence in Institutions,* available online at <http://www.gallup.com/poll/indicators/indconfidence.asp> (visited Feb 23, 2001).

17. Id.

18. Over the past ten years, the percentage of respondents who indicated that they had a "great deal" or "quite a lot" of confidence averages to 45.8 percent, with a low of 39 percent, and a high of 50 percent. Id.

19. Wendy W. Simmons, *Election Controversy Apparently Drove Partisan Wedge into Attitudes Towards Supreme Court,* available online at <http://www.gallup.com/poll/releases/pr010116.asp> (visited Feb 23, 2001).

20. Id.

21. Id. A tentative study of public opinion on the Supreme Court and the 2000 election conducted by political scientists reaches similar conclusions. They find that a majority of Americans approve of the Court's decision and believe it to have been fair. They also find that Democrats are far more likely to disapprove of the Court's decision and to

ward the Court will undermine the Court's legitimacy, I think it more likely that the drop in Democratic opinions toward the Court will prove to be a temporary blip, for the reasons that follow.

II. LEGITIMACY AS HISTORY

A second way to approach the question of legitimacy would be to compare *Bush v Gore* to other historical periods in which the Court's authority has come into question. If the Court's actions today were similar in significant ways to earlier moments of challenge to judicial legitimacy, then we might predict that the changes in the immediate polling data may augur a more sustained attack on the Court. Evaluating *Bush v Gore* in light of earlier historical periods, however, suggests that any sustained assault on the Court's legitimacy is unlikely to arise. The Court's authority has come under serious question four times in our history: the Marshall Court, the Taney Court's decision in *Dred Scott*, the Court's early resistance to the New Deal, and the Warren Court's fight against segregation and its expansion of individual liberties. Close inspection of these periods show that they bear little resemblance to *Bush v Gore*.

The defining characteristic of several of these periods was the persistent, central role of the Court in the political disputes of the day. The New Deal period is perhaps the most obvious in this regard. In an effort to end the Great Depression, President Franklin Roosevelt and a Democratic Congress enacted economic regulatory legislation that sought to impose national solutions on the crisis. In cases such as *A.L.A. Schechter Poultry Corp v*

---

view it as unfair than Republicans. See James L. Gibson, Gregory A. Caldeira, and Lester K. Spence, *The Supreme Court and the 2000 Presidential Election*, unpublished manuscript, available online at <http://artsci.wustl.edu/~legit/research.html> (visited Apr 27, 2001). Another study by the same authors finds that the Court has not damaged its legitimacy with *Bush v Gore*. After the Court's decision, they find that more than 80 percent of the public remains supportive of the Court, that more than 75 percent believe the Court can be trusted, and that about 85 percent would obey the Court even if they disagreed with its decisions. The authors compared their data to 1987 and 1995 polls and found that, if anything, support among the public for the Court has increased. See James L. Gibson, Gregory A. Caldeira, and Lester K. Spence, *The Legitimacy of the U.S. Supreme Court*, unpublished manuscript, available online at <http://artsci.wustl.edu/~legit/research.html> (visited Apr 27, 2001). As these political scientists conclude from the polling data, "support for the Court does not seem to have been depressed by its involvement in the 2000 presidential election." Id.

United States[22] and *Carter v Carter Coal Co,*[23] the Court invalidated New Deal laws as beyond Congress's Commerce Clause power. These cases followed upon a series of decisions during the Progressive Era that also had restricted the scope of Congress's powers to regulate the economy.[24] By the time of the 1936 presidential election, the Court had struck down six federal laws that formed part of FDR's effort to bring about economic recovery. The Supreme Court came to be seen as one of the last obstacles. Similarly, during the Warren Court period, the Court not only decided *Brown v Board of Education,*[25] but also remained in the forefront of the public's attention with other desegregation cases.[26]

In both periods, the Court intervened into the most pressing substantive issues of the day—economic depression and race, among others—and did so repeatedly over a course of years. Even during the Marshall Court period, in which the decisions might be considered more structural—the existence of judicial review,[27] Congress's Necessary and Proper Clause power,[28] the Commerce Clause power[29]—than substantive, the Court remained at the center stage of national politics for several years. Only in *Dred Scott*[30] can the Court be said to have decisively acted only once to settle a national issue. In invalidating the Missouri Compromise, however, that one intrusion represented the Court's effort to end a divisive national debate that had been the central issue in American politics for several generations.

The nature of the Court's interference in these issues almost inevitably sparked a response by the other actors in the political system. In the case of the Marshall Court, it was Jefferson's muttered threats to defy judicial orders.[31] With the Taney Court, it was Abraham Lincoln's attacks on *Dred Scott*

22. 295 US 495 (1935).

23. 298 US 238 (1936).

24. See, for example, *Hammer v Dagenhart,* 247 US 251 (1918).

25. 347 US 483 (1954).

26. *Brown v Board of Education ("Brown II"),* 349 US 294 (1955); *Bolling v Sharpe,* 347 US 497 (1954); *Cooper v Aaron,* 358 US 1 (1958); *Griffin v County School Board,* 377 US 218 (1964); *Green v County School Board,* 391 US 430 (1968).

27. *Marbury v Madison,* 5 US (1 Cranch) 137 (1803).

28. *M'Culloch v Maryland,* 17 US (4 Wheat) 316 (1819).

29. *Gibbons v Ogden,* 22 US (9 Wheat) 1 (1824).

30. *Scott v Sanford ("Dred Scott"),* 60 US 393 (1857).

31. For my own discussion of one instance during this period, see John C. Yoo, *The First Claim: The Burr Trial,* United States v. Nixon, *and Presidential Power,* 83 Minn L Rev 1435, 1451 (1999).

and, ultimately, the coming of the Civil War.[32] With the New Deal Court, President Roosevelt responded by campaigning against the Court and introducing his famous Court-packing plan.[33] With the Warren Court, it was resistance throughout the southern states, criticism in Congress, and criticism from presidential candidates.[34] The response of the political branches or the states demonstrates that the Court had acted in a manner that threatened its own legitimacy. Because the Court had sought to foreclose society (or parts of it) from using the lawmaking process to achieve certain ends, and because those ends were of such intense importance to the people, the chief if not only way for the people (or interest groups, if one prefers a public choice approach to the political process) to pursue their policy preferences was to attack the Court. In other words, the other political actors had to undermine the Court's legitimacy as an institution so as to convince the electorate to support efforts to evade or overturn its decisions.

Contrast these periods with *Bush v Gore*. In *Bush v Gore*, the Court sought to resolve a narrow legal issue involving the selection of presidential electors. The question bears no constitutional implications for the resolution of any significant and ongoing social issues of today—abortion, race relations, education, social security, defense. The decision poses no bar to a society that seeks to use the democratic process to resolve any pressing social problems. While the Democratic party has reason to be dissatisfied with the outcome of *Bush v Gore*, it has no interest in challenging the legal reasoning of the decision in the future. It is highly unlikely that the Court will remain a central player in future presidential election contests. Indeed, the Court's members were last involved in a disputed presidential election more than a century ago. Further, in *Bush v Gore*, the Court was not truly deciding a question of constitutional substance on a par with the scope of abortion rights or the national government's power to enforce civil rights. Instead, it was only clarifying the rules of the game for selecting the only federal official elected by

32. See, for example, *The Dred Scott Decision: Speech at Springfield, Illinois, June 26, 1857*, in Roy P. Basler, ed, *Abraham Lincoln: His Speeches and Writings* 354–65 (World 1946).

33. William E. Leuchtenburg, *The Supreme Court Reborn: The Constitutional Revolution in the Age of Roosevelt* 82–162 (Oxford 1995).

34. Such resistance prevented school desegregation from taking hold in the South for more than a decade after *Brown*. See Gerald Rosenberg, *The Hollow Hope: Can Courts Bring About Social Change?* 74–93 (Chicago 1991). Recent work suggests that the Warren Court did not act out of step with the political branches. See Lucas A. Powe, *The Warren Court and American Politics* 160–78 (Harvard 2000).

the whole nation. It is difficult to conceive of a constitutional question that is more of a pure question of constitutional structure, rather than of substantive constitutional rights. Indeed, the Court perhaps was best suited, as a rational decisionmaker, to settle questions involving rules of constitutional process that may stalemate the other branches of government.

III. LEGITIMACY AS IMPARTIALITY

A third way to examine whether *Bush v Gore* is likely to undermine the Court's legitimacy is to look at current theories of the sources of the Court's authority. The Court itself has sought to give content to its "legitimacy" in *Planned Parenthood of Southeastern Pennsylvania v Casey*.[35] In refusing to overrule *Roe v Wade*,[36] a plurality explained that reversing its precedent would undermine the Court's legitimacy, which it saw as the very source of the judiciary's authority. "As Americans of each succeeding generation are rightly told, the Court cannot buy support for its decisions by spending money and, except to a minor degree, it cannot independently coerce obedience to its decrees."[37] Thus, the judiciary's power is distinguished from the use of force or finances, which are the tools of the political branches. "The Court's power lies, rather, in its legitimacy, a product of substance and perception that shows itself in the people's acceptance of the Judiciary as fit to determine what the Nation's law means and to declare what it demands."[38] Without the sword or purse, the *Casey* plurality believes, the Court's authority derives from the public's acceptance of its power to interpret the Constitution.

How does the Court maintain this legitimacy? According to the *Casey* plurality, the Court receives its public support by "making legally principled decisions under circumstances in which their principled character is sufficiently plausible to be accepted by the Nation."[39] In other words, only by acting in a manner that suggests that its decisions are the product of law rather than politics can the Court maintain its legitimacy. Therefore, the Court must adhere to settled precedent, lest the public believe that the Court is merely just another political actor. "[T]o overrule under fire in the absence of the most compelling reason to reexamine a watershed decision

35. 505 US 833 (1992) (plurality opinion).
36. 410 US 113 (1973).
37. *Casey*, 505 US at 865.
38. Id.
39. Id at 866.

would subvert the Court's legitimacy beyond any serious question."[40] Without this legitimacy, the Court would be unable to perform its role as interpreter of the Constitution, which at times may require the Court to act against the popular will in favor of individual rights.

Leading social scientists appear to agree with the *Casey* plurality's notion of judicial legitimacy. The Court's institutional legitimacy both enhances the legitimacy of particular decisions and increases the voluntary acceptance of unpopular decisions.[41] Valuable as it is, however, legitimacy is hard to come by. Political scientists have emphasized the limited ability of the federal courts to enforce their decisions, and hence have turned to the Court's legitimacy as an explanation for compliance.[42] The Court's standing is further complicated because it lacks any electoral basis for its legitimacy.[43] The way to acquire this legitimacy, many scholars seem to believe, is for the Court to appear to act neutrally,[44] objectively,[45] or fairly[46] by following standards of procedural justice or by making decisions that follow principled rules.

Thus, the question for judging the Court's legitimacy is to evaluate claims that the Rehnquist Court was so intent on achieving partisan ends in *Bush v Gore* that it violated or ignored its own guiding principles. Two claims are prominently made to suggest that *Bush v Gore* was inconsistent with the Court's earlier decisions. First, the Court was acting out of character when it exercised federal power to intervene in the core state function of running elections. Second, a Court that has criticized judicial "activism" suddenly interfered in an especially political process, one fraught with partisanship, and imposed its own unappealable solution upon the problem. The rest of this essay will examine whether these claims of judicial hypocrisy ring true.

40. Id at 867.

41. Tyler and Mitchell, 43 Duke L J at 723 (cited in note 11).

42. See, for example, Murphy and Tanenhaus, 84 Nw U L Rev at 992 (cited in note 14).

43. Gregory A. Caldeira and James L. Gibson, *The Etiology of Public Support for the Supreme Court*, 36 Am J Pol Sci 635, 635 (1992).

44. Marshall, *Public Opinion* at 133 (cited in note 15) ("Justices are viewed as fair, neutral, and even-handed.").

45. Owen M. Fiss, *Objectivity and Interpretation*, 34 Stan L Rev 739, 744–45 (1982) (questioning "whether any judicial interpretation can achieve the measure of objectivity required by the idea of law").

46. Tyler and Mitchell, 43 Duke L J at 746 (cited in note 11) ("[T]he key factor affecting the perceived legitimacy of authorities is procedural fairness.").

Federalism has become the defining issue of the Rehnquist Court. To the extent that the current Court has changed American constitutional law, its activities in redefining the balance of power between the national government and the states will likely prove to be what the Rehnquist Court is best known for. Much of the Court's recent activity has been in the sphere of state sovereignty—protecting states as institutions from federal judicial power through state immunity from damages actions in federal court[47] and from federal legislative power through anti-commandeering principles.[48] Last Term's *United States v Morrison*[49] underscored yet another element of the Court's federalism project. In invalidating portions of the Violence Against Women Act,[50] *Morrison* indicates that the Court is serious about limiting national power itself, regardless of a law's effect on states as institutions. While the Court has made some important decisions restricting Congress's powers to expand individual constitutional rights in ways that cannot be abrogated by states,[51] *Morrison* declares the Court's firm intention to restore limits on Congress's basic power to regulate interstate commerce as well.[52]

A principled adherence to federalism, however, does not require the

47. See, for example, *Alden v Maine*, 527 US 706 (1999) (holding that the Eleventh Amendment gives states immunity from suits in state court arising under federal law issued pursuant to Congress's Article I powers); *Seminole Tribe v Florida*, 517 US 44 (1995) (holding that the previously established congressional power to abrogate state immunity is limited to implementation of the Fourteenth Amendment).

48. See, for example, *Printz v United States*, 521 US 898 (1997) (striking down a portion of the Brady Bill on grounds that it conscripted state officials to execute federal law); *New York v United States*, 505 US 144 (1992) (overturning a law that required the states either to enact radioactive waste legislation or take title to the waste).

49. 120 S Ct 1740 (2000).

50. Pub L No 103-322, 108 Stat 1941, codified at 42 USC § 13981 (1994).

51. See, for example, *Kimel v Florida Board of Regents*, 528 US 62 (2000) (holding that states were not subject to the Age Discrimination in Employment Act under the Eleventh Amendment); *College Savings Bank v Florida Prepaid Postsecondary Education Expense Board*, 527 US 666 (1999) (limiting Congress's power to unilaterally abrogate states' sovereign immunity through legislation designed to remediate or prevent constitutional violations under Section 5 of the Fourteenth Amendment); *City of Boerne v Flores*, 521 US 507 (1997) (invalidating the Religious Freedom Restoration Act as impermissibly expanding the scope of Fourteenth Amendment protections).

52. While the Court in *United States v Lopez*, 514 US 549 (1995), struck down a law on Commerce Clause grounds, many commentators were unsure whether this was to be a one-time event, given certain deficiencies in the federal law at issue there.

Court to refuse to review the presidential election procedures used by the states. Federalism does not create a free-fire zone where states may do anything they please. Rather, federalism is about the appropriate balance of power between federal and state authority, so that neither government abuses its own power at the expense of the rights of the people.[53] By dividing power between the federal and state governments, and then subjecting each to the separation of powers, James Madison wrote in Federalist 51, "a double security arises to the rights of the people. The different governments will controul each other; at the same time that each will be controuled by itself."[54]

This is nowhere truer than in the area of voting. The Constitution certainly accords substantial leeway to the states to manage voting in their own way. As we now know, Article II, Section 1 of the Constitution declares: "each State shall appoint, in such Manner as the Legislature Thereof May Direct, a Number of Electors."[55] Nonetheless, our constitutional system today permits substantial federal intervention into state elections. Congress, for example, has required states to use single-member districts for congressional elections since 1842.[56] The Fourteenth and Fifteenth Amendments to the Constitution guarantee the individual right of each citizen to vote on an equal basis and prohibit states from attempting to discriminate against protected groups by denying them access to the voting booth.[57] *Bush v Gore's* per curiam holding found that the Fourteenth Amendment's guarantee of equal treatment in voting applied not just to access to the ballot box, but also to a state's treatment of a vote after it is cast.[58]

Federal courts and the federal government have engaged in sweeping intervention into state voting procedures. In decisions such as *Baker v Carr*[59] and *Reynolds v Sims,*[60] the Court established the principle of one-person, one-vote. In its recent redistricting cases, such as *Shaw v Reno,*[61] the

53. See John C. Yoo, *The Judicial Safeguards of Federalism,* 70 S Cal L Rev 1311, 1402–4 (1997).

54. Federalist 51 (Madison), in Jacob E. Cooke, ed, *The Federalist* 351 (Wesleyan 1961).

55. US Const Art II, § 1.

56. Act of June 25, 1842 § 2, 5 Stat 491, codified at 2 USC § 2c (1994).

57. US Const Amend XIV–XV.

58. 121 S Ct at 530.

59. 369 US 186 (1962).

60. 377 US 533 (1964).

61. 509 US 630 (1993).

Court has held that states cannot use race as a primary factor in drawing voting districts. Congress has also gotten into the game. Today, in many areas of the nation, the Voting Rights Act of 1965 prevents states from changing *any* voting standard, practice, or procedure without the permission of the Attorney General or a federal court in Washington, D.C.[62] Under this mix of federal laws and judicial precedents, the Court will hear claims that states have engaged in "vote dilution," where election procedures or redistricting essentially gives more political power to some districts over others.[63]

Beyond the general federal involvement in state voting procedures, presidential elections specifically implicate a mix of federal and state laws. The Constitution overrides state constitutions and their allocation of functions by delegating to state legislatures, specifically, the power to establish the rules for choosing presidential electors.[64] Federal law establishes the date on which the presidential election will be held in every state,[65] it allows state legislatures to choose alternative methods if a choice is not made,[66] and federal law explains how Congress will count a state's electoral votes that undergo a challenge.[67] While a state may use judicial methods to resolve these disputes, they must proceed by rules enacted before the election (the essence of the *Bush* suit before the U.S. Supreme Court). Finally, Congress has established December 18 as the date that the electors must meet in each state and send their votes to Washington.

So federal judicial review of state election procedures is nothing new, not even to the Rehnquist Court. It is certainly not the direct threat to our federal system of government that some have claimed, unless they believe that national intervention into state electoral systems violates the basic structure of our federal system of government. Indeed, the Court's intervention in the presidential election dispute was not completely without precedent. While it is true that states have the discretion to set the manner of the state's appointment of presidential electors, electors are federal, not state, officials chosen in a federal, not a state, election. When states select officers that play a federal role, as the Supreme Court announced in *U.S.*

---

62. Voting Rights Act, 42 USC §§ 1973 et seq (1994).
63. *Shaw,* 509 US at 641.
64. *McPherson v Blacker,* 146 US 1, 27 (1892).
65. 3 USC § 1 (1997).
66. Id § 2.
67. Id §§ 5, 15.

Term Limits v Thornton,[68] they have a reduced ability to interfere with their activities or method of selection. In *Term Limits,* for example, the Court rejected arguments that a state's constitutional power to control the "Times, Places, and Manner" of holding congressional elections allowed it to prevent incumbents from appearing on the ballot.[69] This suggests that the state's power over the manner of the selection of presidential electors cannot go far beyond procedural matters such as when and where an election is to be held. Once a state began to use procedures, as in Florida, that may have advantaged one candidate over another, federal principles justified judicial preservation of the integrity of the electoral process.

Even if federalism principles did not prevent the Court from resolving *Bush v Gore,* some may criticize the justices because of their intervention into a deeply political dispute. If not by its deeds, certainly by its rhetoric, the Rehnquist Court has promoted the idea of judicial restraint. While yet another phrase that is often used but seldom defined, judicial restraint can be seen generally as a response to the countermajoritarian difficulty.[70] Because judges are not elected and legislators are, judges should exercise such an undemocratic power as sparingly as possible—how sparingly and on what subjects, of course, remains the subject of great debate.[71] The last paragraph of the *Bush v Gore* per curiam genuflects to this ideal. "None are more conscious of the vital limits on judicial authority than are the members of this Court, and none stand more in admiration of the Constitution's design to leave the selection of the President to the people, through their legislatures, and to the political sphere."[72]

Of course, the majority ran right into the political thickets anyway. Proponents of judicial restraint might have found the Court's interference surprising, if not wholly unjustified. The Court had available any number of opportunities to exercise Alexander Bickel's "passive virtues"[73] to avoid de-

68. 514 US 779 (1995).

69. Id at 829.

70. For well-known efforts to define and grapple with the countermajoritarian difficulty, see generally Jesse H. Choper, *Judicial Review and the National Political Process: A Functional Reconsideration of the Role of the Supreme Court* (Chicago 1980); John Hart Ely, *Democracy and Distrust: A Theory of Judicial Review* (Harvard 1980); Alexander M. Bickel, *The Least Dangerous Branch: The Supreme Court at the Bar of Politics* (Yale 2d ed 1986).

71. For a discussion and criticism of the leading theories, see Terri Jennings Peretti, *In Defense of a Political Court* 36–54 (Princeton 1999).

72. *Bush v Gore,* 121 S Ct at 533.

73. Bickel, *Least Dangerous Branch* at 111–98 (cited in note 70).

ciding the case, including denying certiorari in the first Florida election case to come before it,[74] or denying the stay and certiorari in *Bush v Gore.* Nonetheless, the Court invoked its duty to decide federal question cases as justification. According to the Court, "[w]hen contending parties invoke the process of the courts, however, it becomes our unsought responsibility to resolve the federal and constitutional issues the judicial system has been forced to confront."[75] Unfortunately, this statement is so vague as to carry almost no meaning, as it encompasses any number of cases that the Rehnquist Court would be only too happy to dismiss on grounds of standing[76] or the political question doctrine.[77]

Critics of *Bush v Gore,* however, should not have been surprised by the Court's lack of restraint. This Court has done everything but hide behind the passive virtues. It has reaffirmed the right to abortion[78] and has placed limits on religion in the public sphere.[79] In the federalism area, it has invalidated a series of federal laws in order both to protect state sovereignty and to limit the powers of the national government. One of the laws, the Violence Against Women Act, passed Congress by large majorities in both houses of Congress. In the race area, the Court has invalidated affirmative action in federal contracting[80] and struck down redistricting that sought to maximize minority representation.[81] On the First Amendment, the Court has invalidated federal laws so as to expand commercial speech[82] and to protect indecent or pornographic material.[83] It has risked confrontation with the political branches by striking down federal laws solely on the

---

74. *Bush v Palm Beach County Canvassing Board,* 121 S Ct 471 (2000) (per curiam).

75. *Bush v Gore,* 121 S Ct at 533.

76. See *Lujan v Defenders of Wildlife,* 504 US 555, 573–78 (1992).

77. *Nixon v United States,* 506 US 224, 228 (1993).

78. *Casey,* 505 US 833.

79. *Lee v Weisman,* 505 US 577, 592–93 (1992). The Court, however, also has sought to give religious groups an equal footing in its participation in government aid programs. *Mitchell v Helms,* 530 US 793 (2000) (holding that taxpayer money could be used to buy computers and other instructional materials for religious schools); *Agostini v Felton,* 521 US 203 (1997) (allowing publicly paid teachers to be provided to parochial schools to assist disabled students with remedial, secular education).

80. *Adarand Constructors, Inc v Pena,* 515 US 200 (1995).

81. *Shaw v Reno,* 509 US 630 (1993).

82. See, for example, *44 Liquormart, Inc v Rhode Island,* 517 US 484 (1996).

83. See, for example, *United States v Playboy Entertainment Group,* 120 S Ct 1878, 1893 (2000); *Reno v American Civil Liberties Union,* 521 US 844 (1997).

ground that they violate the separation of powers. Hence, the Court has invalidated the Line Item Veto Act[84] and reversed an effort to expand religious freedoms that the Court had cut back.[85] This Court has been anything but shy in flexing its powers of judicial review to intervene in some of the most contentious issues of the day.

What is important about the Court's recent track record is not just the frequency of the uses of judicial review, but their quality. Initially, the Marshall Court in *Marbury v Madison* grounded judicial review in the Court's unique function in deciding cases or controversies that arise under federal law.[86] As Thomas Jefferson argued, this basis for judicial review leaves ample room for the coordinate branches of government to interpret the Constitution in the course of performing their own constitutional functions.[87] Under the Rehnquist Court, this limited vision of judicial review has steadily been supplanted by assertions of judicial supremacy—that the Supreme Court is not just *an* interpreter of the Constitution, but *the* interpreter of the Constitution.[88] To be sure, the Court's move toward claiming that its readings of the Constitution were final, and that they bound the other branches, truly began with the Burger Court's decision in *United States v Nixon*,[89] if not before.[90] Under the Rehnquist Court, however, the justices

84. *Clinton v New York*, 524 US 417 (1998).

85. *Flores*, 521 US 507.

86. 5 US (1 Cranch) 137, 176 (1803). See also Robert Lowry Clinton, *Marbury v. Madison and Judicial Review* 15–17 (University Press of Kansas 1989); Christopher Wolfe, *The Rise of Modern Judicial Review: From Constitutional Interpretation to Judge-Made Law* 80–89 (Basic 1986).

87. See, for example, Letter from Thomas Jefferson to Abigail Adams, Sept 11, 1804, in Paul L. Ford, ed, 10 *Works of Thomas Jefferson* 89 n 1 (G.P. Putnam's Sons 1905).

88. For my account of this development, see John C. Yoo, Book Review, *Choosing Justices: A Political Appointments Process and the Wages of Judicial Supremacy*, 98 Mich L Rev 1436, 1458–61 (2000).

89. 418 US 683 (1974). For sharp criticism of this vision of judicial review, see Michael Stokes Paulsen, *The Most Dangerous Branch: Executive Power to Say What the Law Is*, 83 Georgetown L J 217, 228–38, 255–62 (1994).

90. Some might argue that the Court first proclaimed its supremacy in *Cooper v Aaron*, 358 US 1 (1958), in which the Court declared that not only were the Court's opinions the "supreme Law of the Land," but that the Court was "supreme in the exposition" of the Constitution. Id at 18. *Cooper*, however, was aimed not at the other branches of government, but at forcing state officials to follow federal interpretation of the Constitution. See Daniel A. Farber, *The Supreme Court and the Rule of Law: Cooper v. Aaron Revisited*, 1982 U Ill L Rev 387, 398–403.

have rapidly expanded their claims to supremacy. In *City of Boerne v Flores*,[91] the Court unanimously declared that Congress could not use its power to enforce Fourteenth Amendment rights inconsistently with the Court's interpretation of the scope of those rights. Several cases have followed that make clear the justices' intentions to stand by *Flores*'s core holding.[92]

Such assertions of judicial supremacy belie any notions that the Rehnquist Court generally has followed a course of restraint. If the Court is willing to go so far as to declare that its power to interpret the Constitution is supreme over the other branches, certainly it is no greater a step to intervene in a dispute about non-substantive, rarely-used election procedures. Nor should critics of *Bush v Gore* express dismay at the role the Court took upon itself in settling the presidential election dispute. Claims to judicial supremacy bespeak an arrogance that the Court has a special role in the American political system, one borne not just out of its unique function in deciding cases or controversies, but out of some vague vision of itself as a final resolver of national issues. The justices, in other words, have truly come to believe in Justice Jackson's famous aphorism that "[w]e are not final because we are infallible, but we are infallible only because we are final."[93] Judicial supremacy has led the Court to view itself not only as the final interpreter of the Constitution, but also—since as Tocqueville noted, many political disputes in America eventually become legal ones—as the nation's final oracle on divisive national controversies.

This should have been apparent from a close reading of *Casey*, the same case in which the plurality of Justices O'Connor, Kennedy, and Souter articulated their theory about the Court's own legitimacy. In declaring its refusal to overrule *Roe v Wade*, the plurality equated the Court's power to interpret the Constitution with the authority to end divisive national controversies. It is worth quoting the plurality on this point:

> Where, in the performance of its judicial duties, the Court decides a case in such a way as to resolve the sort of intensely divisive controversy reflected in *Roe* and those rare, comparable cases, its decision has a dimen-

91. 521 US 507 (1997).

92. See, for example, *Dickerson v United States*, 530 US 428 (2000) (holding Congress could not alter *Miranda* rights); *Morrison*, 120 S Ct 1740 (striking down the Violence Against Women Act); *Kimel*, 528 US 62 (preventing enforcement of the ADA against the states); *Florida Prepaid Postsecondary Education Expense Board v College Savings Bank*, 527 US 627 (1999) (holding Congress cannot abrogate state sovereign immunity from patent claims).

93. *Brown v Allen*, 344 US 443, 540 (1953) (Jackson concurring).

sion that the resolution of the normal case does not carry. It is the dimension present whenever the Court's interpretation of the Constitution calls the contending sides of a national controversy to end their national division by accepting a common mandate rooted in the Constitution.[94]

As *Casey* suggests, the Court's drive for supremacy reveals an image of itself as a great healer of national divisions. One need only have replaced "abortion" with "presidential election" to see that the Court would intervene in *Bush v Gore*.

By reviewing the case, the Supreme Court believed that it could finally bring an end to the destructive partisan struggle over the presidential election, and could do it in a way that would allow the nation to accept the final winner's own legitimacy. A look at the alternatives shows that events threatened to spiral out of control. Any Bush victory that resulted from the intervention of the Florida legislature or Congress, while legal, would undoubtedly have been questioned as driven purely by partisanship. On the other hand, Republicans would have rejected a Gore victory as the result of ever-changing, subjective dimple-counting practices of a few local party hacks or the decisions of a political state judiciary. All of the institutions that could control the outcome of the election—the legislature, the Florida Secretary of State, the Florida Supreme Court, the local election officials and Congress—were subject to charges of partisan bias. Although these institutions are popularly elected, their partisan nature might have allowed the election process to drag on—certainly both Republicans and Democrats demonstrated a willingness in Florida to fight on through each stage of the electoral college process. No doubt the Court believed that only it could intervene so as to bring the national election controversy to an end in a manner that would be accepted by the nation, as indeed it has been.[95]

This is not to say that the precise reasoning of the per curiam was utterly correct. I vastly prefer the theory put forward by the Chief Justice's concurrence: Florida's judiciary had so rewritten the state's electoral laws that it

94. *Casey*, 505 US at 866–67.

95. On December 10, CNN reported that 61 percent of those polled preferred that the United States Supreme Court make the final decision on the selection of the next President, as compared to 17 percent who believed Congress should make the final decision, 9 percent who believed that the Florida State Supreme Court should make the final decision, and only 7 percent who believed the Florida legislature should make the final decision. See <http://www.cnn.com/2000/ALLPOLITICS/stories/12/10/cnn.poll> (visited Feb 24, 2001).

had violated Article II's delegation of authority to the state legislatures to choose the method for selecting presidential electors.[96] Indeed, the per curiam's sudden introduction of the December 12 cutoff date for a remedy—based on the assumption that the Florida legislature intended to adopt the safe harbor date for the selection of presidential electors provided for by 3 USC § 5—makes almost no sense at all unless read in light of the concurrence's structural analysis. What all of this goes to show, rather, is that in deciding *Bush v Gore* the Court was not acting in a hypocritical or partisan fashion. Instead of contradicting its own cases on federalism or judicial restraint, the Court acted in keeping with the general trends of its own jurisprudence over the last decade. The Court's declaration of its role in *Casey* might even have made the justices' intervention in the election dispute somewhat predictable. Consistency of action constitutes a core feature of theories about the Court's legitimacy. The Court's adherence to its own principles makes it all the more difficult, then, to conclude that *Bush v Gore* will undermine the judiciary's legitimacy.

CONCLUSION

Many in legal academia welcomed *Planned Parenthood v Casey* when it first appeared.[97] I would hazard a guess that many of these same supporters of *Casey* have not rushed to embrace *Bush v Gore*. Yet, *Casey* contained the seeds—the claims to judicial supremacy and the aggrandized notions of the Court's role in American society—that would blossom in *Bush v Gore*. Indeed, one can even view the emergence of the per curiam opinion—clearly the work of Justices Kennedy and O'Connor—as evidence of an ultimately failed effort to rebuild the coalition that had produced the unprecedented *Casey* plurality. As in *Casey,* in *Bush v Gore* the Court sought to end a national debate that it feared was tearing the country apart. In fact, the Court's chances of success were much higher in the presidential contest, in which the political system needed a final decision on process rules, than in the abortion debate, which has remained a controversial issue of intense importance to many Americans for decades. It seems that if the Court could intervene into such a contentious political debate as abortion, and survive with its legitimacy more or less intact, then it could safely bring the election dispute to a final conclusion as well.

96. *Bush v Gore*, 121 S Ct at 533–35.

97. See, for example, Kathleen Sullivan, *The Supreme Court, 1991 Term Forward: The Justices of Rules and Standards,* 106 Harv L Rev 22, 24–25 (1992).

Afterword

Whither Electoral Reforms in the Wake of *Bush v Gore*?

RICHARD A. EPSTEIN

This collection of essays does little if it does not establish the wide range of opinions about the epic 2000 presidential election contest, which dominated the news for the five weeks after the election. In one sense, of course, the immediate controversy was definitively resolved by the United States Supreme Court's decision in *Bush v Gore,*[1] which paved the way to the uneventful inauguration of George W. Bush as the forty-third president of the United States. In this sense, the battle over the 2000 election reached its happiest conclusion, which is taken for granted in the United States, but not everywhere else—the orderly transition of power from one administration to another on the appointed day.

It would be, however, a mistake to assume that the closure of this election struggle was followed by a placid return to the status quo ante with respect to the understandings that Americans have of their own political process. The Bush-Gore election contest has already ushered in a period of reconsideration of the full range of practices, both large and small, that surround elections in general—and presidential elections in particular. No institution or practice from the structure of the electoral college to the use of punch ballots will prove resistant to review. In this brief afterword, I will touch upon some of these calls for reform via legislation or perhaps constitutional litigation.

Let us start with a point that now seems far more obvious than it did before the Bush-Gore dispute erupted. The administration of any electoral system is big business, even for those who regard themselves as defenders of a system of small gov-

1. 121 S Ct 525 (2000).

ernment. In ticking off the necessary functions of government within a modern democratic state, it is customary to begin with the prevention of force and fraud in ordinary human affairs, with the provision of infrastructure, and with the control of monopoly behavior. Defenders of the modern, post–New Deal welfare state can think of additional functions that government should discharge, whether they involve intervention in certain market transactions or creation of various programs designed to guarantee minimum levels of social support to the less privileged of our citizens. But one point that both sides to the larger political debate have largely overlooked is that every lofty democratic superstructure rests on a nitty-gritty infrastructure. It is taken for granted that a nation's elections choose the people who will both determine and execute its policies; it is often forgotten that the phrase "hold an election" conceals the thousand grubby, but challenging tasks needed to convert this uncontroversial proposition into a working reality. At the very least, someone has to keep a list of all the eligible voters within a community, which is no mean task when we realize how dynamic these lists are. Each year large numbers of people move from one location to another, for all or part of the calendar year; many voters come of age and leave home; others marry, some of whom change their names; some become incapacitated or die; still others are removed from the rolls for cause; some may be eligible to register at more than one location; still others live outside the United States, while retaining their legal domicile at some former address. The ever greater mobility of American citizens puts immense strains on the simplest tasks of running an election.

Matters, of course, get no simpler in dealing with the actual operation of an election campaign as candidates wind their way through the process of getting their names on the ballot and participating in primaries and general elections. Most of the academic scholarship on voting has concentrated on the grand theoretical issues that make the field so challenging: What is the correct rule for aggregating preferences and choosing electoral winners? What rules should govern the apportionment of voters among various districts when it becomes necessary to balance the demands for equal representation with the demands of various groups, often defined along racial and ethnic lines, for special districts that will allow them to achieve representation in Congress, state legislatures, or local bodies?[2] Elections on the ground raise mundane matters that test these general conceptions. It

2. See, for example, *Shaw v Reno*, 509 US 630 (1993).

does not take much imagination to see that the ever-present need to collect, collate, and count ballots opens up endless vistas for potential fraud. Yet it is difficult to clamp down on that fraud without trenching on the rights of individuals to cast their ballots in an easy and convenient fashion. The easier we make it for ordinary citizens to register, the easier we make it for them to register twice.

For the most part, we as a nation are content to allow these anomalies to run their course because in most cases we do not think that they make much of a difference in choosing the winner. But *Bush v Gore* highlighted this soft underbelly of American elections, just as it threw into high relief the peculiar operations of our electoral college. It showed that different types of voting machines had patterns of different sorts of failure rates. It elicited from the Supreme Court a decision in which seven justices at least decided that the differential levels of participation were sufficient (with vastly different consequences) to sustain equal protection challenges to practices that heretofore had passed well underneath the constitutional radar. At the same time, *Bush v Gore* placed into high relief some of the peculiar constitutional features of the distinctively American system of presidential selection. Both these topics deserve some parting observations. I shall begin with some observations about the reform of presidential elections and then move on to the impact that *Bush v Gore* may have on electoral practices generally.

PRESIDENTIAL ELECTIONS: THE CONSTITUTIONAL FRAMEWORK

The single most important political compromise at the Constitutional Convention concerned the division of power between the large and small states. The key element of that compromise was that each state, regardless of size, was given two votes in the Senate or upper chamber, while the seats in the House of Representatives or lower chamber were apportioned in accordance with population. The compromise was deemed necessary to prevent the larger states from swamping the smaller ones at the federal level. The consequence, however, has been that the small states tend to do better on a per capita basis than do the large states in the constant struggle for appropriation of federal funds.[3] But whether it be for better or worse, the right of each state to have two senators is entrenched firmly in the Consti-

---

3. See, for example, Lynn A. Baker, *The Spending Power and the Federalist Revival*, 4 Chapman L Rev 195 (2001).

tution and, in principle at least, cannot be overridden by ordinary constitutional amendments, which themselves require supermajorities to pass under the various provisions of Article V. The consent of each state is required individually, and no one thinks that is forthcoming.

The terms of the great compromise over the composition of Congress heavily influenced the shape of the rules for presidential elections. These are not held by direct popular vote. Rather, Article II, Section 1, Clause 2 provides that the number of electors in each state shall be "equal to the whole number of Senators and Representatives to which the State may be entitled in the Congress." The imbalances that are explicitly preserved for the Senate are carried over, albeit in attenuated form, into what is commonly, but misleadingly, called the electoral college. Indeed, that same section does not even call for the direct election of state electors, but rather allows them to be "appointed" in the manner that the legislature thereof may direct—a provision that at the very least allows for variation in the method by which electors are chosen in each state, of which the popular vote is only one. In the initial understanding, moreover, the electors, once appointed, had a deliberative function: "The Electors shall meet in their Respective States, and vote by Ballot for two persons." The meeting took place at the state level, not the national level, in an obvious effort to keep state power great in the selection of the president. In addition, it was clearly contemplated that the electors could vote their individual consciences for whatever candidates they deemed appropriate. It was only with the passage of time that electors were selected (not appointed, mind you) by popular vote within the state and pledged to the slate on whose behalf they ran.

ABOLISHING THE ELECTORAL COLLEGE

Given this background, it is correct, but somewhat anomalous, to say that the entire system of the electoral college contemplates an outcome in which the candidate with the majority of the popular vote nationwide could nonetheless fall short in the electoral college. A more accurate statement of the initial understanding was that it was unlikely to have anything so simple as a popular vote for presidential candidates in the first place. The framers were not apostles of popular democracy, but devout believers in the need for Byzantine electoral structures to prevent the masses from taking over the reins of political power. But the legislative reforms uniformly undertaken under the constitutional umbrella have made explicit the possible inconsistent outcomes between the electoral and popular votes. In fact, the

2000 Bush-Gore campaign was the first since the Hayes-Tilden campaign of 1876 in which the candidate who had the majority of the popular vote did not carry the electoral college. It is therefore not surprising that proposals to eliminate the electoral college have surfaced in both the academic and the public debates, including a proposal to that effect by the junior senator from New York, Hillary Rodham Clinton. Those proposals will not go through because they will be opposed in the amendment process by the small states, who stand to lose influence under it.

On balance, the voting system of the electoral college, however, may have more than inertia to defend it. One way to see the point is to note, first, that the number of cases in which the electoral vote diverges from the popular vote is small, so that the tension in contemporary legitimacy is not a commonplace occurrence. In addition, the weighted voting scheme of the electoral college does fit within the original constitutional framework. Although the importance of states qua states has dwindled in recent years, it would be a mistake to assume that it has disappeared altogether. If the greater imbalances that are found in the Senate, with their profound budgetary and political processes, are widely accepted, then it seems odd to focus on the voting anomalies in presidential elections that produce much smaller distortions in popular outcomes.

In addition, the changes in the conduct of the presidential election through the abolition of the electoral college would be profound. At the very least, the entire structure of political campaigns would change as both candidates would now seek to wage a multifront war in order to secure that vital popular majority. Under the current system, George Bush and Al Gore could give a discreet pass to New York and Texas, respectively, because Gore had a lock in the first and Bush had a lock in the second. But once the popular vote is all that matters, then a vote is a vote wherever it may be. The next Gore will go to Texas to pare down the next Bush's lead, and the favor will be returned in New York. Large population centers will draw all the attention. The smaller states and less populated regions will be left to fend for themselves. The fears that animated the initial constitutional compromise will be borne out in the contemporary setting.

All that may or may not be a good thing, but one feature of a nationwide popular vote should put dread in the hearts of the most ardent reformer. *Bush v Gore* was an extraordinary occurrence because the closeness of the vote in one state held the entire election in the balance. But now ask what would happen if a nationwide recount were required because of the overall closeness of the popular vote: about 600,000 popular votes separated the candidates, and in some future election, it could easily be closer. How would the recount process look if the anomalies of Palm Beach County turned up in fifteen other states? Illinois, for example, had a real flap that turned out not to matter when many voters in DuPage County who had registered under the state's motor-voter registration system arrived at the polls on election day to find no record of their registration. The great unanticipated benefit of the electoral college system is quite simply that it puts into place fifty or so firewalls that localize the mistakes and irregularities to the state in which they occur. We can ignore, as it were, the mistakes in both New York and Texas because they did not affect the outcome in either place. But put both states in the same hopper, and who knows how the individual recounts and the flurry of lawsuits would sort themselves out.

At the very least, it seems clear that we should have to adopt uniform standards for the governance of nationwide federal elections to prevent political embarrassment and ubiquitous equal protection challenges. Yet it then becomes unclear whether a single election could cover state and federal offices. These transitional matters are not easily negotiated, particularly since we can be confident that no one will agree on what these uniform standards should be or how they should be implemented. In sum, it seems on this score best to leave the overall system alone. The odds of a nationwide recount for popular vote seem small, but the turmoil such a recount could create seems too large. Better one stick on this point with the status quo ante than to flee to ills of which we are but dimly aware.

STATISTICAL TIES AND PROPORTIONATE VOTING

The closeness of the Florida contest also fed the common observation that the outcome in the Bush-Gore contest was so close that it should be treated as though it was a statistical tie. Here that position rests on the sensible observation that the differences in the final tallies (which are numbers below one thousand) are small enough to lie within any margin of error. The question, however, is this: what follows from that observation? One common response is to apportion the votes between the candidates. In contrast, it seems as though the best answer is nothing at all. The difficulty here starts with the necessities of a case. The Constitution calls for one president of the United States. No matter what system of selection is used, it is always possible to find an election contest so close that a single vote could change its outcome. But so long as we cannot divide the office between two candidates, then we must find a way to choose one president even when the vote is an exact tie.

In the electoral college, of course, it is possible to finesse this ultimate truth by dividing, say, the votes of Florida evenly between the candidates (perhaps giving the odd vote to the candidate with the small majority). But this clever solution does not obviate the need for recounts in close cases. Let us suppose, as was the case in Florida, that we treat as a statistical tie any count that shows that the two leading candidates are within 0.5 percent of each other in the vote totals—the actual percentage is unimportant for what follows. Under the old system, we have one tipping point at 50 percent. Thus, a recount is called for if the tallies show that the two candidates are 0.499 percent apart, but not if the difference is 0.501 percent. There is only one margin that matters. To be sure, the likelihood that the recount will be more reliable than the original count is unproved, so whether we stick with the initial count or go to the revised count, we have not obviated the philosophical angst that a single miscounted vote could give the election to the wrong candidate.

But what happens if we decide to split the vote in the event of the statistical tie—say, when the candidates are within 1 percent of each other? Now there are two boundary lines: the first has candidate A ahead of candidate B by around 0.5 percent; the second has candidate B ahead of candidate A by about the same amount. But in each case, what are we to do if the votes are within 0.5 percent of either of these boundaries? It turns out that in a two-person election we have to conduct a recount if the final outcome is between 49 and 51 percent for each candidate. The range of doubt expands because we operate along two margins, even if the stakes drop somewhat— that is, the choice is now between all and one-half of the electoral votes, instead of all or none of the electoral vote. More challenges at lower stakes: it hardly is clear whether this profile is better than the current system, which tolerates a single discontinuity on which more turns. It is easy after the fact to note that an election is really a statistical tie when nothing turns on that sage observation. It is a lot harder to devise any sensible system of electoral recounts to police the border between a divided vote and an all-or-nothing split. The sharp discontinuities in outcomes do not disappear so long as the selection of a president requires at least some all-or-nothing choices. A single vote can still make the difference. In *Bush v Gore*, for example, Gore would have won the election if the votes had been split because of a statistical tie, while Bush would have won it if they were not. The next time around, therefore, a small shift in the popular vote totals could lead to a similar impasse at a different margin, hardly a reform worth inviting.

These observations should be sufficient to dispel another possibility—namely, that votes should be prorated between the candidates in each state so as to get rid of any pretense of the winner-take-all outcome. But as before, this effort to temporize only creates newer problems as it eliminates older ones. In cases like Florida, a recount of the 2000 popular vote would apparently be of little consequence because only a single electoral vote would hang in the balance.

Just as with statistical ties, however, there is a price to pay for moving away from all-or-nothing outcomes. There are simply more cases in which recounts will be required, for the number of election counts that hover close to a boundary line would sharply increase. In Florida, with 25 votes, we could conceivably ask for a limited recount if the total vote is uncertain within one-half of a percent of one of these 24 dividing lines: that is, if one candidate gets between 3.75 and $4.25 + 4n$ percent, where n runs from 0 to 23. There are thus many more inflection points, even if each counts for a single electoral vote. As before, this new regime reduces the stakes for a recount only in a single state. It does not reduce the likelihood of a recount in an election where the popular vote is close. Then we shall have to have recounts in many states at the same time. After all, what should be done if ten electoral votes separate two candidates and twenty states have vote counts that hover near one of these forbidden lines? We simply swap one form of pandemonium for another, and we still are left with the possibility that tiny swings in the popular vote can shift the outcome in an all-or-nothing election.

In light of these alternatives, there seems then to be no reason to depart from the current practice, notwithstanding its evident infirmity. The odds are against a quick recurrence of the Florida impasse, where the state count was close and the outcome of the national election hung in the balance. It is best therefore not to react overmuch to past situations. It is better to improve the use of voting machines so that the counts become more reliable, at which point the problem will in most instances take care of itself.

CLEANING UP THE ELECTORAL MACHINERY

Thus far, I have rejected major changes in the operation of the electoral system in response to the late unpleasantness of the Florida election. But the unsettled nature of that dispute does suggest one line of reform of constitutional dimensions that should receive more serious play in the general public debate. Quite simply, there is no reason to keep human electors at all. A numerical tally seems quite superior. The first reason is that today the electors serve no function at all. Yet they are capable of misbehaving and violating their pledges. In the Bush-Gore election, one Washington, D.C., Democratic elector simply did not bother to vote at all because he was disenchanted with Al Gore. Nothing turned on that symbolic gesture, but matters could have been more dramatic if some Bush electors had defected to Gore, believing that the popular vote should prevail or disapproving of the actions of the United States Supreme Court. A switch of two votes could have thrown the election into the Congress. A switch of three votes could have put the outcome over to Gore.

Given these stakes, it seems odd that the entire matter should be governed by a loose sense of custom. A rule that just awards the electoral votes to the state in accordance with the electoral tally obviates the risk, without altering the balance of power between large and small states. In addition, this reform eliminates some of the pressure from postelection disputes. Since there are no electors who have to meet, the December deadline for the meeting of the electoral college is eliminated, thus removing at least one aspect of the transition problem. That said, there still remains the risk of a tie vote in the electoral college, which should in turn be obviated by a simple reform at the next Census: add an additional seat in the House of Representatives so that the total number of electors is odd. That reform, at least, should lie within our institutional grasp.

GENERAL ELECTORAL REFORMS

As a matter of practical politics, any systematic reform of the presidential election process will require a constitutional amendment and thus has to move at a very slow pace. The same cannot be said of the raft of challenges to the current electoral system that have come hard on the heels of *Bush v Gore*. None of these challenges rests on the Article II argument that the election was not held in accordance with the rules laid down by the Florida legislature. That rationale commanded the support of only three of the justices and thus could not serve as the launching pad for the challenge. But even if it had the support of five justices, it would have been a nonstarter for comprehensive constitutional litigation. The Article II argument does not depend on the identification of some external standard to which all state elections must conform. Rather, by its terms, it is confined to presidential elections, and as to those, it demands only that the system that is used be that which was put in place by the legislature in the first place. So long as the electoral practices follow the letter of the law, no Article II challenge can be mounted, no matter how ill-advised that system appears to be.

The aftermath of the Supreme Court's equal protection argument is, of course, far broader. At its root, an argument that questions any differential effectiveness of the vote of an individual gives rise to a question of constitutional dimension, wholly apart from any claim of discrimination on grounds of race or ethnicity. Since, moreover, some of the least-reliable voting equipment is concentrated in the poorest districts, which are heavily African-American and Latino, a traditional race-based classification can sometimes be added into the mix. Just that has been done, for example, in the current litigation pending in Illinois. *Black v McGuffage* [4] and *del Valle v McGuffage* [5] both press the equal protection claim in the context of municipal elections.

The situation in Illinois is similar to those in many other states and gives some focus to the issues. It can be briefly summarized as follows.[6] At present, Illinois uses five different voting methods. The most reliable system is the optical scan system, which allows for a vote count to be made on an in-precinct basis. Under current practice, this system screens for overvotes and for ballot defects, but not for undervotes. This system is in use in ten counties within the state. Next, in three counties, the same optical scan system is used, but here the counts are done centrally, and not within the precincts. Third, there are punch card jurisdictions where votes are counted in the precincts. These have the capability of notifying voters of errors, but under current Illinois law, these reports cannot be made. These systems are used chiefly in the city of Chicago and the nearby suburban counties. Fourth, elsewhere in the state the votes are done by punch cards and counted separately; again, error notification is possible, but not done. Finally, the state has a system of absentee ballots, which precludes, of course, any system of error notification.

The results in Illinois are surely typical throughout in other states: the

4. Civil Action No 01C 0208 (filed ND Ill 1/11/2001). McGuffage is the chairman of the Chicago Board of Election Commissioners. All his co-commissioners were joined in both suits.

5. Civil Action No 01C 0796 (filed ND Ill 2/5/2001).

6. My thanks to Thomas Ioppolo of the Illinois State's Attorney's Office for his summary of the relevant Illinois law.

rates of vote failure are far higher in the punch card jurisdictions than in the optical scanning jurisdictions. In Illinois, the failure rate was about 0.5 percent for optical scanners, against a statewide failure rate for all systems of about 3.85 percent and a failure rate for punch cards in predominantly Latino or African-American wards of about 7 percent.[7] Wholly apart from any constitutional questions, these differences properly give rise to real concerns, for they suggest that many of these harms are avoidable by simple technologies that protect individuals against the consequences of their own haste, confusion, or sloppiness. But the harder questions are whether these differential patterns reveal an equal protection violation under the logic of *Bush v Gore* and, if they do, what the appropriate remedy for those defects should be.

One simple response to the problem is to say that *Bush v Gore* was a one-ride pony and that its principles do not apply to any ordinary and routine election—without quite saying why. That approach, of course, runs into the obvious objection that individual cases should be decided in accordance with general legal principles, which by definition must apply to more than the case before the Court. It also would only lend credibility to charges of the political nature of the Court's eleventh-hour intervention. So the question quickly shifts to whether some more-principled ground of decision could be found. The most promising line of analysis for these newer claims starts with the proposition that the equal protection violation in *Bush v Gore* was premised not only on differential failure rates between the optical scan and punch card regimes, but also on Florida's failure to adopt a single standard across the different counties for dealing with dimpled and hanging chads. The overall analysis thus turns not only on differences in effective participation levels, but also on the low systemwide costs needed to eliminate the manifest disparity.

Given this simple balancing framework, the key defect in the Florida procedures was that they tolerated countywide differences in interpretation even though it would have taken only a stroke of the administrative pen to have adopted a uniform rule for reading chads. Indeed, the Florida election law gave the secretary of state the power to interpret its statutory provisions in order to achieve the requisite level of uniformity. Transposed to the Illinois suit, the initial question is whether the same can be said about the refusal to activate the unused error notification technology available in

7. See Civil Action No 01C 0796k, at ¶ 24.

the punch card systems. Here some evidence should be taken to determine whether the use of that technology would introduce new problems of its own. But at least in the abstract, it seems hard to imagine exactly what those problems would be, so under the heightened form of scrutiny invited by *Bush v Gore*, that change could well be constitutionally required.

Where this leaves the absentee ballots, which cannot be checked before they are submitted, is somewhat unclear. But it does seem unlikely that any higher error rate in these ballots should form the basis of a successful constitutional challenge because here it looks to be virtually impossible to incorporate any error notification technology. Absentee ballots have always been subject to a higher rate of failure, if only because there are higher rates of slipups in any system that operates at a distance, especially when strong administrative safeguards are needed to prevent the higher risk of electoral fraud. The process itself is more complex. It would be odd if the results were every bit as good.

Next, there seems to be little constitutional difficulty with respect to one other distinction within the Illinois system—the use of in-precinct counts for some counties and out-precinct counts in others. Here the expected likelihood that the vote will be properly cast is the same no matter where it is counted. Presumably, the different counting systems reflect the population densities in the various precincts and the level of technical expertise available at the precinct level. So long as no invidious distinctions creep into the analysis, it seems unlikely that these differences in administration should be thought to raise an equal protection problem under *Bush v Gore*, especially if the proposed remedy decreases the reliability of the overall system.

The case is far closer when it comes to the central question in these suits—whether all counties should be equipped with optical scanning equipment with its error notification technology. Clearly, a good deal turns on the level of scrutiny that is brought to the inquiry. If it is just a matter of one voter being treated differently from another, then it becomes doubtful whether the current Supreme Court would apply the strict scrutiny standard. In an effort to overcome that difficulty, both Illinois cases have alleged a disparate impact by virtue of race, but have not been able to present credible evidence that the differentiated treatment was motivated by any desire to advance political interests along racial lines. Just where this leaves the standard of review is not quite clear, but the hornbook law looks with suspicion on calls for evaluating race-based discrimination claims on a strict liability basis.[8] It seems difficult to impute any discriminatory purpose to the current state of affairs.

The installation of uniform voting machines, however, raises very different issues in that here it requires the state, or its various voting districts, to make substantial outlays of wealth in order to avoid the stain of a constitutional violation. The Illinois litigation, for example, was raised by a request for the immediate installation of optical scanners for aldermanic elections; that took place in February 2001 (the case was compromised out on statutory grounds), where the costs of compliance would have only been greater. The poorer counties may be hard-pressed, particularly on a tight time schedule, to find the funds for these appropriations. While it is too early to make confident predictions, it seems likely that the equal protection claims will put additional pressures on the states to both fund and administer the entire electoral system (both state and federal) in a more centralized fashion. The roles of the counties to set policy could be reduced, and cross-subsidies (such as those increasingly found in statewide education programs) could become the order of the day.

Exactly how will all this play out? It is too early to say. But no matter what the final path, there seems little doubt that the equal protection theory fashioned by the five conservative justices of the United States Supreme Court seems ripe to be pressed into the service of causes that are championed by their more liberal brethren. The complex inner workings of our electoral system have been brought to the surface, where it seems likely they will remain for some time, at both the constitutional and the political levels. Presidents come and go. Structural reforms endure. In that simple observation perhaps we may find the central lesson of *Bush v Gore*.

8. *Washington v Davis*, 426 US 229 (1976).

INDEX

Note: United States Supreme Court is abbreviated as USSC, and the Florida Supreme Court is abbreviated as FSC.